"He who knows not the world,

knows not his own place in it."

MARCUS AURELIUS

# The Unicorn
# BOOK of
# 1953

*Prepared under the Editorial Direction of*

**JOSEPH LAFFAN MORSE, Sc.B., LL.B.**

*Editor in Chief*

THE NEW FUNK & WAGNALLS ENCYCLOPEDIA

UNICORN BOOKS, INC., NEW YORK

# STAFF

**Joseph L. Morse,** Editor in Chief
**Richard M. Gordon,** Executive Editor
**Clayton Rawson,** Art Director
**Homer Cable,** Picture Research
**John Hackett,** Consultant

**WRITERS:** Val Adams • George A. W. Boehm • Emory Lewis
David Dempsey • Martin Fass • Terry Ferrer • Karl Hess
Harrison Forman • Lewis Funke • Harry B. Murkland
Gordon C. Hamilton • Joseph Roddy • Stanley W. Page
Sherwin D. Smith • Judith Murphy • George A. W. Boehm
Samuel T. Williamson • Morris Weeks, Jr. • Jesse Zunser

**PRODUCTION:** James Allen • Natalie Raymond • Marjorie Rose
Mimi Chen Mi Chu • Annabelle Nemser

# Preface

THIS—THE SECOND VOLUME IN OUR ANNUAL series—gives us opportunity to report on the reception accorded to our *Unicorn Book of 1952*, issued just a year ago.

Everyone who saw the book, within our limited acquaintance, praised it. We heard from readers, and from friends of readers, who wanted to know where they could buy a copy of it. Some few book critics saw it, and wrote reviews about it. Altogether, what people had to say warmed the hearts of our staff members. The book was handsomely designed; it was dramatically illustrated; it was fascinating to read; it was a valuable addition to any library.

What greater praise could one ask? These were the goals we had tried to achieve, and people said, with some enthusiasm, that we had achieved them.

Well, here we are again, and this time we hope and believe we have done better than last time. We think you will find the writing more even in quality and the whole work better balanced. These virtues are in natural consequence of a more experienced, more smoothly working organization. That there is room for improvement, of course we admit, and expect to do even better next year. But this much is *good*, we think, and we know you will enjoy the volume at least as much as last year's.

Reading the copy submitted by our various writers, I was struck with a kind of nostalgia that you, too, must feel on looking back over the great events of 1953. There is a quiet thrill, different from any other, in reliving the emotions felt months ago on reading the original news dispatches. Even the little events, peppered here and there throughout the book, we remember, and experience a small surprise that we store away so much from our daily reading, and unconscious of our riches, can recall some tiny item of it instantaneously and with ease.

In such reactions lies a large part of the charm of this book. Nearly unique, we believe that charm to be, in a basic reference work.

Again we of the staff wish you pleasure in our new book, and I, as chief editor, want to call your attention to its principal architects, listed on the opposite page. Special mention again must go to Clayton Rawson, for the job he did with type and layout, to John Hackett, for his advice on text and pictures, and to Richard M. Gordon, for bringing the whole book into being.

JOSEPH LAFFAN MORSE
Editor-in-Chief

# Contents

# THE UNICORN

# BOOK OF 1953

HAPPY BIRTHDAY, IKE!

# Mood of the Year

IN WASHINGTON AN OLD SOLDIER BECAME President of the United States. In London a young Queen was crowned. In Moscow a tyrant died and was succeeded by a poker-faced fat man. These three events of 1953 highlighted a year of change.

Fighting stopped in Korea, but peace talks bogged down. The Soviet Union tried out an H-bomb, yet seemed neither ready for war nor willing for peace. Armed Communists infiltrated farther into Indochina. The cold war continued.

Yet there were bright spots for the West. World Communism suffered some moral defeats. Only a handful of North Korean and Chinese prisoners of war elected to go home. In East Germany, proletarian workers demonstrated against their "proletarian" rulers—and the years' most heroic gesture was that of unarmed Berlin workingmen stoning Soviet tanks.

Elsewhere there was tension and terror. In the Middle East, Israel and the Arab nations waged murderous truce. In Iran, wily, weeping Mohammed Mossadegh fled Teheran mobs and the premiership.

The African continent was in ferment. Egyptians kept twisting the British Lion's tail. In North Africa, nationalistic Algerians and Moroccans badgered the French. In East Africa, fanatical anti-white Mau Maus continued to chop British settlers to pieces. In South Africa old Daniel Malan, the stiff-necked Prime Minister, won a new mandate for his white-supremacy program.

Malan and Mossadegh were two old men who, in their seventies, headed governments during 1953. Another was stubborn Syngman Rhee, President of South Korea. Still an-

other, a giant of our times, recovered from a slight stroke, resumed his brandy and black cigars, received the Nobel Prize for literature, and became Sir Winston Churchill, Knight of the Most Noble Order of the Garter.

Nature during this twelvemonth was as eccentric as ever. Earthquakes shook Turkey and the isles' of Greece. Abnormally high spring tides flooded the coasts of Britain and the Low Countries, and 2000 lost their lives. Flash floods hurt Japan. Tornadoes killed 400 in the U.S.

In 1953 an average of 115 persons a month were killed in flying accidents, and in Japan the worst disaster in aviation history occurred when 129 servicemen died in a crash of an Air Force Globemaster.

But not all 1953 events will echo down time's corridors. Rita Hayworth married again, and so, for the fifth time, did Barbara Hutton. She married Porfirio Rubirosa, the ex-husband of Doris Duke. Zoologist Alfred C. Kinsey reported on the American female.

In 1953 man climbed higher, dived deeper, and flew faster than ever before. A New Zealand beekeeper, Edmond Hillary, and Tenzing Norkay, a stocky Sherpa tribesman, scaled Mt. Everest, 29,141 feet and the world's highest mountain. In the Mediterranean, Auguste Piccard and son Jacques descended 10,334 feet in a steel diving ball. And Air Force Major Charles (Chuck) Jeager flew through the stratosphere at 1650 miles an hour, two and one-half times the speed of sound.

Yet it was only yesterday that man broke through the "unbreakable" sound barrier.

NATIONAL

AFFAIRS

**SOMETHING FUNNY** struck Defense Sec. Wilson and wife as this photo was snapped. He was less amused later, when Congress insisted he sell all his General Motors stock

# Ike's First Year

AN ERA ENDED WHEN 1953 BEGAN AND THE first Republican President in twenty years took office. Dwight D. Eisenhower's first year in the White House was a year of beginning to get ready to start.

Even so, there were signs of change in Washington. Fearing job cuts, federal employees curtailed department-store installment purchases. Credit requirements tightened. Fewer government workers slipped away from their desks for a mid-morning coffee break. Coffee consumption at cafeterias and snack bars in federal buildings fell from 43,000 to 34,000 pounds a month.

The new President was at his desk at 8 A.M. and ready for conferences a half hour later. Legislators and high officials, accustomed to 10 A.M. meetings, grumbled at having to gobble breakfast and be at the White House at 8:30 A.M. At Burning Tree Golf Club, greens fees were

raised from $5 to $10 on Wednesdays and Saturdays, the usual Eisenhower golfing days, and members were asked not to bring guests from Washington.

Although the Eisenhowers gave the required number of state dinners and official receptions, they seldom went out in the evening. Their idea of a day's perfect end was to watch television in their second-floor sitting room with steak dinners on trays before them.

It was some time before new high officials and their wives became captives, like their predecessors, of Washington's social system. Until then, hostesses who snagged members of the incoming administration for parties were dismayed when the honored guests left early for home and bed. "I've never worked so hard in my life," one Cabinet member remarked.

In his 1952 campaign, Eisenhower had promised a "new positive approach". But he had to take over the government's executive branch first. He also had to maintain friendly relations with a Congress whose razor-thin Republican majorities were led by experienced politicians who had opposed Ike's nomination and distrusted his "internationalism". In particular, there was a senator named Taft.

And another senator named McCarthy.

Most important of all was the task of ending the costly, unpopular war in Korea, and of avoiding World War III by keeping the cold war in Europe from developing into a shooting one. At home there were other problems: cutting the cost of government without sacrificing military security and easing government controls over prices and wages without disrupting the economy.

On the day of his inauguration, the new President faced these problems confidently. Probably no incoming administration had been so thoroughly briefed

before taking over. And for little courtesies between new and outgoing Presidents there was no historical parallel.

When, on Inauguration Day, Dwight D. Eisenhower set the gents-furnishings world agog by rejecting the ceremonial stovepipe hat for a dressy black homburg, President Truman, when he emerged from the White House to ride to the Capitol with his successor, also wore a homburg. When the Trumans motored to Union Station after the inaugural, they boarded the presidential private car, which Eisenhower had provided for their return to Independence, Mo.

The only Eisenhower dissatisfied with Inauguration Day courtesies was Major John. The Eisenhowers' soldier son was with his Third Division unit at the Korean front when orders came for him to report for temporary duty in Washington. On their ride to the Capitol, President-elect Eisenhower asked President Truman who had given the order, because John, who wanted no favoritism shown him, "was raising hell about it".

"Just tell him," said Mr. Truman, "that contrary old man in the White House did it."

The new President was sworn in before 250,000 onlookers. The 2400-word inaugural address, during which Mr. Truman patted his hands in approval, was second only to George Washington's 134 words as the shortest on record.

Domestic problems, said President Eisenhower, were dwarfed by foreign ones. He was soon to find the domestic dwarfs just as hard to overcome as the foreign giants. However, his address appeared to please nearly everyone, including highly placed Europeans and labor leader Walter Reuther, head of the Congress of Industrial Organizations (C.I.O.).

"A great and inspiring speech," said Senate Majority Leader Taft.

"A very good statement of the Democratic problems of the last twenty years," said Senate Minority Leader Johnson.

During thirty-seven years of married life, the Eisenhowers had never lived in a home of their own. Even the Gettysburg farm they acquired after World War II, in anticipation of retirement, had seldom been occupied. Consequently they pulled up no roots when they moved into the White House.

They did not see much of their new home on the day of occupancy. First came a five-hour inaugural parade. Then came not one but two inaugural balls, in preparation for which, a friend reported, the new President was confronted by his first crisis. "Mamie!" he cried. "Where the hell is my monkey suit?"

Furious search failed to locate the presidential white tie and tails. Then someone recalled it had been left in some baggage on the special train that took the Eisenhowers to Washington, and a hell-for-leather ride retrieved it from Union Station. Finally, off to the balls a little late, the President wore his new black homburg. So many Eisenhower Republicans did likewise that Washington haberdashers had to call upon Baltimore, Philadelphia, and New York for help.

Since Mrs. Eisenhower wore pink, many inaugural ball gowns were also "Mamie pink". Beauty salons had special prices for "Mamie bangs"—a $2 hairdo using one's own curls; $10 to $17.50 for removable bangs using rented curls.

Not since Theodore Roosevelt, exponent of the "strenuous life", has there been such an active, restless President as Eisenhower. He even dictates while waggling a golf iron or half sitting on the edge of his desk, swinging a foot. Rumors about his being in poor health were pretty well discounted by year's end.

His day begins shortly before 7 A.M. Like most soldiers, he is a quick dresser—shave, shower, and into his clothes in less than twenty minutes. Ex-Sergeant John Moaney, a soft-spoken Negro from Maryland's Eastern Shore who has served General Eisenhower in and out of the Army, brings breakfast to the dressing room. At this time the President skims through morning newspapers—three New York, two Washington, and one Baltimore. Then he leaves for his office.

He returns to the White House for lunch—he's not an eat-at-the-desk executive—and usually returns again an hour before dinner. Few of his White House intimates belong to his official family, and the same goes for his golf and bridge mates.

Life in the White House is something like occupying the second floor of a museum. Unlike Mrs. Truman, Mrs. Eisenhower enjoys it. Unlike Mrs. Roosevelt, the new First Lady spends most of her time there. She likes people, and people take quickly to her. Once she tried to answer all her mail personally; now she can't. She has her own circle of friends, most of whom date back to the three years she lived in Washington while her husband was away at war. She doesn't share Ike's fondness for bridge; her game is canasta.

By midyear, many syndicated newspaper pundits and air-wave oracles had abandoned their hosannas to "a strong new President". They began asking: "When will Ike turn on the heat?" "When will he cut Senator McCarthy down to size?" "When will he whip the Old Guard Republicans into line?"

And the C.I.O., dedicated to the forty-hour week, totted up the hours the President spent away from his desk whamming golf balls.

He whammed some in the company of Senator Taft, whose onetime nickname of "Mr. Republican" gave way to another, "Mr. Congress". The predicted split between winner and loser of the 1952 Republican nomination did not occur; instead, the two men drew closer.

The G.O.P., Eisenhower once told a press conference, is divided into groups who think differently. His job, as he saw

**ALL THE EISENHOWERS** beam in unison at the Washington inaugural ball; Major John and wife, Mrs. John Doud (Mamie's mother), Mamie, Ike

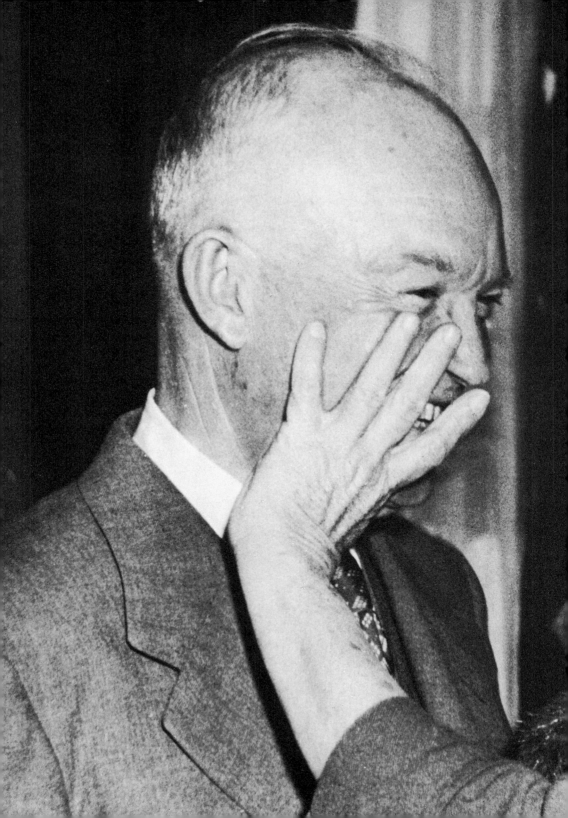

**"SEEING"** the President's face with her sensitive fingers, the famous deaf-and-blind Helen Keller forms her own impression of Ike: "He has a wonderful smile"

it, was to bring people together in order to achieve progress. He avoided head-on clashes with Congress. He conferred with legislative leaders each Monday morning, and every member of Congress—Republican and Democrat—sat at the White House luncheon table before the end of the session.

A professional soldier most of his life, he applies military methods of work in the White House. As Commander in Chief of Allied Forces in Europe, he had welded a team out of American, British, and French commanders and staff officers. As President he attempted to weld another team.

White House assistants correspond to the general staff at Supreme Headquarters. As heads of departments, Cabinet members correspond to army commanders in the field. And Congress corresponds to wartime Washington, whence came General Eisenhower's authority and to which he applied for things needed—men, money, and supplies.

Ever since he assumed high command, Eisenhower has had a chief of staff who was a demon for work and who did not mind injuring others' feelings by saying "no". In 1953, if the screams of anguish which sometimes came from congressmen and politicians were any indication, Sherman Adams, Assistant to the President, qualified for the post. He was also chief blametaker.

A former governor of New Hampshire and close Eisenhower campaign adviser, Adams runs the White House staff. He is on the job shortly after 7 A.M. At 8:30 A.M. he holds a crisp, businesslike staff meeting, when decision is made on what matters can be handled without the President and what must be brought to his attention. Then Adams and the staff members in whose provinces the weighty matters lie are ready to brief Ike.

Another feature of the Eisenhower ad-

ministration developed when Congress, facing an election year in 1954, showed itself unwilling to grapple with one issue after another. The President turned these policy issues over to bipartisan commissions and committees, indicating that he would accept their group decisions.

By the time Congress adjourned early in August, many policy-making bodies were at work: on universal military training, tax revision, antitrust law enforcement, Taft-Hartley labor-law revision, foreign trade, and a farm program.

Critics termed this "government by postponement" and "face saving". They called Ike a weak President and deplored "lack of leadership". Right-wingers demanded greater turnaway from policies of previous administrations.

Toward the end of the year there were signs of restiveness among the voters. The Democrats won two elections, in Wisconsin and New Jersey, to fill vacant congressional seats that had long been Republican. A Democratic governor was elected in New Jersey.

"As of today," said Republican National Chairman Hall, "we are in trouble."

"I've lost skirmishes before," said the President.

And so he had. In 1943 in North Africa, he had bogged down at Kasserine Pass and nearly lost his job. After his nomination, his campaign had so slowed down in August that the pro-Eisenhower *New York World Telegram* declared ". . . Ike is running like a dry creek".

Said one of his friends: "I had misgivings during the pre-convention campaign and between August and October, when Eisenhower and Stevenson were campaigning for the presidency. But each time, after I thought the twelfth hour was about to strike, Ike suddenly moved with force and confidence. He looks long at problems before he decides. But after he decides, he is an express train."

**IKE'S FAVORITE PHOTO:** Golfing in Augusta, Ga., he formally greets his grandson Dwight, 5

MEMBERS OF THE CABINET COMPRISE THE Eisenhower "first team". At the end of his inaugural address the new Chief Executive turned to kiss his wife, then went to the President's Room, a glass-chandeliered marble horror in the Senate wing of the Capitol. There he signed his first executive order, a message to the Senate nominating eight first-team members:

Secretary of State: John Foster Dulles of New York

Secretary of the Treasury: George M. Humphrey of Ohio

Attorney General: Herbert Brownell Jr. of New York

Postmaster General: Arthur E. Summerfield of Michigan

Secretary of the Interior: Douglas McKay of Oregon

Secretary of Agriculture: Ezra Taft Benson of Utah

Secretary of Commerce: Sinclair Weeks of Massachusetts

Secretary of Labor: Martin P. Durkin of Maryland

Nomination of the ninth member, Charles E. Wilson of Michigan, to become Secretary of Defense, was postponed. Mr. Wilson and the Senate Armed Services Committee, which was expected to recommend his confirmation, were in a pickle.

Choice of Wilson, president of General Motors, world's largest corporation, to

# TEAM

**IKE'S FIRST CABINET** arrives for his inauguration. The Secretaries by number: 1) Dulles (State), 2) Humphrey (Treasury), 3) Wilson (Defense), 4) Brownell (Justice), 5) Summerfield (Post Office), 6) McKay (Interior), 7) Benson (Agriculture), 8) Weeks (Commerce), 9) Durkin (Labor), 10) Lodge (Ambassador to U.N.), 11) Hobby (Health, Education and Welfare)

head the government's biggest, freest-spending department seemed to most senators a happy one. But, asked Senator Byrd of Virginia, what about Section 433, Title 18, U.S. Code?

Apparently no one had given it much thought. Section 433 plainly says that any government official who does business with a firm in which he has an interest, or from which he draws a profit, faces two years in jail and a $2,000 fine.

The Defense Department is General Motors' biggest customer—$5 billion in orders were then on the books. Although Wilson had severed all official connection with G.M. before his nomination, his G.M. stockholdings and forthcoming bonuses would add up to about $2.7 million.

Mr. Wilson balked at casting all this loose. Committee members didn't see why he should be beyond the law. If the occasion arose, Senator Hendrickson asked, could he make a decision "adverse" to General Motors?

"Yes, sir, I could," he said, then added some inept words which returned to plague him throughout 1953.

"I cannot conceive of one, however, because for years I have thought that what was good for our country was good for General Motors, and vice versa."

The white-haired industrialist, seething after many hours of senatorial questioning, finally boiled over. "I really feel you are giving me quite a pushing around," he said. "My God, I am making a great sacrifice to come down here!"

This outburst won him no friends on the committee, for many senators also go to Washington at financial sacrifice. Republican senators called at the White House. Make Wilson sell his stock, they said, or withdraw his nomination. Wilson sold his stock. Six days after inauguration, he was confirmed.

In the Wilson affair, the Eisenhower team fumbled at the kickoff in what it ex-

pected would be one of its strongest plays: businesslike operation of the executive branch by big businessmen. When a friendly congressman remarked that "Charlie Wilson is a lousy politician", he was also describing the new team's other business members. Their fundamental weakness was lack of political savvy and knowledge of how to deal with Congress. Their impatient or arrogant answers to questions in congressional committees were damaging.

Ultimately these officials found that government cannot be run like a corporation. In their own businesses, the high-

**EAGER HELPER** James Hagerty, the President's press secretary, awaits answer to message he brought Ike on speaker's platform at Massachusetts exposition

salaried executives had met with boards of directors once a month. As government officials, they had to spend long hours away from their desks, conferring with boards of directors—committees of Congress. During his first four months in office, Secretary Wilson spent thirty-one hours before congressional committees and 183 hours preparing his testimony. That added up to twenty-three eight-hour days. Nothing like that had happened at General Motors.

The businessmen in the new Cabinet had had to satisfy stockholders once a year at annual meetings. Now press and

radio would report their activities to the stockholders—the general public—every day. It was hard for some of them to learn that they must work and live in a goldfish bowl of public scrutiny.

When Secretary of the Treasury Humphrey was head of a big corporation, one job of the firm's public-relations department was allegedly to keep the boss's name out of the papers. In Washington, Humphrey was inaccessible to the press until a newspaperman wrote him, "I predict that soon you will find you need me as much as I need you."

Yet the two first-team members who

**PRIVATE LIFE:** Top-hatted Sec. Dulles adjusts tie before attending formal White House dinner

were in the hottest water with congressmen and politicians had already spent some years in Washington. They were the ministerial-looking Secretary of State Dulles, and Secretary of Agriculture Benson, one of the Twelve Apostles of the Mormon Church. The State Department has ever been a tempting target for congressmen. "Advice and consent" of the Senate are required to ratify the department's treaties and confirm its ambassadors and high officials; and senators are more generous with advice than they are with consent.

Dulles had been an international lawyer, United States senator, ambassador-at-large to the United Nations. He had drafted the post-World War II treaty with Japan. Two of his relatives had been secretaries of state: Grandfather John Foster, under Benjamin Harrison, and Uncle Robert Lansing, under Woodrow Wilson.

Consequently, when he took over his department, he knew what he was up against.

One fact aggravated his difficulties: it was his responsibility to formulate Republican foreign policy, and the Republican party was part internationalist and part isolationist.

**PUBLIC LIFE:** Bespectacled Sec. Hobby offers views on education to a House subcommittee

There was also fear in the State Department. Some officials were panicky over Senator Joe McCarthy, whose mildest criticism was that the department still followed the old Truman-Acheson line.

In two important respects, Dulles abandoned that line. He rejected the old policy of "containment" of the Soviet Union, and allowed its author, George Kennan, to retire. In its place he held out hope of the "liberation" of Russia's satellite peoples, though not by force.

Dean Acheson, Dulles' elegant predecessor, had been suave in dealing with foreign ministers. Dulles was irritatingly blunt, especially when expressing American impatience with Western Europe's snail-like progress toward unity, but by the end of the year, predictions that he would resign and be replaced by Governor Dewey of New York had died down.

## Benson's "Heresy"

However, resignation rumors continued regarding big, rawboned Secretary of Agriculture Ezra Taft Benson.

Less than three weeks after inauguration, a storm burst around Benson. It began when he told livestock men in St. Paul that lower farm prices would help stabilize the market, that government price supports should not "encourage uneconomic production" and cause heavy surpluses, and that subsidies should merely "provide insurance against disaster".

"Heresy!" farm statesmen in Congress fumed. Republicans like Senator Young of North Dakota demanded Benson's scalp. Democrats, from Russell of Georgia to Humphrey of Minnesota, were indignant in words but happy in the hope that Benson's policies would help elect a Democratic Congress in 1954.

Meantime, Benson had to administer the parity law (rigid crop control and price support), which had more than a year to go. When early-summer drought parched feed lots in the cattle country, the New-Dealish Farmers' Union mobilized small stock raisers for a futile "march" on Washington. In Wisconsin a Republican farm district elected its first Democratic congressman. And the American Farm Bureau Federation, biggest farm organization in the country, which had supported Benson, showed signs of wavering at its December convention.

To avoid adding to the storm, Benson's subordinates worked out two stock leads for press releases from his office. Lead No. 1 broke bad news to farmers in this manner: "The Department of Agriculture reported". Lead No. 2 brought good news in this way: "Secretary Benson announced".

Although there was more to "report" than "announce", Benson predicted a new approach to the agricultural problem that would satisfy the farmers.

Benson is a praying man, leads his family in daily prayers, and prays silently during the day. From some quarters came the cynical gibe, "less piety and more parity". But Benson had spent nearly ten years in Washington as secretary of the National Council of Farmer Cooperatives, and he knows agriculture from the ground up. Whether he was to win or lose was for 1954 to decide.

One Eisenhower Cabinet member lost during 1953, and resigned. Thus ended the Democrats' quip that "Ike's Cabinet has several millionaires and one plumber". Secretary of Labor Martin Durkin, a Stevenson supporter and head of the A.F.L. Plumbing and Pipe Fitting Industry union, was not deliriously happy in his job. He complained to friends that, when he entered a room, other officials "all stop talking". Durkin's chief ambition was to go before the A.F.L. convention in September with an administration-backed revision of the Taft-Hartley labor law. He did go before the convention, but as ex-Secretary of Labor, and with a charge that Eisenhower had repudiated his endorsement of proposed Taft-Hartley revisions.

When Vice President Nixon tried to assure the convention that a "misunderstanding" had caused Durkin's resignation, he was drowned out by mocking laughter. The unhappy Mr. Durkin returned to his plumbers' union. His successor was a management man, James P. Mitchell, vice president in charge of personnel and labor relations for Bloomingdale's department store in New York City.

## Humphrey Gives Thanks

Less dust was raised around George Magoffin Humphrey. "When I say my prayers," said the new Secretary of the Treasury, "I thank my Maker I'm not Ezra Benson." All Humphrey had to do was collect taxes, borrow money, pay the government's bills, and see to it that none of these complex operations fouled the national economy. He did everything he was supposed to do during 1953 with few voices uplifted in anger against him.

There were some grumbles in the spring when the Treasury began borrowing and refunding at higher interest rates. And late in July Humphrey failed to convince Congress that the federal debt limit should be raised from $275 billion to an all-time high of $290 billion.

Humphrey had been head of the M. A. Hanna Company, a Cleveland steelmaking firm with a flock of subsidiaries ranging from Great Lakes shipping to coal and iron mines and textiles. Except for "raising money for all of Bob Taft's campaigns", he had never mixed in politics, and it was "against all my beliefs for

businessmen to go into government". He was looking forward to retirement at his Holiday Hill Farm outside Cleveland when he was tapped for the Treasury.

General Lucius Clay, Eisenhower's chief talent scout, had been impressed by Humphrey's incisiveness and had recommended him. When the President-elect sized him up for the Treasury post, the two men took an instant liking to each other. "I see you part your hair the same way I do," said Eisenhower to the equally bald Humphrey.

There are similarities in the backgrounds of four other Cabinet members—Attorney General Brownell, Postmaster General Summerfield, Secretary of the Interior McKay, and Secretary of Commerce Weeks. All four had participated in politics. McKay had been governor of Oregon. Brownell and Summerfield had been chairmen of the Republican National Committee. Weeks had been its treasurer, and had raised $6 million for the Eisenhower campaign. All four had been for Eisenhower before the Chicago convention.

McKay and Summerfield had started as office boys, ultimately became automobile dealers. Summerfield had the biggest Chevrolet agency in Michigan; McKay's Chevrolet agency was biggest in Oregon. Counting Wilson, that made three Cabinet members with General Motors connections.

When the Post Office Department planned a 3¢ stamp celebrating fifty years of the trucking industry, Summerfield recognized the truck in the stamp design —a Reo. He ordered the stamp redesigned with a truck looking like no other.

New Cabinet heads had troubles both with pressure groups and congressional critics. Secretary of Commerce Weeks fired, then took back, Director Allen V. Astin of the National Bureau of Standards, in a hassle over the bureau's tests

**VICE PRESIDENT** Nixon and wife pose for family portrait with daughters Patricia (left) and Julie

of a storage-battery additive. Secretary of the Interior McKay, who believes in encouraging taxable, private electric power, was the target of public-ownership groups.

The tenth member of the Eisenhower Cabinet arrived when Congress created the Department of Health, Education and Welfare. This was carved out of the Social Security Administration and includes the Public Health Service—with the biggest of all medical research centers—and the Office of Education. It affects the lives of 67,000,000 people and disburses some $4 billion a year.

## Mrs. Secretary Hobby

The department is headed by a woman whose first name is Indian for "forget". Oveta Culp Hobby, 48, wife of a former governor of Texas, 75, and owner of the *Houston Post*, is the second woman to hold Cabinet rank. Unlike Frances Perkins, who was "Madam Secretary" of F.D.R.'s Department of Labor, Mrs. Hobby prefers to be addressed as "Mrs. Secretary". Eisenhower had known her when she was World War II commander of the W.A.C.'s. She had supported him in the Texas pre-convention primaries, and had headed "Democrats for Eisenhower" during the 1952 presidential campaign.

Mrs. Hobby's Cabinet rank wrinkled the brows of Washington hostesses. What was the dinner-table precedence for her husband? Eventually it was decided that, since a Cabinet officer's wife assumes her husband's rank, a Cabinet officer's husband should have the same honor. So Will Hobby sits at table above and not below the salt.

Between Cabinet and Congress there might have been greater friction but for a young man named Richard Nixon.

Death has dealt Vice Presidents even hands: seven have died in office; seven have inherited the presidency. A Vice President's traditional duties are not the pace that kills. Daytimes, he presides over the Senate, with little to say beyond: "The clerk will call the roll." Nighttimes, he is the administration's official diner-out. A Vice President in the prime of life should be able to jump into dinner-coat work clothes in five minutes.

Richard M. Nixon, thirty-sixth Vice President, still goes out four or five nights a week to dine for his country. Daytimes, he soon became the most useful member of the Eisenhower team.

Dictionaries define "vice president" as a substitute or deputy. Dwight Eisenhower is the first Chief Executive to take that definition literally. In place of the President, Nixon presides over the National Security Council, an inner cabinet in which defense and international policies are hammered out before State and Defense departments carry them out.

Since solemn Calvin Coolidge, Vice Presidents have attended Cabinet meetings, but only Nixon has conducted them, sitting at the head of the long elliptical Cabinet table when Ike was out of town. This 40-year-old California Quaker, with a nose like Bob Hope's and a grin like Larry Parks', is actually Assistant President.

Not all this was planned. Nixon merely stepped into a vacuum. He was the only experienced politician on a green team. Except for Dulles and Weeks, who had sat briefly in the Senate, no Eisenhower Cabineteer had had Washington legislative experience. In his ten-year legislative career, Nixon had been both representative and senator, and he knows Republican and Democratic leaders of both houses intimately.

Before the Eighty-third Congress was a month old, Nixon discovered sentiment among new congressmen for the Bricker

Amendment, which would limit the Executive's treaty-making powers, and advised the White House not to buck it but to dilute it. He found two powerful Democratic senators in a slow boil over being ignored in supposedly bipartisan foreign policy. Nixon suggested a White House luncheon invitation, and everything was dandy with Georgia's Russell and George.

When Nixon was on the House Un-American Activities Committee, he had trapped highly placed Alger Hiss into admissions which had sent him to jail. That feat gave him a spy-catching reputation above that of later probers. Twice he deflected impetuous Red-hunting Representative Velde from embarrassing the G.O.P., and twice steered McCarthy from open breaks with the administration.

### "Niku San" in Asia

In 1953, a fact-finding, friend-winning trip through Asia, at Eisenhower's order, added to Nixon's prestige. Twelve months before, disclosures of his "California fund" had put his political career on the brink of ruin. His dramatic TV explanation of his personal finances and the uses to which he had put money raised by California friends saved the day and kept him on the Republican ticket, with Eisenhower's reassuring: "He's my boy!"

There have been few tours like the round-the-world-in-seventy-days flight of Dick Nixon and Pat, his trim, redheaded wife. With stop-offs from New Zealand to Libya, they visited nineteen countries on their 45,000-mile journey. In each country Nixon saw business people and labor leaders, as well as top government officials. He was briefed by American embassy officials; then went about largely on his own to mingle with humbler folk.

"Old Asia hands" told him such behavior "just isn't done", that natives would laugh at it. And laugh they did—with pleasure. The Vice President traveled through Asia shaking hands like a congressman up for re-election. Crowds in Japan, Malaya, Indonesia, and India had never seen the like before, and they loved it.

In Malaya, Nixon held up a reception line of starchy British officials to clasp hands with a barefoot boy peering at the goings on through a wire fence. In Singapore, inhabitants of the most caste-conscious white settlement in Asia gagged over their gin and quinine at a newspaper photograph of Nixon in a crowd of natives, and the caption: NIXON GREETS THE COMMON MAN.

A photograph of him shaking hands with a Chinese boy preceded him to Hong Kong, where he made an unscheduled visit to a slum district and was almost mobbed by friendly Chinese who recognized him from his pictures. At Osaka, in Japan, "Niku-San" drew bigger crowds than the Emperor, because, said Japanese, "he shakes hands with people". The Nixons estimate they pumped 100,-000 hands during their tour.

There were a few Communist demonstrations in Australia, Japan, and Burma. At Pegu, near Rangoon, a welcoming crowd included Communists bearing placards: "Go Back, Warmonger, Valet of Wall Street". The Vice President walked up to one demonstrator, saying, "I notice these cards are addressed to Mr. Nixon. I am Nixon and I'm glad to know you."

Nixon returned to this country convinced that there is more liking for America among Asians than their leaders express. One good-will trip alone may not have altered American-Asian relations, but it did raise a question: had there been more aloof headshaking than cordial handshaking in our Asia policy?

Fitzpatrick in
the St. Louis
Post-Dispatch

**HEARTBREAK RIDGES ON THE HOME FRONT**

# CONGRESS

WHEN THE NEW EIGHTY-THIRD CONGRESS met on Jan. 3, 1953, Republicans had one more Senate seat than Democrats and ten more House seats. Grizzled Democrat Sam Rayburn of Texas yielded Speakership of the House to Republican Joe Martin of Massachusetts and became House Minority Leader.

"Time will tell whether they can really run a government," Rayburn said of the Republicans. "Any jackass can kick a barn door down, but it takes a carpenter to build it back."

The new Congress did both. Three investigating committees, hunting both Reds and publicity, continued to kick holes in the Truman administration. But

Congress also did some carpentering. Out of 10,695 bills introduced, only 515 became laws, ranging from appropriations to a measure modernizing the charter of the Washington Gas Light Company.

Congress cut $3.4 billion from the Eisenhower budget. It also extended the excess-profits tax through 1953, gave title to offshore tidelands to the states, authorized sending surplus food to needy nations, and approved creation of a new Federal Department of Health, Education and Welfare.

In doing what they did, senators and representatives uttered 16,000,000 words. In support of the 515 bills they passed,

**REPUBLICAN SYMBOLS**—globe, elephant (carried by House Speaker Martin), portrait of Gen. Douglas MacArthur—accompany the party's return to power

**THE FAMILIAR FACE** of Ohio's Sen. Robert Taft is captured in this candid photograph, taken at a press conference some months before his death

or in viewing them with alarm, they filled 11,420 pages of the *Congressional Record,* at a printing cost of $84 a page.

The President did not get all he wanted in taxes or in foreign aid. Congress took no action at all on such recommended legislation as prompt revision of the Taft-Hartley Act, a new farm program based on flexible rather than rigid price supports, extension of Social Security, overhaul of the McCarran Immigration Act, and statehood for Hawaii.

Longest talk on the Senate floor during 1953 was by slight, bulletheaded Wayne Morse of Oregon, a former law-school dean. Elected as a Republican, he turned "Independent" in protest against the Eisenhower campaign platform.

In the Eighty-third Congress, Morse was given no important committee posts. He therefore took the floor almost every Friday afternoon to deliver an hour-long "report of the Independent party" on the week's legislative doings.

One April forenoon Morse walked into the Senate chamber wearing a freshly pressed blue suit with a pink rose in one lapel. At 11:40 he took the floor to denounce a bill which would extend state title to offshore lands and resources (oil) from 3 to 10½ miles. At dinnertime he was still denouncing. When the dawn's early light filtered through the Senate chamber's glass ceiling, he was still on his feet, discussing states' rights, horseback riding, and boloney.

At 10 A.M. he sat down, suit rumpled, pink rose wilted, and vastly pleased with himself. He had spoken for twenty-two hours and twenty-six minutes without once leaving the Senate floor. It cost $7000 to print his 100,000 words in the *Record*.

Morse's performance beat the long-distance speaking record made back in 1908 by Senator "Fighting Bob" La Follette (18 hrs., 23 min.). It was also the year's most spectacular—and most futile—opposition in Congress to a measure backed by the White House.

Early in 1952 the Supreme Court had declared that rights to offshore oil lands belong to the federal government. Eisenhower favored state ownership, delighting powerful oil interests and the revenue-hungry offshore-oil states of Texas, California, and Louisiana.

Four days before leaving the White House, President Truman had issued an executive order setting aside offshore oil lands as a naval oil reserve. Congress reversed him and gave these lands to the states, but not without delaying tactics by Morse and others.

On April 1 a little band of liberals in the Senate began dragging their feet against this measure. They talked for thirty-five days, and then let the Senate pass the bill. In the House the measure went through in forty minutes.

Less spectacular but more stubborn opposition to Eisenhower-backed legislation came from 77-year-old Dan Reed, a New York Republican congressman from the Concord-grape country along Lake Erie. He had been in Congress since 1918, and when the Republicans took over in 1953 he became chairman of the powerful House Ways and Means Com-

**THE BELOVED CAPITOL** where Taft served so long is the backdrop as an honor guard bears his body down the steps following funeral services

**REPUBLICAN** against Ike: Rep. Reed of New York argues loudly, but in vain, for lower taxes

mittee, where all money-raising bills originate. The first day of the new Congress, he introduced a tax-cut measure which Republican members of his committee endorsed 15 to 0.

It provoked frowns at the White House and Treasury. The new team was just realizing that it wasn't so easy to balance the budget, after all. Also, the excess-profits tax was due to expire on June 30. Although Republicans had denounced this tax as "bad" during the campaign, it brought in $800 million every half year. Word went to the Capitol that the administration wanted E.P.T. extended until Jan. 1, 1954.

"No," said Dan Reed, setting a granite-like chin. "Tax reduction was a campaign promise."

"Yes, but—" said White House people.

"No," said Dan Reed.

The super-powerful House Rules Committee refused to allow the Ways and Means Committee's tax-cut bill to come before the House. Whereupon Dan Reed refused to call his committee together to act upon extending E.P.T. Speaker Joe Martin visited stubborn Dan, who now had a new nickname, "Syngman Reed", after an equally stubborn old gentleman in Korea.

"We were one word apart," said Speaker Joe. "He said 'no'. I said 'yes'."

Time was running out. Dan Reed was invited to the White House. "Dan," said the President, turning on the Eisenhower charm, "all I'm asking you to do is call a meeting of your committee to consider E.P.T.—and let the democratic processes work."

"I'm afraid, Mr. President," said Reed coldly, "you don't understand how democratic processes work in Congress."

Perhaps Dan Reed, for all his experience, didn't understand, either. Speaker Martin sought to line up the Rules Committee to bring the E.P.T. bill to the floor and thus circumvent Reed's committee. As legislative manners, this course was rude. But Speaker Joe, though he had plumped for either Taft or MacArthur for President, would go down the line for any President who was a Republican. He pushed aside his forelock and said, "This is war."

The war didn't last long. Martin didn't have to persuade the Rules Committee to act. He found enough Ways and Means committeemen willing to extend E.P.T., and Reed finally capitulated and called his committee together after a sit-down of nearly five months. When the vote was taken in the House, Reed's was one of the 77 against. "I'm not surrendering," he said in his trumpeting baritone. Republicans and Democrats alike stood up and cheered.

Eisenhower's nomination of Charles ("Chip") Bohlen as Ambassador to Moscow was also forced down reluctant senatorial throats. Chip Bohlen, 48, with twenty-five years in the Foreign Service, is one of the few American diplomats who speak Russian fluently. He had been translator for F.D.R. at the Yalta conference with Churchill and Stalin during World War II, and for Truman and Byrnes at the Potsdam conference following the surrender of Germany. For playing this role he was suspect by hardshell senators.

Secretary Dulles said he found nothing against Bohlen that adversely affected his usefulness in Moscow. Senator Knowland of California supported Dulles—whereupon Joe McCarthy of Wisconsin questioned the honesty of both. When McCarthy suggested a lie-detector test for

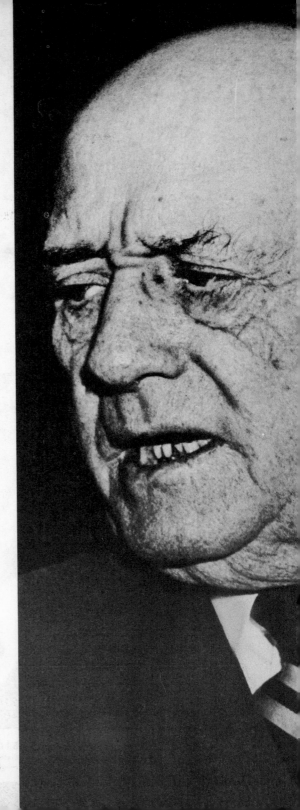

**DEMOCRAT** against Ike: House Minority Leader Rayburn of Texas speaks for wait-and-see element

**BIG SMILE** of Atty. Gen. Brownell as he is kissed by Washington "Cherry Blossom Queen" also might bespeak his pride in G.O.P. accomplishments

Bohlen and expressed further distrust of Dulles, Senator Taft, then Senate Majority Leader, took the floor. His face was red with anger, and in a voice as harsh as a crosscut saw he termed McCarthy's proposal "ridiculous".

Taft did not question Dulles' judgment about Bohlen, but suggested that two senators go over the Bohlen file and report their findings. The Senate agreed, and Taft and Senator Sparkman of Alabama, Democratic vice presidential nominee in 1952, were named. They reported that they found nothing even remotely suggesting that Bohlen might be a security risk.

McCarthy, with Senator McCarran, his Democratic ally, now said Bohlen should be rejected because he was "one of the Acheson gang".

Then came sounds from the White House. The President told a press conference he knew Bohlen well. He had high regard for him and his ability. Moreover, he was the man best qualified for the Moscow post. It was because he was best that his name had gone to the Senate in the first place. The next day Bohlen was confirmed by a large majority, 74 to 13.

Largely through Taft's prestige, Republican senators of diverse purpose and philosophy were kept from open breaks with the White House. But within a few weeks after the Bohlen affair, Eisenhower was to lose Bob Taft's support—for a reason more serious and lasting than mere disagreement.

## The Death of Taft

Late in June, 1953, a tall, bespectacled man in his middle 60's, wearing a rumpled suit, hobbled on crutches into New York Hospital. He was registered as "Howard Roberts Jr." and put to bed. Across the street was Memorial Center for Cancer and Allied Diseases. The patient might have been taken there, but didn't wish to be.

As it was, top specialists from Memorial visited him. He was given X-ray treatments to ease his pains, and received transfusions for anemia. Early in July he was wheeled into an operating room, and surgeons found incurable malignant tumors. After the patient was sewed up, a score of specialists agreed that nothing more could be done except to make him comfortable. On Friday morning, July 31, he died.

In Washington that morning, a Senate debate over raising the federal debt limit was interrupted for a quorum call. Trooping in from offices and committee rooms, ninety-one senators answered to their names and heard Senator John W. Bricker of Ohio, in faltering tones of deep emotion, announce the death of Robert A. Taft.

Taft had entered the New York Hospital as "Mr. Roberts" so that news of his being there would be kept temporarily from his invalid wife. A medical checkup the year before, on the eve of his pre-convention campaign for the 1952 presidential nomination, had found nothing wrong.

But in April, 1953, while playing golf with President Eisenhower at Augusta, Ga., Taft complained of pains in the legs. Between hospital tests, he returned to Washington in June for a few hours in the Senate.

"Bill," he said to Senator Knowland of California, "I have to stay off my feet a good deal for the rest of the session. I'd like you to act as floor leader."

Then he turned to Minority Leader Lyndon Johnson and said, "I'll be back in January," and, leaning on his crutches, he walked out of the Senate for the last time. And he knew it was the last time.

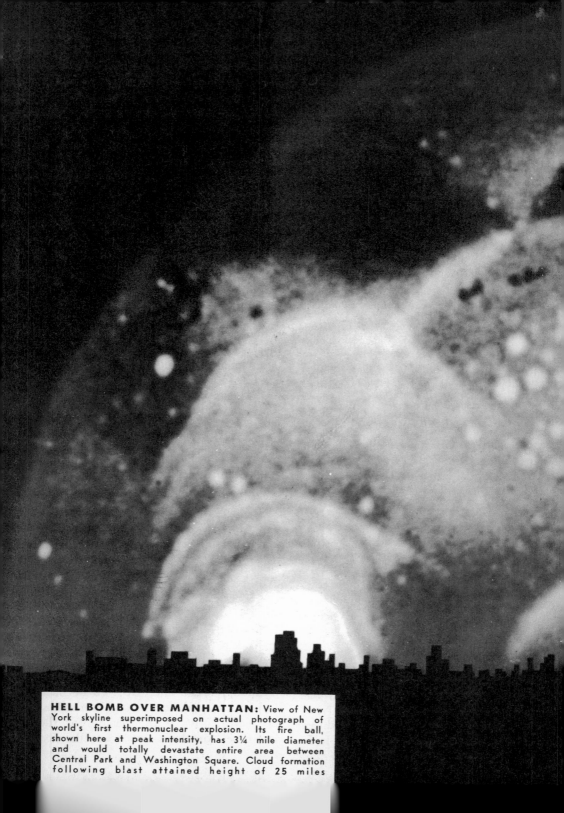

**HELL BOMB OVER MANHATTAN:** View of New York skyline superimposed on actual photograph of world's first thermonuclear explosion. Its fire ball, shown here at peak intensity, has 3¼ mile diameter and would totally devastate entire area between Central Park and Washington Square. Cloud formation following blast attained height of 25 miles

# DEFENSE

A HALF HOUR AFTER BEING SWORN IN AS Secretary of Defense, Charles E. Wilson walked into his huge Pentagon office. Against his white "security" telephone he propped a framed motto he had brought from Detroit—"Nullo Bastardo Carborundum", which is illegitimate Latin for "Don't let the bastards wear you down". Then, with cigarette dangling from a corner of his mouth and spilling ashes on his coat lapels, he punched a buzzer and said to a Marine Corps aide, "Let's go to work."

He had plenty to do. His orders were to produce more defense for less money. According to a Pentagon wisecrack, what was wanted was "a bigger bang for a buck".

The armed services got a bigger bang. More mushroom-shaped clouds rose over the Nevada desert. Atomic artillery became a reality. Fantastic new guided missiles were in production. By the end of 1953 an atomic submarine awaited christening by Mrs. Eisenhower.

The armed services also got fewer bucks. Yet, like a fat man forced on a diet by doctor's orders, they seemed healthier, even stronger. By the end of 1953, U.S. defense was considered so strong that a potential aggressor would think twice before starting anything.

To be Deputy Secretary of Defense, Wilson brought with him quick-thinking Roger M. Kyes, who had been his chief assistant at General Motors. He gave Kyes a free hand and the toughest, meanest job in the department: budget and upper-level administrative reorganization.

Kyes was 47, tall (6 ft. 4 in.), and conscious of having a face like a medieval gargoyle. "I'm the ugliest-looking man in Washington since Abe Lincoln," he admitted.

Wilson and Kyes found the Pentagon swarming with 950 committees and boards. ("A board," runs an old Navy saying, "is long, narrow, and wooden.") Wilson got seven new assistant secretaries, who rode herd on what boards, committees, and commissions he couldn't abolish.

"There's a yowl every time I look into something," Wilson commented. He and Kyes looked into Defense Department research. They found 8000 different projects, with appropriations amounting to more than $1.25 billion a year. Even to take inventory of them and describe their work would cost $125,000. But Wilson and Kyes shucked as many unimportant research projects as they could, including an inquiry into what makes potatoes brown.

The services were top-heavy with generals and admirals. The Air Force had two generals for every five second lieutenants, and more colonels than first and second lieutenants combined. On V.E. Day, 1945, the Army had 1074 generals for 6,000,000 men; on Ike Day, 1953, it had 499 generals for 1,500,000 men. Wilson and Talbott found the Air Force had 109 military bands—one group of musicians to every 9000 airmen. They cut the number to forty-seven.

A reported shortage of ammunition in Korea was blowing up into a scandal. Under the Army's antiquated accounting system, ordnance people once thought they had no money, when actually they had $2 billion of unexpended funds. Contracts meandered through forty-two offices and over 200 desks before manufacturers got word to go ahead.

Wilson and Kyes found that the cost of merely preparing a defense budget was $30 million. They turned for help to a quiet, blond Iowan who had been

**RESEARCH,** essential to U.S. defense, is aided by devices like this: a wind tunnel with vanes allowing air to make a smooth right-angle turn at 60 m.p.h.

**MEN ON GUARD:** In these emergency suits, made to supply proper pressure to the wearer if cabin pressurization fails, U.S. pilots now fly above 50,000 ft.

**MACHINES ON GUARD:** Air Force jets streak over a long-range radar station, part of our "advance" defense line

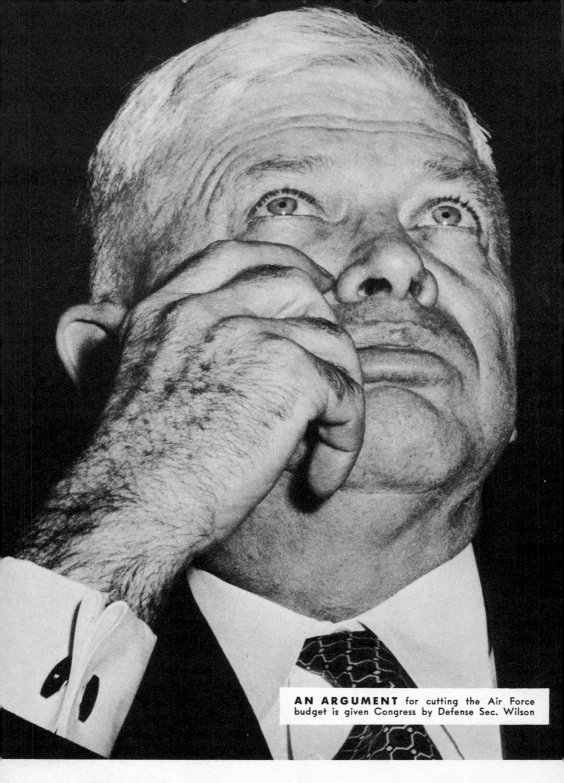

**AN ARGUMENT** for cutting the Air Force budget is given Congress by Defense Sec. Wilson

## CONGRESSIONAL CONCERN is dramatized by "dummy" N. Y. newspaper

Comptroller and Assistant Secretary of Defense ever since the three armed services merged in 1947. What figures Wilfred J. McNeil didn't carry in his head, he could find in a little black book always within reach.

McNeil convinced Wilson and Kyes that $5 billion could be lopped off the $16.5 billion Air Force item in the Truman budget. Among other things, the cut meant reducing the 143-wing program to 120 wings. McNeil argued that there was no need of appropriating for the larger force until air bases and trained personnel were available to handle it. His little black book showed the Air Force already overfinanced in aircraft production, and asking for money to replace planes that hadn't yet been built.

When the new defense budget of $34.4 billion came out with the Air Force cutback, Air Force officers solemnly warned Congress that any figure less than 143 wings would imperil the nation. At a White House bridge table the President turned a cold eye on Air Secretary Talbott. "I understand you're not supporting the budget," he said. Talbott hastily assured his host that he would go along.

During a July-August fortnight, Congress passed the Eisenhower defense budget, fighting stopped in Korea, Malenkov said the Russians had the hydrogen bomb, and new chiefs of staff moved into the Pentagon.

The new Joint Chiefs were instructed to re-examine the whole scheme of American defense from the point of view of immediate danger, of a long period of international tension, and of economy. In October they made their recommendation: increase the armed forces at an annual cost of one third more than the current defense budget. Budget people hit the ceiling; the Joint Chiefs were reminded that they were to indicate cuts, not increased spending.

When civilian listeners came down from the ceiling, the Chairman of the Joint Chiefs of Staff, Admiral Arthur W. Radford, spoke. The prime obstacle to defense economy, he said in effect, was that the military had never been told what sort of war to prepare for. Consequently they had to guess and plan for anything, anywhere, any time.

This guessing was expensive. For example, policy makers had limited the scope and nature of the Korean War.

New weapons had not been used. But, concluded Radford, if the policy people would confide to the military what kind of warfare—atomic or conventional big war, conventional or atomic small war—we would wage in case of trouble, then the Joint Chiefs could take a "new look" at the problem.

The National Security Council (top advisory body on national-defense matters) did just that. It told the Joint Chiefs that, since new weapons comprise a big military advantage for the U.S., our defense plans should center around their use.

Each arm of the service had received a proportionate share of the defense dollar. Now the Joint Chiefs formulated a new concept. It called for regrouping the armed services around atomic weapons and guided-missile striking power. There would be a new balance of forces in which the importance of revolutionary new weapons would be fully recognized.

Greater emphasis would be placed upon air power, but the $5 billion Air Force cut would not be restored. Army and Navy strength would be reduced later on. Despite protests by General Ridgway and Admiral Carney, a budget based upon the new concept was approved by the National Security Council in December.

Never before had administration policy people committed themselves to the extent of advising the military what sort of war to get ready for.

Civilian control meant knocking a few heads together. One general talked back to Roger Kyes. "Look," said "Jolly Roger", flipping the starred insigne on the officer's shoulder strap, "I didn't come down here to shovel snow but to pluck stars."

When Navy Secretary Anderson called upon bureau chiefs for detailed reports, he was reminded that civilian Secretaries customarily had concerned themselves with broad policies and had left details to the admirals. When Anderson repeated his request for procurement details from the Bureau of Ships and got the same general answer, he relieved the bureau chief, Rear Admiral Homer N. Wallin, of his post.

Wallin figured in an ugly Navy feud over promotion of Hyman G. Rickover, the brainy, hard-driving engineering officer who developed the *Nautilus,* the world's first atomic-powered submarine. Shortly after the sub's keel was laid in

**SURPRISE MANEUVER:** After plane (right) hit sea on takeoff from carrier in background, Navy pilot is temporarily stuck between his parachute and rescue helicopter

1952, the Navy awarded Rickover, then a captain, the Legion of Merit medal for "the most important piece of development in the history of the Navy".

A day later, a selection board of nine admirals passed over Rickover and made two captains junior to him rear admirals. This decision was made in face of recommendations from the Secretary of the Navy and the Atomic Energy Commission, and was the second time Rickover had been turned down. Having been denied promotion twice in successive years,

he would have been forced to retire in June, 1953, after thirty years in the Navy.

When other Navy men had shied from appointment to Oak Ridge, the government's atomic plant in Tennessee, Rickover wangled a detail to study nuclear energy there. Dedicated to the idea of an atomic submarine, he returned to a Navy in which airmen, who had won ascendancy over surface men, had small interest in undersurface craft, except to destroy enemy ones. But old submariner Admiral Chester Nimitz was still Chief of Naval

Operations. He signed a letter, written by Rickover, endorsing the atomic submarine, and the first hurdle was passed.

After authorization, all that remained to be done was to devise an atomic steam plant—a spectacular development—solve a few previously unsolved problems of metallurgy and radiant activity, and launch a nuclear-powered submarine in January, 1954. Under Rickover, all these objectives were achieved.

Meanwhile, two big-circulation magazines carried articles by admirals who hailed the birth of the atomic submarine but failed to give credit to the man who developed it. One author was Admiral Wallin, who had become chief of the bureau in which Rickover's Nuclear Power Division reposed. When, in late 1953, a storm broke in Congress over this cavalier treatment of Rickover, the White House got busy, and Captain Rickover became a rear admiral before his retirement deadline.

Even then not all inhabitants of "Navy Country" in the Pentagon gave up. A few days before Mrs. Mamie Eisenhower was to whack a bottle of upstate New York champagne over the blunt bow of the *Nautilus,* somebody leaked to the press a statement that the new sub wasn't much, merely a "test vehicle".

That brought wire-burning telephone calls from the White House and Atomic Energy Commission, and a few hours of desk pounding in Secretary Wilson's office. The next day the officer suspected of the leak ate humble pie in the Pentagon pressroom. And thus was launched the age of atomic ship propulsion.

**GUIDED MISSILES** figure in current defense plans of all the Western allies. This high-speed antiaircraft rocket is being launched at a test station in Australia

**BY REMOTE CONTROL** the Nike, an Army guided missile, comes in at 1,500 m.p.h. to knock down a B-17 target plane. Radar-guided, Nike has range of 30 miles

# The OPPOSITION

AFTER HIS DEFEAT IN THE LAST PRESI-dential election, Adlai Stevenson expressed Democratic party hopes in golfing terms: "We're interested in the figure 108—out in '52, back in '56."

Actually, Democrats are hopeful of coming back in the '54 congressional elections. At the end of 1953 they had a majority of one in the Senate but needed three or four more seats to control the House. Since 1900, in fifteen out of sixteen congressional elections in non-presidential years, the party out of power has gained seats.

During 1953, Democrats in Congress behaved as though they had elected Eisenhower. Democratic votes in Congress made possible most of the Eisenhower-backed legislation that was enacted. In the Senate, Charles Bohlen was confirmed as Ambassador to Russia only because five more Democrats than Republicans voted for him. Only two Democrats opposed him.

In the House, foreign aid was opposed by 40 percent of the Republicans and would have failed but for Democratic

**IN KOREA** Stevenson wears Navy flier's helmet and immersion suit for a flight in a dive bomber

enhower came not from Democrats but Republicans. Said Pennsylvania's Representative Hugh Scott, a former chairman of the Republican National Committee: "A number of our Republican 'ins' are still acting as if they were 'outs'. Having spent twenty years in opposition, they snipe at the administration from habit."

Senator Wiley, chairman of the Foreign Relations Committee and a Wisconsin colleague of Joe McCarthy, warned against his party's "saboteurs, malcontents, and gold bricks". The core of Republican opposition to Eisenhower consisted of a dozen senators and between two and three dozen representatives belonging to the party's extreme right wing.

The members of the right wing supported McCarthy. They endorsed the Bricker Amendment, which would have tinkered with the President's treaty-making power. They saw no difference between Dulles and Acheson. Said one news commentator, "To them a security risk is any Democrat holding a government job." To Representative Scott and his friends, they are "old fuds", most of whom come from "safe" districts which return them to Washington time and again and thus enable them, under the seniority system, to occupy powerful committee chairmanships.

During the 1953 session, Democratic legislators took their cue from House Democratic Leader Sam Rayburn, who has served longer in the House than any other member and was Speaker longer than any other legislator in history.

He laid down a policy of "constructive opposition". Let the Republicans squabble among themselves, but don't let a good measure die merely because it is introduced by the G.O.P. In the spring when Republican conservatives blocked a six-months' extension of the excess-profits tax, Rayburn mustered enough

votes. There were eighty-three roll-call votes on Eisenhower legislation in Congress. Fifty-eight would have been lost without the aid of Democrats. Said Adlai Stevenson: "The greatest beneficiary of the Democratic party these last few months has been President Eisenhower."

The most relentless opposition to Eis-

Democratic votes to get the bill passed.

His strategy was paralleled in the Senate partially because its Minority Leader, Lyndon Johnson, was a Rayburn protégé when he first went to Congress. Also, both Democratic leaders would be up for re-election in 1954 in Texas, a State which plumped for Eisenhower, though it returned Democrats to Congress.

Johnson, 44, is the youngest man ever to become a party leader in the upper house. He is seldom on the floor, and a Senate speech by him is rarer still. Most of his work is done in the Democratic cloakroom. At a June party-unity dinner in Mississippi, where Ike carried fourteen counties, he urged Democrats to "save" Eisenhower from the Republicans. Johnson charged that the Republican Old Guard was sabotaging the President's legislative program. "The American people," he said, "elected President Eisenhower to preserve the strength, the prosperity, and the freedom of America. That platform will be realized only if they give him a Democratic Congress in 1954. . . ."

Complicating an already strange political situation, at the end of 1953 New York Governor Thomas Dewey and Attorney General Herbert Brownell made some startling accusations. In 1948, Dewey, whose campaign manager was Brownell, was so confident of winning the presidential election that he lost it. At that time the Dewey-Brownell strategy was to speak softly and not be nasty to the Democrats. But in the late fall of 1953, shortly before Eisenhower announced a legislative program which

**IN INDIA** two dancers clad as "monkey guards" join our No. 1 Democrat at an official reception

would need Democratic support, Brownell and Dewey cut loose.

Brownell charged that Harry Dexter White "was known to be a Communist spy by the very people who appointed him". Although Brownell later explained he did not mean to accuse ex-President Truman of malfeasance, his attack angered Democrats who were counted upon to vote for Ike's program.

A month later, Dewey delivered a brass-knuckled speech. He recalled to Connecticut Republicans "two and a half years of horror" in Korea during the Truman administration. "Whenever anybody mentions the words Truman and Democrats to you," he said, "for the rest of your lives remember those words are synonymous with Americans dying, thousands of miles from home, because they didn't have the ammunition to defend themselves. Remember that the words Truman and Democrat mean diplomatic failure, death, and a government infested with spies and traitors."

Democrats resented that speech, said plenty, but did not know how to retaliate. In late 1953 they still lacked a first-rate issue. They would have liked to exploit farm discontent, but, aside from the South, their party's main strength lies in the cities, whose populations are consumers, not farmers. If they supported Eisenhower's legislative program they would help build up a record of Republican achievement. If they opposed it, they would be denounced as obstructionists.

The Republicans also lacked issues on which they could unite. They were divided over Taft-Hartley, foreign trade, farm-price support, taxes, and especially "McCarthyism". Yet the Republicans cannot afford another congressional session as barren of achievement as the last one.

It seemed to Republican Senator Ralph Flanders of Vermont that Republicans were ". . . devoting too much time to making a record against the Truman administration. Are we really going to hitch our buggy to that old nag and expect to get anywhere by flogging it? Great Godfrey! That horse is dead."

Apparently someone in the Washington post office had the same idea. At the end of 1953 a copy of Northeast Airlines' annual report was mailed to shareholder "Harry S. Truman, 1600 Pennsylvania Avenue, Washington, D.C." Back it came, the envelope stamped "Moved. Address Unknown."

But Harry Truman had not disappeared. When he left the White House on Jan. 20, 1953, a couple of trucks preceded him. They contained several-score

filing cabinets, personal records, a neatly catalogued library, thirty suits of clothes, Margaret Truman's piano, and Mrs. Truman's TV set and demitasse collection. The records went to storage in Kansas City Court House to be consulted during preparation of forthcoming Truman memoirs. The remainder of the goods went to the high-ceilinged mid-Victorian Truman home in Independence, Mo.

No recent President left the White House in such a carefree state of mind. Mr. Truman suffered neither from ill-health nor gnawing bitterness of defeat. Crowds no longer pestered him, merely friendly well-wishers. Elective office had no more attraction; the word was "no" to suggestions that he run for senator.

In nearly all political matters Harry Truman deferred to Adlai Stevenson, for "After all, I'm the man who pushed him into this business in the first place."

Whether Stevenson would be "pushed into this business" again was problematical in 1953. He declined Secretary of State Dulles' invitation to join the U.S. delegation to the United Nations.

Stevenson's six-month round-the-world trip was an energetic, fact-finding tour. It also astonished many foreign Stevenson admirers who expected—and some hoped —to hear denunciation of the Eisenhower administration and McCarthyism. Instead, ". . . while abroad I never criticized the handling of our foreign affairs; rather I have sought to explain American attitudes and positions when I had to as best I could".

To questions, at home and abroad, whether he would again seek presidential nomination, he repeated, "I don't know, and if I did, I wouldn't tell you."

**CONVICTED RED** Robert Thompson, captured after two years in hiding, starts for jail at last

**CONVICTED SPIES** Julius and Ethel Rosenberg: they were executed

# COMMUNISM

IN 1953, TWO CONVICTED SPIES DIED IN THE electric chair; thirty dedicated Communists were sentenced to jail; a former U.S. Treasury official, five years dead, was the cause of the year's liveliest political controversy; the nation's most popular TV actress revealed that she had once registered as a Communist to please her grandfather; and, for "security reasons", 1456 persons were fired from the government.

The most dramatic event of the year was the execution of the Rosenbergs. An electrician ended the lives of the Rosenbergs one evening in June. He earned $300 by twice pulling a switch in Sing

Sing prison. He also ended more than two years of legal maneuvers as well as world-wide agitation to commute the Rosenbergs' sentences.

In the twenty-six months between conviction and execution, the defense made eight court appeals, raised over twenty points of law in petitions for writs, and sent three formal appeals to the White House.

In the view of most Americans the Rosenbergs' guilt had been established beyond the shadow of a doubt. As President Eisenhower stated in explanation of his final denial of executive clemency: ". . . The Rosenbergs have received the benefit of every safeguard which American justice can provide . . . Their original trial and the long series of appeals constitute the fullest measure of justice and due process of law. . . ."

There was no letup, however, in Communist vilification of American justice. Yet, in East Germany, only one day before the execution of the Rosenbergs, Communist authorities had imposed the death penalty on a German house painter named Willi Göttling. He died less than twenty-four hours after his arrest. His crime: participation in the East Berlin riots against Red rule.

The Rosenbergs, who had two young children, were the first U.S. civilians to be put to death for espionage by order of a civil court. Their crime: conspiracy to commit espionage and supply atomic data to the Soviet Union. To the end they maintained that they were innocent—despite official promises of clemency in exchange for information.

Their 1950 arrest and conviction were aftermaths of the spectacular Canadian-spy-ring cases, which had implicated U.S. Army Sergeant David Greenglass, once stationed at the atom-bomb development plant in Los Alamos, N. Mex.

Greenglass testified that his sister Ethel, and her husband Julius Rosenberg, had recruited him to smuggle sketches from the plant.

The Rosenbergs were born and raised on New York's shabby Lower East Side, and during eight years of marriage had lived in a three-room apartment in Knickerbocker Village, a low-rent Manhattan housing project.

Ethel Rosenberg did her own housework and shared her engineer husband's outlook on the world. It was she who produced the code sign (torn halves of a box of raspberry Jello) which enabled David Greenglass and a courier, Harry Gold, to identify each other.

The Jello box was only one link in the damning chain of evidence against the Rosenbergs. Others were testimony that Greenglass had supplied the Rosenbergs with a cross-sectional diagram of, and a ten-page report on, the atomic bomb; testimony that the Rosenbergs had furnished Greenglass with $4000 for the purpose of financing his escape to Mexico; testimony that the Rosenbergs had procured passport photos as part of a plan to flee to France; and testimony that Julius Rosenberg had solicited antiaircraft and fire-control secrets from an engineer employed by the Navy Department.

Soon after Judge Irving R. Kaufman imposed death sentences on the Rosenbergs, describing their crime as "worse than murder", Communists the world over organized "Save the Rosenbergs" demonstrations. They charged not only that the Rosenbergs had been framed but that they were victims of anti-Semitism—though trial judge, and prosecutor, were Jews.

Many non-Communists rallied to slogans of "Clemency for the Rosenbergs". In January, 1500 American clergymen besought President Eisenhower for mercy. In France and Italy, pro-Rosenberg and anti-U.S. sentiment flared high, though few Frenchmen expressed themselves as bitterly as the eminent philosopher Jean-Paul Sartre, who wrote: "Do not be surprised if we scream from one end of Europe to the other: 'Watch out! America has rabies. Cut all ties which bind us to her; otherwise we in turn will be bitten and run mad.'"

French priests, veterans, politicians, labor leaders, and the entire press, both Left and Right, pleaded for clemency. Twice the Vatican sent word that the Pope had received urgent appeals from

**INNOCENT BYSTANDERS:** The Rosenberg boys follow their parents' case in the newspapers

many European Catholics on behalf of the condemned pair.

Three stays of execution were granted. And because of extraordinary developments, the Rosenbergs lived a day beyond June 18, the fourth date set for their execution.

On Monday of the final tense week the Supreme Court, having again refused to review the case or stay the execution, adjourned for the summer. At this juncture two obscure lawyers, who had been snubbed by counsel for the Rosenbergs, submitted a petition in handwriting to Associate Justice William O. Douglas which raised a point of law not previously brought before the court. On Wednesday came the electrifying news that Justice Douglas had granted an indefinite stay of execution pending a review of the legal technicality.

After making his decision, Justice Douglas, a liberal jurist who climbs mountains, shoots lions, and writes books, drove off for the Pacific Northwest. But the next day, after being located at a Midwest motel, he was haled back for an extraordinary session of the Supreme Court, convened at the request of the Attorney General.

By noon Friday the Supreme Court, holding that the legal question at issue was "not substantial", vacated the stay: the Rosenbergs must die. An hour later, President Eisenhower refused a last request for executive clemency. Before sundown the Rosenbergs were electrocuted, Julius first, his wife ten minutes later.

In 1953, government action against Communist party leaders was carried out under the Smith Act of 1947, which penalizes conspiracy to teach or advocate forcible overthrow of the government. After trials lasting from seven to nine weeks, thirty C.P. leaders were convicted. Eighteen more were indicted. All were "second-string" leaders, with the exception of rotund, 62-year-old Elizabeth Gurley Flynn, member of the National Committee of the Communist party.

Other familiar names associated with Communism popped up during the year. The former high State Department official, Alger Hiss, was denied parole from his five-year prison term. Hiss had been convicted of perjury in 1950 for having denied that he gave government secrets to Whittaker Chambers, former courier for a Communist spy ring. According to unofficial reports, Hiss has been a model prisoner and well liked by his fellow inmates. Apart from legal counsel, his only visitor has been Mrs. Hiss, an employee in a Manhattan book shop.

The U.S. Court of Appeals also rejected the appeal of William Remington, former government economist accused of Communist activity and, like Hiss, convicted of perjury.

Except for these cases, congressional investigations into subversion were responsible for headline news about Communism. Intimately involved in the headline news was Republican Senator Joseph Raymond McCarthy of Appleton, Wis. And connected with most of the year's bristling security activities was the phenomenon called, by his enemies and by McCarthy himself, "McCarthyism". In 1953 it became an international word.

Returning from a world tour, Adlai Stevenson, Democratic candidate for President in 1952, reported that it was the topic most frequently raised with him abroad.

McCarthy's methods inspired both praise and dispraise. To some, McCarthy was a hero; to others, a heel.

McCarthyism meant different things to different people. To some it meant distortion of truth by innuendo. It meant also contempt for fair play, and unsupported accusation of American citizens, in the name of Americanism.

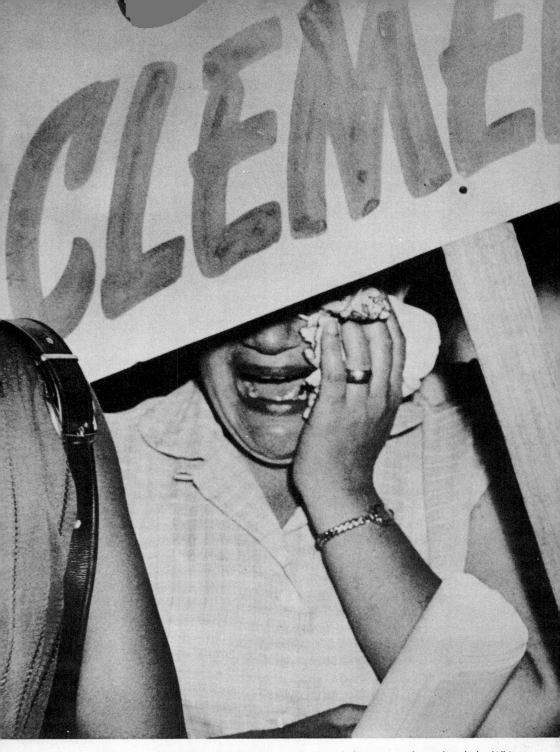

**USELESS TEARS** are shed by one of the women who picketed the White House until the last moment, asking presidential clemency for the Rosenbergs

To others McCarthyism meant relentless exposure of Communists and Communist sympathizers who infested the government and defense plants. It meant also exposure of teachers who could subvert the young. Senator McCarthy once sought to freeze the meaning of the word "McCarthyism" by giving this title to a book he wrote eulogizing himself.

As the year began, a Senate Rules subcommittee of three Democrats, after an eighteen-month investigation, issued a 400-page report on McCarthy. It described "devious financial dealings" by the Wisconsin senator. It pronounced "highly improper" a $10,000 fee he had received for a 10,000-word pamphlet he had written for the Lustron Corporation, then a manufacturer of prefabricated houses and in need of federal aid.

"A new low in dishonesty and smear," McCarthy replied.

In 1953, Senator McCarthy undoubtedly exercised more power of intimidation than any other man in the United States. Throughout the year, President Eisenhower declined to contradict him by name.

Another Eisenhower was not so reticent. One of the President's brothers, Arthur B. Eisenhower, a Kansas City banker, termed the Wisconsin senator "the most dangerous menace to America".

"When I think of McCarthy," he said, "I automatically think of Hitler."

Said McCarthy, "I can't hold Ike responsible for what his relatives say."

The Senator, always on the go, investigated tirelessly. He created a mass following through talks to packed halls and by radio-TV appearances; and he obtained potent backing from Texas oil barons, influential right-wing journalists, socialites, and politicians.

In the midst of it all, he found time to get married, although he had once said "there is no place in my kind of life for a wife". After an on-again-off-again romance, he made place for Jean Frazier Kerr, 29, voted the most beautiful girl at George Washington University in 1945. It was "Jeannie" with the blue-green eyes who had done research for McCarthy off and on for four years and who had

**DEFENDING** his university against charges voiced by Sen. McCarthy, Harvard Pres. Pusey says he knows of no Reds on the faculty

The Harvard Crimson

Princeton Tigers Will Defend Big Three Title
Against Underdog Varsity in Stadium Today

**MOST VOCAL** of America's anti-Communists, McCarthy in 1953 tangled with (among others) the State Department, the Army, various Democrats

**TIME OUT FOR LOVE:** Sen. McCarthy, who once said his life had "no place" for a wife, is snapped in traditional groom's pose cutting wedding cake with his bride

helped prepare his 1950 West Virginia speech, in which he accused the State Department of harboring Communists. It was that speech which vaulted the Senator out of obscurity.

More than a thousand persons filled Washington's St. Matthew's Cathedral for the wedding. Vice President and Mrs. Nixon were among the guests. The Eisenhowers sent regrets, but the White House was represented by Sherman Adams and General Wilton Persons, assistants to the President. Also in attendance were Arthur Summerfield (Postmaster General), Allen Dulles (chief of the Central Intelligence Agency), Harold E. Stassen (Foreign Operations Administrator), and many senators and representatives.

The first sight of McCarthy conducting an investigation surprised most observers, for despite the awe and fear in which he was held, he was a smiler and a back-slapper.

His technique was first to examine a witness in secret session. If the testimony proved promising, it was repeated in open hearing before spectators and packed press tables. If it had possibilities of sensationalism, radio and TV might be mobilized.

Dozens of witnesses before McCarthy fell silent after parroting, "I refuse to answer on the ground that it might incriminate me." Thus they wrapped themselves in the immunity furnished by the Constitution's Fifth Amendment, which contains provisions that no witness may be forced to testify against himself. "Fifth Amendment Communists", McCarthy called them.

At hearings, McCarthy usually listened with half-shut eyes, staring at the ceiling, seldom looking at the witness. He put questions in a low, sleepy-sounding voice that turned to a snarl when replies irked him. Witnesses were allowed to bring counsel and consult freely before answer-

ing. When a witness was through, McCarthy summed up. Often his summation drew protests of "distortion".

During 1953, McCarthy hunted subversives in the Government Printing Office, the Army Signal Corps, the United Nations, Harvard University, the General Electric Company. He continued to ride herd on the State Department, despite the departure of his archfoe, former Secretary of State Dean Acheson, making the Voice of America program his special target.

He early showed displeasure with President Eisenhower for appointing Dr. James B. Conant, former president of Harvard University, as High Commissioner to Germany, and Charles Bohlen as Ambassador to Russia. From that point on, the year was a chaos of forays and retreats, of threats and promises, but it was usually McCarthy who called the turns.

The administration faced him down, however, when he attempted to investigate the Central Intelligence Agency, which is concerned with counter-espionage and is the most hush-hush arm of the government.

In March the junior Senator from Wisconsin turned his attention to the problem of Allied trade with Red China, North Korea, and Soviet ports in the Far East. Before he had finished many diplomats began to wonder who was running U.S. foreign affairs, McCarthy or Secretary of State Dulles. On March 27 McCarthy announced that his representatives and a group of Greek shipowners had concluded an agreement under which trade with the Red areas would be halted. Shortly thereafter Secretary Dulles reminded McCarthy that ". . . Congressional committees [do not enter] the field of foreign relations. . . ."

In May the Senator again took up the question of trade with the Reds. He

called it a "shocking policy of fighting the enemy on the one hand and trading with him on the other". Singling out the British for his heaviest broadsides, he charged that two British-owned vessels had been used in 1951-52 to transport Communist Chinese troops. The British pointed out that the vessels were under Panamanian registry. McCarthy later produced data on the extent of British trade with Red China. As a remedy he suggested, among other things, that the U.S. sink "all the accursed ships" trading with China. Critics charged that the China-trade furor had been timed to divert attention from the Matthews episode.

In the summer of 1953 he had hired as his subcommittee executive director one Joseph B. Matthews, a former Protestant minister, missionary, and college professor who had been associated with American Communists during the 1920's and early 1930's. He had been a headlined darling of the Communist *Daily Worker*, and had written the semi-autobiographical *Odyssey of a Fellow Traveler*. Of late, he had become a professional Red-hunter.

A few days after McCarthy hired him, *The American Mercury* published an article by Matthews: "Reds and Our Churches". The first sentence read: "The largest single group supporting the Communist apparatus in the United States today is composed of Protestant clergymen."

In the resultant indignant outcry over "slanders against men of God", President Eisenhower, without naming names, denounced such generalized attacks. When the smoke cleared, Matthews had resigned and the three Democratic members of McCarthy's subcommittee had walked out, not to return by year's end. Meanwhile, many of the subcommittee hearings were held with McCarthy as sole inquisitor.

For five months McCarthy belabored the Voice of America and the overseas libraries of the U.S. Information Service (U.S.I.S.), then under the supervision of the State Department. He went all out to prove that the Voice was riddled with Communists and "Communist thinkers", and that the libraries were rife with pro-Communist literature. This brought to world attention two new McCarthy investigators, Roy M. Cohn and G. David Schine, both youths of 26.

Cohn, son of a New York judge and leading Democrat, was a brilliant student who won his law degree at twenty. As an assistant U.S. attorney, he helped prepare the government's case against Julius and Ethel Rosenberg. Schine, handsome, Harvard-educated heir to the Schine hotel chain (the Roney Plaza of Miami Beach, the Ambassador of Los Angeles), secured appointment to the McCarthy staff, as an unpaid consultant, by virtue of his friendship with Cohn. Schine's qualifications as a specialist in the antisubversive field became evident when he wrote *Definition of Communism*, a pamphlet free for the taking in all Schine hotels.

These two hopped abroad in April to riffle through U.S.I.S. library shelves. Including press conferences, sleep, sightseeing, sampling the best in local cookery, and actual investigative work, the "quiz kids" (a label given them by European newsmen) spent 40 hours in Paris, 17 in Bonn, 41 in Vienna, 25 in Rome. Their youth, assurance, slapdash speed, and off-the-cuff pronouncements flabbergasted European newsmen.

During their six hours in London they spent a few minutes with dignified U.S. Ambassador Winthrop Aldrich, former

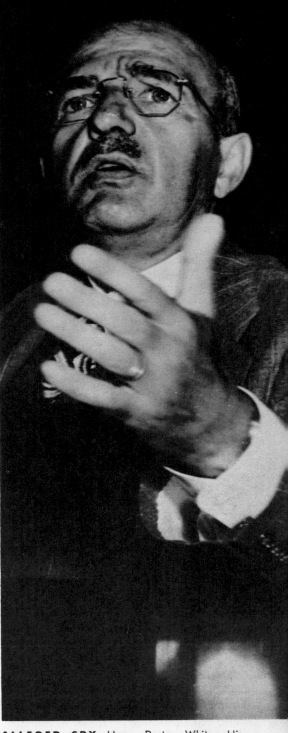

**ALLEGED SPY** Harry Dexter White. His case created a furor five years after his death

board chairman of the world's largest bank, and gave him high marks: ". . . for a man who has been here only two months, he seems to have grasped the problems very well".

McCarthy's attack rattled the State Department, which sent ten separate and often contradictory directives to the libraries. One resulted in the tossing out of *The Thin Man* and other detective stories by Dashiell Hammett, an alleged Communist, but still one of President Eisenhower's favorite murder-mystery writers. Another inspired at least one library to give the heave-ho to *Witness*, a book written by Whittaker Chambers, onetime Communist and the nemesis of Alger Hiss.

### "The Book Burners"

Policy stabilized when the President intervened: books, regardless of authorship, which furthered understanding of America and her cause would remain.

The President's intervention came in a folksy speech to the Dartmouth graduating class. "Don't join the book burners," he said. "Don't be afraid to go into your library and read every book, as long as any document does not offend [your] own ideas of decency." And again: "How will we defeat Communism unless we know what it is?" The impromptu words were taken as a slam at McCarthy.

"He couldn't very well have been referring to me," the Senator said. "I have burned no books." To critics of Cohn and Schine, he snapped: "Anti-Semitism!"

Toward the end of the year, McCarthy tempestuously investigated the Army's radar center at Fort Monmouth, N.J. Despite sensational allegations, little evidence of espionage came from his one-man hearings. But there were indications that he was planning to attack the Army, as he had the State Department.

By this time McCarthy was making bigger and better headlines by getting hip-deep into the Harry Dexter White case. However, two rival watchdogs of security got there first: Representative Velde of Illinois, and Senator Jenner of Indiana.

In the House of Representatives, the principal scourge of subversion was Harold Himmel Velde, a tall, handsome lawyer and ex-F.B.I. man, Republican chairman of the Un-American Activities Committee.

Mr. Velde had a tendency to sound off without consulting his committee members. In March, 1953, he stated that "inquiry into Communist infiltration" in churches was "entirely possible". In the ensuing din, Republican leaders "talked" to Velde, who then announced that no such investigation was contemplated at the moment.

In the Senate, the Internal Security Subcommittee was also Red-hunting, under Republican Senator William E. Jenner of Indiana, the first World War II veteran to reach the Senate.

Jenner is a product of the hard school of Indiana politics. He got his first taste of Washington as a law student and $4-a-day elevator operator in the House Office Building. Such swing-from-the-floor speeches as the one in which he called General George C. Marshall a "front for traitors" won him the title of "Bush League McCarthy" and the obvious dislike of Dwight Eisenhower. Nonetheless, it was the Jenner subcommittee that got the nod when the administration, in late 1953, decided to raise the ghost of Harry Dexter White.

White had gone to work for Henry Morgenthau's Treasury Department in 1934, and had helped draw up the Morgenthau Plan, which sought to transform postwar Germany into a pastoral country. During the Truman administration he was promoted first to be Assistant Secretary of the Treasury and then U.S. Executive Director of the International Monetary Fund. White resigned because of poor health in 1947.

In 1948, Elizabeth Bentley, self-confessed former courier for Communist spy rings operating in the government, testified that she had received secret documents from White. Summoned before the House Un-American Activities Committee, White paid tribute to democracy and denied all charges. Three days later he died from a heart attack. In the years following, his name cropped up frequently in congressional investigations, notably in testimony by Whittaker Chambers.

On Nov. 6 Attorney General Herbert Brownell, talking to a Chicago luncheon club on "ethics in government", flatly asserted: ". . . Harry Dexter White was a Russian spy". Then he threw a bombshell.

"White," said Brownell, "was known to be a Communist spy by the very people who appointed him to the most sensitive and important position he ever held in government service." His "spying activities . . . were reported in detail by the F.B.I. to the White House."

The storm broke. Headlines shrieked the charge that Harry Truman, then President, had knowingly promoted a spy. Mr. Truman angrily denied it, and made several off-the-cuff retorts he later had to amend.

"That Brownell," said President Eisenhower, "he can sure stir things up." Brownell later said he had never meant to question Mr. Truman's loyalty, only his blindness to the Communist menace.

Besides Mr. Truman and his military aide, General Harry Vaughn, Brownell added, other high officials were privy to White's treachery, including Attorney General Tom Clark (now a Supreme

Court Justice) and Secretary of State James Byrnes (now Governor of South Carolina). Quick confirmation came from Governor Byrnes, no longer a Truman crony.

Promptly Senator Jenner's subcommittee called Vaughn and others, arranged for a telegraphic interview with Byrnes, and set a later date for Brownell.

## Truman Subpoenaed

At this point, Mr. Velde, alone in his home in Pekin, Ill., was pondering. Finally, at 5 A.M., he grabbed a telephone, called Washington, and ordered subpoenas for Truman, Clark, and Byrnes—a former President, a justice of the Supreme Court, and a governor of a sovereign state. "We should get in the act," his committee counsel was quoted as saying.

The following day President Eisenhower said that (1) he did not think Truman had knowingly appointed a spy; and (2) he himself would not have issued the subpoenas.

Velde decided to "postpone" the hearings. Meantime Messrs. Truman, Clark, and Byrnes had rejected the subpoenas, though Governor Byrnes said he would receive the committee in his office.

Ten days after the original Brownell charge, Mr. Truman presented his answer over nationwide radio-TV. Brownell, he said, had "lied to the American people" in a "sordid . . . attack on the loyalty of a former President".

In substance, his rebuttal was that he had learned of the F.B.I. report on White too late to stop Senate confirmation of the appointment, and that he had let it go through so that other F.B.I. probes would not be endangered. "Any unusual action . . . might well have alerted all the persons involved. . . ."

Some of Truman's intimates said the White case had been handled "according to a plan worked out by the F.B.I." Mr. Truman did not say quite that.

For sixteen hours after Truman's address, it looked as if he had knocked Mr. Brownell into a cocked hat. But the next afternoon Mr. Brownell, before a televised hearing of the Jenner subcommittee, testified that the record did not bear out the Truman version.

Then came another bombshell: the F.B.I.'s formidable J. Edgar Hoover took the stand. Mr. Hoover, alert, florid, his bifocals big as headlights, said he had been informed of, but did not approve, the Truman plan for handling the White problem; and that White's transfer to the International Monetary Fund had hindered, not helped, the F.B.I.'s check on his activities.

Up to this point Senator Joseph McCarthy had scarcely managed to get in a word edgewise. Now it was his turn to talk.

In his radio-TV speech, Mr. Truman had charged the Eisenhower administration with having embraced "mccarthyism" (the typescript of his speech omitted the capital letters). The reference occupied forty seconds of a half-hour broadcast; whereupon McCarthy demanded, and got, "equal time" from the networks: a half hour, or $300,000 worth of free time, in which to reply.

Before Mr. Truman spoke, President Eisenhower had expressed the hope that the 1954 elections might be fought out on legislative issues; that by then the Communists-in-government controversy would be history.

Taking to the air late in November, McCarthy dealt with Mr. Truman in the expected manner. Then he suddenly shifted his bludgeon to the Eisenhower administration, charging it with failure to do an adequate job in eradicating Communists, and with coddling our Allies on the China-trade issue. But the

real gauntlet he seemed to fling down was this: the 1954 campaign would be fought on his terms, not the President's; and his continued drive against Communists and Communist sympathizers— not the President's program—would be the principal issue.

One White House aide called the speech "a declaration of war against the President". Where all this left McCarthy as the year ended was far from clear, either to the administration or to the country at large.

Another moot question was the administration's record in ridding the government of "disloyal" persons. Previously a distinction had been made between

"loyalty" and "security" dismissals; now a new order was inaugurated, in which all unreliable persons were lumped together as "security risks". Unreliables were not only subversives, but also alcoholics, homosexuals, and blabbermouths. In October the White House announced that during the preceding four months, 1456 persons had been fired from government office; Republican orators implied or asserted that all or mostly all were subversives. But when figures from individual government departments were demanded and published, it looked as if the administration had been caught with its statistics down, for the 1456 total included resignations, firings for economy, and firings for many other reasons, including, possibly, subversion.

As 1953 ended, many basic questions about McCarthyism were unresolved. Some people were saying that the McCarthy cure was as bad as the Communist disease itself. Others were asking how much popular support McCarthy and his methods could count on.

A year's-end Gallup poll indicated that 50 out of 100 Americans approved of McCarthy, 29 disapproved, and 21 had no opinion. But as to McCarthy's methods, 38 out of 100 approved, 47 disapproved, and 15 didn't know.

**HEAD PROBERS** in Congress: Velde (House Un-American Activities Committee), Jenner (Senate Internal Security Subcommittee), McCarthy (Senate Permanent Investigating Subcommittee)

**NEGRO BISHOP** Joseph Bowers is consecrated by Francis Cardinal Spellman at solemn high mass in Mississippi. Bowers' Catholic diocese is Accra in British West Africa

# Race Relations

IN MANY AN AMERICAN TOWN, 1953's happiest celebration was a gala homecoming for heroes returned from North Korean prison camps. Parades met them; bands played; mayors made speeches.

Not so in Hopkinsville, Ky., a town of 18,000.

Late in August, Sergeant Frank J. Quarles and Sergeant Clyde Moore, both wearers of many battle stars, both imprisoned for nearly three years, came home. Nothing happened. Quarles and Moore are Negroes.

Nine days later, a Negro civic organization began to plan a welcome for them. At first it met resistance; then the town had a change of heart. Colonel Gil-

mer Bell, a former aide to General Jonathan Wainwright and a survivor of the Bataan death march, offered to speak at a banquet for the two sergeants. Other leading white citizens cooperated.

On Sept. 8, after they had been home two weeks, the two young Negroes were "welcomed" by Hopkinsville. An estimated 9000 citizens, black and white, cheered their parade. And Mayor Koon, white, spoke for the city: "We cannot honor you; you honor us by your presence."

The incident was symbolic of U.S. race relations in 1953. It was not a year of long official strides toward equality; neither was it a year of major violence and

ROCK AND STICK typify white residents' reaction when Negro families move into a Chicago housing project. Police quelled this riot, but feeling remained high

racial unrest. For the second consecutive year there were no lynchings.

That fact, however, was scant consolation to the family of Moses Jones, Negro, shot dead Dec. 28 in Grove City, Ala., by Clarke County Sheriff Jenkins Hill. Sheriff Hill said he had shot in self-defense.

Behind the shooting was a story. Early in the year the sheriff had been accused in a bootlegging conspiracy. When he was tried in September, Moses Jones, himself a smalltime bootlegger, testified that the burly law officer had tried to shake him down for "protection money". The sheriff's trial ended in a hung jury (10 for conviction, 2 against), with a new trial ordered for early 1954. Cautious Moses Jones moved to a neighboring county.

Late in the fall another Negro prosecution witness was shot to death by a co-defendant of Hill. The killer went free, largely on the testimony of Sheriff Hill, who was the only witness.

Then, after Christmas, Hill went after Moses Jones with a fugitive warrant charging him with failure to pay $154.25 in fines for bootlegging and reckless driving. Jones' wife and friends got the

money together, but the sheriff refused to take it. Instead, he handcuffed his prisoner and drove back to the Grove City jail. There Jones died. As the sheriff tells it, he "grabbed me and tried to take my gun away". There were no witnesses.

The biggest race-relations story of 1953 was postponed until 1954. In the spring the Supreme Court had been expected to rule on whether segregation of

**MIXED MARRIAGE** makes headlines in England as Peggy Cripps, daughter of the late Sir Stafford, weds law student Joseph Appiah, son of a Gold Coast (Africa) tribal chieftain

the races in public schools was discriminatory and unconstitutional. Not since
1896, when the doctrine was laid down
that separate public facilities were constitutional if they were equal, had so vital
a case involving human rights been before the court. A decision that segregation was contrary to constitutional guar-
antees would have far-reaching effects
for minorities in this country.

But instead of ruling, the court ordered
new arguments, which were heard in
December. Decision was expected in
1954.

Fearing that the court might declare
Jim Crow schools illegal, South Carolina,
under Governor James Byrnes, and
Georgia, under Governor Herman Tal-
madge, took legislative steps to abolish
"public" education (in case their fears
were justified), and to set up "private",
segregated schools financed by State
money.

In other cases the Supreme Court
handed down a series of decisions which,
with one exception, were regarded as
gains for minority groups. The exception
upheld North Carolina in its use of property and poll-tax lists for jury selection.
For the rest, the court set aside the
death sentence of a Georgia Negro because of racial discrimination in the
selection of his jury, ruled that a home-
owner could not be sued for violating an
agreement not to sell to a non-white, and
upheld an eighty-year-old law barring
discrimination by Washington, D.C.,
restaurants.

As a result of this last ruling, and without incident, most Washington eating
places began to serve all races; Negroes
and whites sat side by side at lunch
counters. Indirectly, the ruling also
cracked segregation in Washington
theaters.

In lower courts, judicial decisions also
provided great gains. In Arizona the

**WITHOUT FANFARE** white musician Lennie
Hayton, Negro singer Lena Horne, stay happily wed

Superior Court of Maricopa County outlawed segregation in the schools of Phoenix. And North Carolina reversed 1952's notorious assault-by-leer conviction, in which Mack Ingram, Negro father of nine, had been convicted of assaulting a 17-year-old white girl by allegedly "leering" at her across a field. The State Supreme Court threw out the conviction.

As in 1952, no important new laws were passed in 1953 to guarantee minority rights. In seventeen state legislatures, bills were introduced to prevent discrimination in private employment. Only in Kansas did one pass, and it lacked teeth.

Although President Eisenhower did not lead Congress to the adoption of any civil-rights laws, he did speak out against second-class citizenship. "I believe the only way to protect my own rights is to protect the rights of others." To see that business firms which have contracts with the government hire their employees without discrimination, he created the Government Contracts Committee.

The President was accused of sitting on both sides of the fence when he named Jane Morrow Spaulding, a Negro, as assistant to the Secretary of Health, Education and Welfare, and then selected Governor Byrnes, an outspoken white supremacist, as a delegate to the United Nations.

### Navy Ends Segregation

Under White House pressure, the Navy ordered segregation ended among civilian employees at forty-three Southern naval installations. This order reversed Navy policy, which had followed the local custom. Although some naval commandants publicly dragged their heels, the Navy announced that by Nov. 11 all "white" and "colored" signs had come down except at Newport News, Va.

When the Defense Department announced that the Navy and Air Force were "completely integrated" and that the Army would be within eight months, no mention was made of the Navy Stewards Branch, composed almost entirely of Negroes. That has long been a sore point with Negro leaders; they say the Navy makes servants of its colored recruits.

The harshest racial clash of the year occurred in Chicago. There Donald Howard, a 25-year-old Negro mail carrier, with his wife and two small children moved into the Trumbull Park housing project. Their arrival was greeted by riots sparked by young toughs who roamed the neighborhood tossing lighted torches at business places rumored to have Negro patrons.

Chicago police acted swiftly to put down the rioting. Both the Howards and the Chicago Housing Authority stood by their anti-segregation guns. But at year's end, headlines continued to tell of stonings, arson, and heavy police guards.

The Negro's struggle for equal status made other news during the year.

In Columbia, S.C., fifty Negro soldiers were arrested Thanksgiving night, following an argument set off when one sat next to a white woman on a bus. The fifty were refused legal counsel and were fined a total of $1773.

In neighboring North Carolina, Catholic Bishop Vincent Waters ordered the Holy Redeemer Church (white) of Newton Grove merged with St. Benedict's (Negro). Before the merger, attendance had averaged 250 whites and seventy-five Negroes. On the first Sunday after the merger it fell to fifty-eight. Outraged white parishioners stood outside making lists of whites who attended.

Bishop Waters answered this intimidation by extending his anti-segregation order to all Catholic churches in North Carolina. Many North Carolina Catholics were displeased, but there was no open defiance.

The dean of New York's Episcopal Cathedral of St. John the Divine, the Very Reverend Dr. James A. Pike, rejected an honorary degree from the University of the South in Sewanee, Tenn., because it did not admit Negroes. "I could not in conscience receive a doctorate in white divinity," Dr. Pike said. Later in the year Sewanee opened its doors to all races.

## Negroes in Office

In politics Negroes made steady gains. Manhattan's new borough president was Negro Hulan Jack, a businessman and former State assemblyman. In deference to the Negro's political power, all the major parties had nominated colored men for this position.

In Atlanta, Ga., Dr. Rufus E. Clement, 52, president of Atlanta University, won a seat on the city's Board of Education by a vote of nearly 2 to 1 over his white opponent.

In North Carolina, twenty Negroes ran for municipal office, and six were elected. Surveys of the 1952 vote in the South showed that Negroes had cast ballots undisturbed in unprecedented numbers.

In New York City a cause of increasing racial tension was the influx of immigrants from Puerto Rico.

Because Puerto Ricans are American citizens, and as free to move north to New York as Hoosiers are to move west to California, they are leaving the poverty of Puerto Rico in ever increasing numbers.

What began as a trickle half a century ago swelled to a flood estimated at 69,-000 in 1953. In New York, where the bulk of them remain, they now total about 450,000—one out of every twenty New Yorkers. However, the Puerto Rican Department of Labor recently reported that, as the U.S. job market tightened, the tide turned. From October on, more Puerto Ricans returned to their island than went north. Whether this trend will continue depends on jobs and housing both in Puerto Rico and in New York City.

The Puerto Rican impact on New York has been enormous. "Se habla español" ("Spanish is spoken") signs blossom in shop windows. Spanish-language newspapers thrive.

Unfortunately, the Puerto Rican also feels the prejudice which a testy city inflicts upon its newest, hence least integrated, citizens.

White New Yorkers often say: "Puerto Ricans get off the plane and head for the nearest relief office," although Welfare Department statistics do not bear out this charge. To Negro New Yorkers, the new Puerto Rican is someone lower in the social and economic scale than he, and also a menace who overcrowds his already substandard housing and vies for his job.

To the Puerto Rican, New York is a wet, cold city where he is cooped up in an overpriced slum. Often paying over $80 a month for a single small room, into which he may have to crowd six of his family, he may also be obliged to share a toilet with as many as ten other families. He works for small wages at a menial job, but he stays because things are even worse "at home". His tuberculosis rate is high, and often he must support a larger family than he can afford. Hence "Rodríguez" or "Gómez" or "Hernández" is a familiar name at city clinics. He poses a school problem, too, for his youngsters usually speak little English

**SQUALID SLUMS** in San Juan, the island's capital, help answer the question: Why do Puerto Ricans leave home?

and may have had haphazard schooling.

But beset as they are, underprivileged Puerto Ricans have advantages over another group of Spanish-speaking migrants: the "wetbacks". They are Mexican peasants, lured across the border illegally to labor, often in near-peonage, as farm hands.

Despite mass deportation—389,000 in the year ended June 30, 1953—wetbacks are still numbered in the hundreds of thousands in the Southwest. After a late-summer tour of the area, Attorney General Brownell called their importation an American racket and moved to strengthen controls along the long open border of Texas.

Immigrants to the U.S. from Europe were officially encouraged. Congress passed a law in midsummer admitting

214,000 displaced persons, mainly from northern Europe, during the three years following its enactment. This was in addition to the usual immigration quotas. But operation of the law was so snarled in red tape that it was Christmas before the first immigrant landed.

The year's racial news was not without humor.

The "Turks", a South Carolina colony of descendants of pre-Revolutionary Arab settlers, became a court case when they refused to let their children attend school with Negroes, while whites refused to let *their* children attend with Turks.

Probably the most absurd note was a vote by the Florida Ku Klux Klan at a Konclave in October. It discarded its racial ban and invited all Florida Negroes to join—in segregated Klaverns!

# CRIME

THE CRIME CURVE TURNED UP IN 1953. IN twelve months, Americans committed more than 2,000,000 major crimes (murder, manslaughter, rape, robbery, assault, burglary, larceny, auto theft), an average of one every 4.3 minutes.

The pattern changed from that of 1952. Prison riots continued into February in two states (Pennsylvania and Oregon), and then stopped. In their place, headlines blazoned a revival of that shocker of the 1930's: kidnapping.

The Midwest got it all. In June a Chicago politician was "snatched"; in November a baby in Evansville, Ind. And in Kansas City, Mo., occurred the year's most appalling case: the Greenlease kidnap-murder.

There, on Sept. 28, six-year-old Robert C. (Bobby) Greenlease Jr. was attending

**BLOODY** but unbowed, Los Angeles bartender Hiram McGuire stands over bandit he shot down when three-man gang tried to hold up his tavern

**DEATH IN DENVER** is the theme of this photo-sequence. Above: Police officer Richard Schippers pleads vainly with Kenneth Stanley to drop pistol he has been brandishing. Right: Felled by Schippers' rifle butt, Stanley fires (arrow), draws blood. Below: Other officers who came to Schippers' aid find they have halted Stanley—for good

the French Institute of Notre Dame de Sion. When a stocky, puffy-eyed woman appeared saying she was Bobby's aunt, sent to fetch him because his mother had suffered a heart attack, a nun let him go. Only later, when a phone call revealed that Mrs. Greenlease was in perfect health, was the tragic truth discovered.

What happened thereafter was a nightmare. The bogus aunt, an alcoholic divorcée of 41 named Bonnie Heady, took Bobby to her accomplice, Carl Hall, 34 (an alcoholic and a morphine addict). They drove across the State line into Kansas, where Hall shot the little boy through the head. Then he sent a ransom note to Bobby's father, coolly demanding $600,000.

The elder Greenlease, a wealthy automobile distributor, undertook to raise the sum—three times more than any other ransom ever paid in America—in $10 and $20 bills, as requested. The money was handed over, and the kidnapers drove off to St. Louis, seemingly scot free.

Their own natures, however, betrayed them. Renting an apartment, they got drunk and quarreled. Hall walked out, carrying a suitcase. When a cab driver steered him to a prostitute, Hall rewarded him with $2500.

Next day the prostitute told the cabbie Hall's suitcase held "a million dollars" in cash. The cab driver, taking fright, called Police Lieutenant Louis Shoulders; he and a patrolman nabbed Hall in another rented apartment. Hall groggily admit-

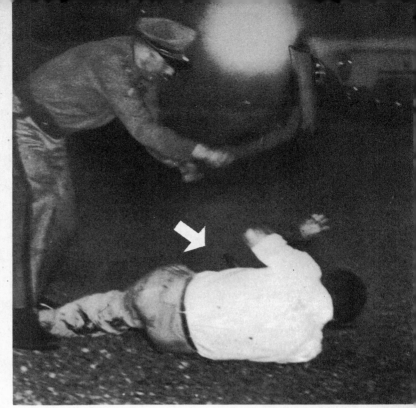

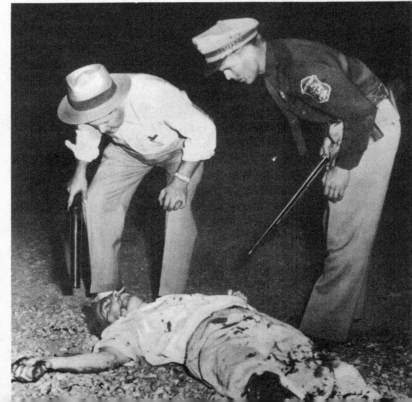

ted his guilt and directed
police to Bonnie Heady,
who, in a drunken stupor,
was still waiting for him.

Hall, son of a prosper-
ous Kansas lawyer, had
been a misfit from child-
hood. During one spell
at military school he
had come to know Paul
Greenlease, Bobby's fos-
ter brother. Years later,
when he found himself
serving a robbery sen-
tence in Missouri, he
remembered the Green-
lease family. Paroled, he
met Bonnie Heady—one-
time respectable house-

wife who inexplicably had turned to liquor and prostitution—and with her plotted the kidnaping.

One detail highlighted the case—and the callousness of their planning. Well in advance, Hall dug a hole outside a bungalow in St. Joseph, Mo., and bought quicklime. In the hole, under the quicklime, Bobby's body lay even as Hall was arranging for delivery of the ransom money from Bobby's father.

As for the money itself, Hall's arrest uncovered $296,280. With what the pair had spent, that left about $300,000 unaccounted for.

Suspicion fell on the policemen who had collared Hall: Lieutenant Shoulders, a veteran of twenty-seven years on the St. Louis force, and Patrolman Elmer Dolan. Shoulders later was suspended, and then indicted by a federal grand jury on charges of perjuring himself in testimony about the case. He had not been tried as the year ended.

Meanwhile two of the ransom bills turned up in Michigan. The rest of the $300,000 was still missing on Dec. 31. If Carl Hall and Bonnie Heady knew anything about it, the knowledge went with them, for on Dec. 18 they paid for their crime in the gas chamber of the Missouri State Prison.

Other murderers also were abroad in 1953. Most alarming was a youth of 18 who, unlike Carl Hall, had shown no sign of emotional instability. Fred Eugene McManus was known as one of the nicest boys in Valley Stream, N.Y. Son of a well-to-do family, he had grown up notably fond of animals and children, an athlete with a shy, polite manner.

In March, 1953, however, Fred came home on a ten-day Marine pass. Two days later he took off for Rochester, N.Y., to meet 16-year-old Diane Marie Weggeland, whom he had met on a vacation trip.

Thinking they could marry in Minnesota without parental consent, they headed west. Fred got a new car for them, plus $58 in cash, by thumbing a ride with a driver and shooting him with his service revolver. Before the young lovers were picked up three days later in Iowa, the revolver had spoken four more times.

The pair's return to Rochester was like a honeymoon. On the plane they laughed, held hands, played canasta. Asked why he had killed five persons in cold blood, Fred said, "I was in love and I needed money." Yet the car and cash from his first victim had been his only loot. And it was for that murder that, after pleading insanity, the nice-looking young Marine was sentenced to life imprisonment, while his sweetheart began a term at a correctional institution.

## A Crime of Passion

Another killing, a crime of passion, had elements that have engrossed many a novelist. It involved 19-year-old Roy Roger Schinagle Jr. of Ohio, and Cynthia Pfeil, also 19, of New York. The two had met a year before at Ohio Wesleyan University, but Cynthia had not registered for the 1953 fall term because of low grades. Instead, in August she ran away from home to be near Roy. A month later her body was found on a country road near Upper Sandusky, Ohio, strangled, stabbed, and battered.

Arrested, Roy admitted killing his sweetheart after a "silly quarrel". But a coroner's report said the girl was pregnant.

In October, when Roy was about to be tried for first-degree murder, he pleaded guilty to a second-degree charge —to which Cynthia's parents agreed—and won a life sentence. As a student Roy had wanted to become a minister. Now, in jail, he said he hoped to become a chaplain's assistant.

A third horrifying murder story broke in New York City in December. Police recounted it as follows:

On an August evening, Dr. and Mrs. William Fraden were sitting in their Bronx apartment when Harlow, their 20-year-old son (and only child) called with good news: he finally had a job. All his life the tall, bespectacled boy had been a problem. His schoolteacher mother had called him lazy, a sissy, even a homosexual. Yet she and her husband had coddled Harlow. Typically, when they turned him out in June in an effort to make him seek work, they gave him $2000 plus a fat allowance.

Thus cushioned, Harlow rented an expensive apartment for himself and a friend, Dennis Wepman, 22. Then the Fradens cut Harlow's allowance. Later he came to tell them his "news", bearing a bottle of champagne with which to toast it.

The job story was a lie. Following a plan he and Wepman had hatched, Harlow poured three glasses of champagne and put potassium cyanide in two. At the first sip, his parents dropped to the floor.

Harlow then called in Wepman, who had waited outside in the corridor. Dr. Fraden was still conscious, and his son forced more cyanide down his throat. Finally the youths left. Two days later Harlow returned, "discovered" the bodies, and called police.

Despite official doubts, the crime was listed as a double suicide. Young Fraden inherited $52,000 and began living high. But to his accomplice, Wepman, he gave only $127. His stinginess led to a quarrel. Then Wepman spilled the whole story to a girl, and it reached the ears of the police.

Fraden was reading poetry when the police picked him up. He sat silently as Wepman gave the details of that August night, but he spoke up when the police accused him of murdering for gain. Ridiculous, he said. He had killed his mother—"that paranoid"—because he hated her, and his father because she had dominated him. He and Wepman were jailed on charges of first-degree murder.

Other crimes of 1953 were mainly unexceptional. Gambling continued to recover from the temporary impact of 1951's Kefauver probes. In Philadelphia, for example, 137 policemen were implicated in graft charges relating to a "numbers game" ring. And robbery held its usual lure, particularly for the gunman who hit a bank in Floral Park, N.Y., for $191,280, probably the biggest one-man bank haul ever.

## Waterfront Violence

But the year's No. 1 crime saga was the sprawling, many-branched tale of murder, racketeering, bribery, and violence that unfolded in the New York-New Jersey area. It involved not only the underworld but businessmen, lawyers, labor leaders, politicians, sportsmen, and others. It fell into two distinct parts, but here and there they touched.

Part I was the waterfront story. It had begun in 1952, when New York and New Jersey crime commissions took their first long, hard look at conditions along New York harbor's 700 miles of docks. What they saw was evidence of a long-festering mess that kept them (and other investigators) calling witnesses and listening to testimony throughout 1953.

The heart of the mess was corrupt labor practices in the International Longshoremen's Association (I.L.A.). This sixty-year affiliate of the American Federation of Labor represented roughly 25,000 men whose living comes from handling cargoes on the New York harbor piers. Aided on occasion by shipping firms, the I.L.A.

**FACING TRIAL** for wanton shooting of five innocent people, 18-year-old Fred McManus unconcernedly cuddles his 16-year-old girl friend Diane Weggeland

ruled with an iron hand the men it purported to represent.

Only in January, 1953, for example, was it revealed that in 1940 I.L.A. Local 824 had been taken over by one Michael (Mickey) Bowers, who held no union office. Thereafter, crime mushroomed to the point where 824 was nicknamed the "pistol local". Neither I.L.A. nor the shippers did anything effective about it.

In 1953 something was finally done.

It began when the New York Crime Commission won admission from I.L.A.'s tough, old (69), lifetime president, Joseph P. Ryan, that he had taken close to $50,000 from his union's "anti-Communist fund" and spent it on clothes, Stork Club lunches, a trip to Guatemala, and other personal items. The I.L.A. announced

that Ryan had a right to the money, but he was indicted for theft of union funds.

Then the A.F.L. put the heat on Ryan to clean up the I.L.A. When nothing much happened, the A.F.L. voted overwhelmingly at its September convention to expel the recalcitrant union. This, its first expulsion for corruption, cast adrift a total of 60,000 men. Driving home its point, the A.F.L. formed a new International Longshoremen's Association to represent all good dock workers.

For a while longer Ryan clung to the $20,000-a-year job he had held since 1927. But in November, under multiple pressures, he resigned and was succeeded by Captain William V. Bradley, 50, head of I.L.A.'s tugboat division.

On October 1 the "old" I.L.A.'s contract

with the New York Shipping Association expired during a wage deadlock. A strike ensued which tied up almost the whole Atlantic coast until President Eisenhower, acting under the Taft-Hartley law, got an eighty-day "moratorium".

Earlier, New York and New Jersey (with federal approval) had created a bi-state waterfront commission designed to purge the whole harbor. The commission first required all longshoremen to register. Then it took aim on two long-standing evils: (1) the shape-up system of hiring under which longshoremen gathered at the piers each morning and were picked by hiring bosses who were both I.L.A. members and company representatives);

and (2) the I.L.A.-controlled public-loading companies (which put cargo on trucks after it has been lifted from the ships' holds to the docks).

The shape-up ended Dec. 1. As of that date, registered longshoremen began reporting to thirteen employment centers, where licensed hiring agents handed out the day's jobs. After a one-day protest strike by the old I.L.A., the new system was accepted by all concerned. Meanwhile, legislation was passed to outlaw the superfluous public loaders.

But a big question remained: which I.L.A. would get the longshoremen? The A.F.L. group was busily signing up recruits when the expiration of the eighty-

**FACING ACCUSER** who charged him with knife and gun attacks, alleged drug addict Andrew Ayala tries to break free from New York police to kick Ralph Alvarez' arm

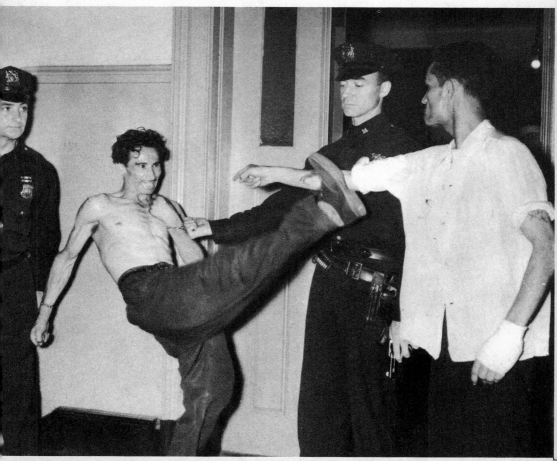

day strike moratorium against the old I.L.A. forced new action. Faced with a probable dock walkout on Christmas Eve, the National Labor Relations Board ordered an election which it hoped would establish the dock workers' union preference and allow prompt resumption of wage negotiations with the shippers.

Unfortunately, the election was a flop. The old I.L.A., buoyed at the last moment by moral support (and a reported $50,-000) from A.F.L.-hating old John L. Lewis of the United Mine Workers, polled 9060 votes against the new I.L.A.'s 7568, and agreed not to call a strike for the time being. But more than 4000 ballots were challenged, some 3000 qualified longshoremen had not voted at all, and the real winner was in doubt. At the year's close, the A.F.L. was demanding a new election.

Part II of the New York-New Jersey saga dealt chiefly with harness-racing scandals. It grew out of the shooting of a union leader outside his Bronx apartment.

The slain man was Thomas F. Lewis, 35, president of Local 32-E of the Building Service Employees' International Union (A.F.L.). His killer, a professional gunman named Edward (Snakes) Ryan, was shot down almost at once by a policeman, and died without saying why he had gone after Lewis. Investigation of Lewis' affairs started something.

First it developed that he was a labor racketeer. His province was Yonkers Raceway, just north of New York City. There, disregarding State regulations, he had brought hoodlums and ex-convicts into the 1000-man labor force his union represented. These included four "trouble shooters", to whom the management had paid $164,500 in three years to ward off phony strikes.

Governor Thomas E. Dewey promptly held up the raceway's fall opening four days while every employee was screened for a criminal record. Meanwhile the newspapers were asking what kind of men were the track owners who allowed Lewis to get away with his expensive game. The answer spotlighted the new role of harness racing as entertainment, business and magnet for unscrupulous men.

Since 1940, races between trotting horses pulling light sulkies have become a big-time attraction. Slick new tracks, night racing under floodlights, and pari-mutuel windows have captured an ever growing public. In 1953, in the twelve states where pari-mutuel wagering was legal, more than 8,000,000 paying spectators bet close to $400 million. And nowhere else has harness racing grown so fast as in New York, where $1 million-bet nights are common.

The owners of Yonkers Raceway included men of dubious connections. Thomas Lewis had no trouble there. Nor, it soon developed, had William de Koning, a similar "operator" at Roosevelt Raceway on Long Island (his alleged specialty: kickbacks from track employees). In fact, both raceways seemed to be controlled by much the same people, who were also revealed to be stockholders in Midwest harness tracks.

In New York, Governor Dewey named a special board to clean up harness racing. Meanwhile, newspapermen found an interesting side light. William de Koning had made regular visits to a certain convict in Sing Sing prison. So, it turned out, had many other newsworthy New Yorkers and New Jerseyites.

The prisoner was Joseph (Joey) Fay, former vice president of the International Union of Operating Engineers (A.F.L.). In 1947, Fay had begun a 7½-to-15-year term for extorting $368,000 on a New York building project. But jail had not removed him from circulation.

During Fay's five years in Sing Sing he

had been visited by labor leaders, politicos, businessmen, and others. N.Y. Senate Majority Leader Arthur H. Wicks, who, as acting president of the senate, had become temporary lieutenant governor on the resignation of Frank C. Moore, explained how it had been in his own case.

He only went to see Fay, he said, "to discuss labor conditions in the counties I represent". For example: a dispute between two unions over whose members should install certain machinery in a power station. When the dispute threatened to tie up an $18 million project, Wicks went to Fay. "Soon the representatives of the two unions met in New York, settled their differences. . . ."

Governor Dewey had Joey transferred to another prison where close tabs could be kept on future callers. Dewey also managed to force Wicks to resign his posts in the State Legislature. Then the Governor got back to harness racing, which was causing him political embarrassment. (Example: his friend and G.O.P. ally, Republican leader J. Russel Sprague, had been shown to own large blocks of raceway stock.)

Late in December, Dewey named George P. Monaghan, former New York City police commissioner, as "czar" of the State's tracks. Monaghan's assignment was to "keep hoodlums and undesirables out of every phase of harness racing".

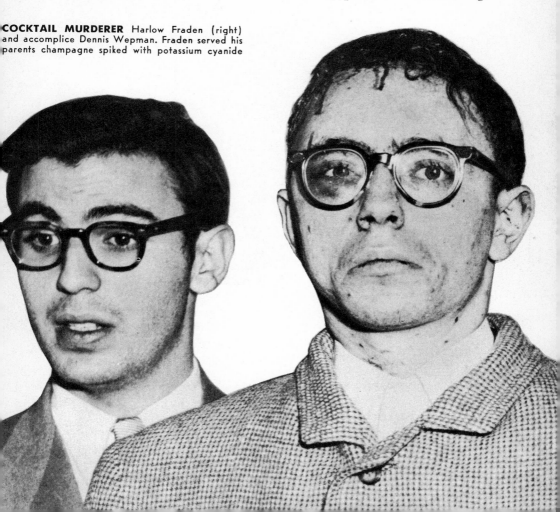

**COCKTAIL MURDERER** Harlow Fraden (right) and accomplice Dennis Wepman. Fraden served his parents champagne spiked with potassium cyanide

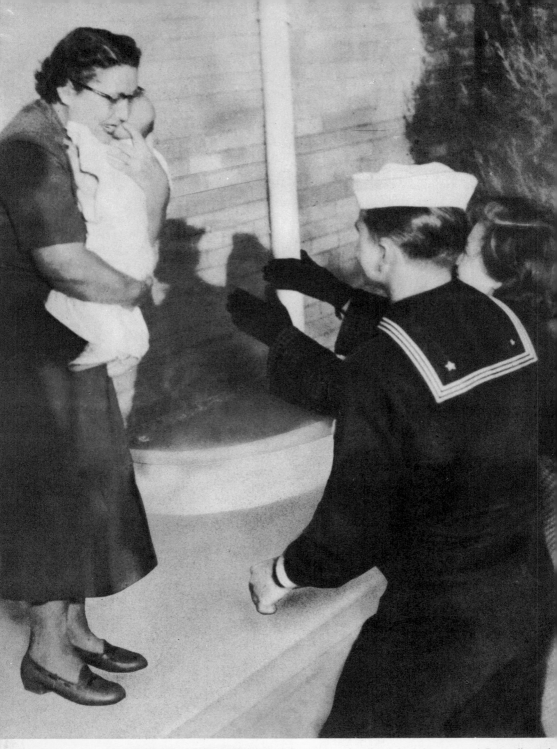

**REUNION IN OKLAHOMA** is joyous for the Robert Stammers of Evansville, Ind., as they reach for baby son kidnaped from their home and recovered unhurt 550 miles away.

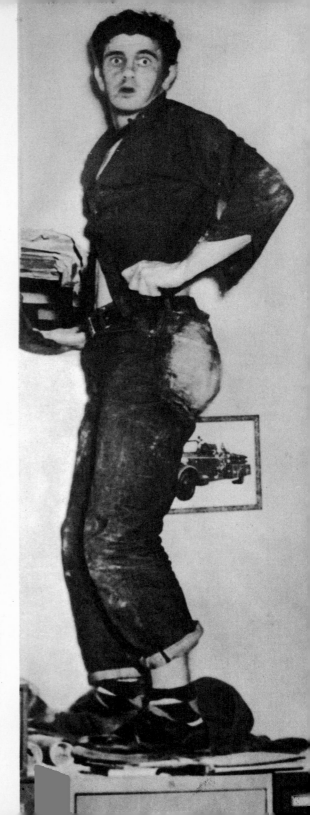

The year 1953 marked the reappearance of several formerly headlined names. Chief among them were the following.

Gambling overlord Frank Costello, who in 1952 was jailed for contempt of Congress. In 1953, freed after serving fourteen months, he faced further imprisonment on charges of income-tax evasion.

Bookmaker Harry Gross, who in 1951 was sentenced to twelve years in a New York jail. In 1953, after three tries, he won a reduction in his sentence to eight years, which, with time off for good behavior, would free him in 1956.

Minot F. (Mickey) Jelke 3d, young oleomargarine heir, whose arrest in 1952 on compulsory-prostitution charges highlighted New York's "café society" season. In 1953, having served most of an eight-month sentence for illegal possession of firearms, he was freed on $50,000 bail, pending appeal of a three-to-six-year sentence on the prostitution charge.

Aldo Icardi of Pittsburgh and Carl Lo-Dolce of Rochester, N.Y., who in 1944 had parachuted into northern Italy with Major William V. Holohan of New York City, to arrange delivery of arms and supplies to Italian partisans. In 1953 an Italian court sentenced them respectively to life imprisonment and seventeen years in jail for Holohan's murder—a sentence that could be enforced only if they voluntarily returned to Italy.

For a lighter note at year's end, America recalled the story of the proprietor of the Busy Bee Café in Dallas, Tex. He finally evolved a way to stop the burglaries that had emptied his till twenty-five times. To blast anyone attempting to jimmy the café's window, he rigged up a shotgun with an automatic tripper. Next day he discovered robbery No. 26. Its loot: the shotgun.

# WORLD AFFAIRS

# The Stalin Era Ends

**MOSCOW MOURNS:** This slow-moving file is on its way to view Joseph Stalin's body as it lies in Lenin's tomb (right)

"ON THE NIGHT OF MARCH 2, 1953, J. V. Stalin had a sudden brain hemorrhage . . . as a result of which he developed a paralysis of the right leg and right arm with loss of consciousness and speech."

The medical bulletin was issued at 2 A.M. on March 4, the first of an hourly series. A later bulletin revealed that Stalin had been given "oxygen . . . camphor compounds, caffeine, and glucose. For the second time, leeches were used to draw blood . . ."

News of the leader's grave illness grapevined through Moscow's snowy streets. About 9 A.M., much later than usual, the March 4 morning papers arrived on the stands, where crowds of readers queued up.

By 10 A.M. a stillness in Red Square indicated the awesome presence of death.

Outside the U.S.S.R., things were not so quiet. In the White House, President Eisenhower hurriedly conferred with Secretary of State John Foster Dulles and British Foreign Secretary Anthony Eden. *The New York Times* hinted at the possibility of war. On Wall Street old Czarist bonds jumped ½ to ¾ points. In the Vatican the Pope said a special prayer for the Russian people.

"One of the greatest persecutors of the Catholic Church . . . since the birth of Christ is dying," said a Vatican official, expressing "profound commiseration for a man who must appear before the tribunal of God under the crushing weight of such frightful guilt".

On March 6 came the final word: "The heart of the comrade and inspired continuer of Lenin's will, the wise leader and teacher of the Communist party and the Soviet people—Joseph Vissarionovich Stalin—has stopped beating."

**WHILE THE WORLD WATCHES,** the fallen dictator makes his farewell appearance in a satin-trimmed coffin lavishly decked with hothouse flowers

The notice that Stalin had died on March 5 had been withheld for six hours. To soothe the suspicious, Stalin's last gasps were affirmed by the party's Central Committee, the Council of Ministers of the U.S.S.R., and the Presidium of the Supreme Soviet.

In Poland "more vodka was drunk that night than at any time since the war," Jan Hajdukiewicz, escaped Pole, was later to relate. "The police had to close the bars and night clubs to curb the celebration."

What manner of man was this whose dying could arouse Pope and President, Wall Street and Warsaw? History may never again witness so powerful a tyrant. On the other hand, it is tragically possible that Stalin was the Tyrant of Tomorrow. The late George Orwell's book

*1984* forecast a world of robots dominated by Big Brother, for whom Stalin was the model. Following is the story of Big Brother's rise to power.

## Up the Ladder

In 1879, few Americans had heard of Georgia, nestled between the Black Sea and the Caucasus Mountains. But on Dec. 21 of that year, in the mountain town of Gori, an event was taking place which would make Georgia almost as well known as the Cracker State. On that day the laundress Ekaterina Djugashvili, wife of the drunken cobbler Vissarion, gave birth to a son.

After much sacrifice, she was able to enroll her Soso (Joey) in the Orthodox Seminary of Tiflis, capital of Georgia, to train him for the priesthood. But Soso developed not faith in God but faith in Marxism. After four years—at the age of 18—the seminary expelled him, reputedly because of his revolutionary activities.

Under the name of "Koba" (The Indomitable), the fiercely mustachioed, beetle-browed, pock-marked youth became a fire-eating labor agitator. Tracked down by the police, he made his first of six trips to prison in Siberia in 1902. In 1913, by that time calling himself "Stalin" (Man of Steel), he was sent to escape-proof Kureika, 20 miles from the Arctic Circle. There he remained until the overthrow of Czar Nicholas II in March of 1917.

Stalin first met Nikolai Lenin, founder of the Bolshevik party, in 1905 and became a devoted Bolshevik. After the 1905 rebellion, when Lenin's party was scattered, demoralized, and impoverished, Stalin robbed banks and turned the loot over to the party.

In 1912 he became a member of the Central Committee and also helped . found the Communist newspaper *Pravda,* whose editorship he resumed after his return from exile. On Nov. 7, 1917, when the Bolsheviks seized power, he was appointed Commissar of Nationalities.

During the years of civil war that followed, Stalin was brought into prolonged contact with more worldly and brilliant comrades. He grew to hate Leon Trotsky, acid-tongued leader of the November *coup d'état.*

Then, in 1922, Stalin was made the first Secretary-General of the Communist party. This post became his passport to power as he filled the party's key positions with men owing him personal allegiance.

By the end of 1922, Lenin warned against the "enormous power" Comrade Stalin had amassed. On March 5, 1923, Lenin, who had suffered a paralytic stroke, informed Stalin that he was severing "all personal and comradely relations" with him. This in no way daunted the man of steel. On the day of Lenin's funeral, having misinformed the vacationing Trotsky as to the exact date of the event, a fur-hatted Stalin, "loyal comrade and true disciple of Lenin", as he was ever after to describe himself, plowed through the snow at the head of the pallbearers.

## A Czar Is Born

In the scramble for power that followed, firebrand Trotsky demanded immediate socialism in the Soviet Union and a resumption of world revolutionary activity. The scholarly Nicolai Bukharin urged an extension of the New Economic Policy—a temporary return to capitalism—introduced by Lenin in 1921. Stalin anathematized both sides.

To isolate Trotsky, he joined with the Bolshevik stalwarts Lev Kamenev and Grigori Zinoviev, Lenin's former cronies.

But once Trotsky was defeated, Stalin stranded his two partners. In 1929 Trotsky was exiled; in 1940, having settled in Mexico City, he was hacked to death in his study, presumably by a Stalin agent.

The first of the Soviet Union's ambitious Five Year Plans was launched in 1928. "The history of Russia," said Stalin, "is the history of defeats due to backwardness. . . . We must no longer be backward."

The years of the first Plan were punctuated by trials of "wreckers" and "saboteurs". People vanished. Some were shot. A piecework speed-up system was instituted. A Donets coal miner named Aleksei Stakhanov was glorified for having exceeded his production norm, and Stakhanovism became a cult.

By the end of 1932 the output of coal, oil, pig iron, and steel had doubled. Immediately after, the second *Piatiletka* (Five Year Plan) was off and running. This at first called for production of consumer goods, desperately needed by the masses. But in 1933, Hitler, an archenemy of Bolshevism, became German Chancellor, and the Plan swerved back to heavy industry.

Then came the collectivization of agriculture. First the poor peasants were roused against the rich. But once these rich "kulaks" had been shipped by the hundreds of thousands to forced-labor camps, the remaining peasants were herded into huge kolkhozes or collective farms.

Many defied Stalin, destroyed their crops, slaughtered their beasts. But collectivization went on. Even the devastating Ukrainian famine of 1932–33 did not stop the process. Altogether, 10,-000,000 persons starved to death.

"How long do you intend to go on killing people?" Lady Astor asked Stalin. "As long as it is necessary," he replied.

In January, 1934, Sergei Kirov, Stalin's protégé, wrote in *Pravda:* "It is difficult . . . to imagine the figure of such a giant as Stalin." Kirov's difficulties were soon over. In December he was assassinated. Stalin, so the story goes, had secret-police chief Henry Yagoda stage the murder.

An alleged plot against Stalin's regime gave Yagoda the pretext for throwing out a huge dragnet, while Georgi M. Malenkov, Stalin's bright young private secretary, made up the dossiers of those whom his boss wanted out of the way. Thousands of small fry were executed. Sixteen top party figures were imprisoned.

## Prosecutor Vishinsky

In August of 1936 the first great "purge" trial took place. Andrei Y. Vishinsky, later the U.S.S.R. delegate to the United Nations, did the prosecuting. Kamenev and Zinoviev, among others, confessed to sabotage and treason, on alleged orders of archvillain Trotsky.

A grim joke, the Stalin constitution, was proclaimed in December of 1936. It promised the Soviet citizen every conceivable freedom. Articles 127 and 128 were the cream of the jest. These guaranteed all citizens inviolability of person and home.

Soon the purge trials were resumed, bigger and bloodier than ever. A surprise victim was Henry Yagoda.

During 1937 and 1938 most of the "heroes of the Bolshevik revolution", among them Bukharin and Aleksei Rykov, Commissar of Communications, took turns at spinning out well-rehearsed confessions and then went to their graves.

Marshal Mikhail Tukhachevski and seven other top army chiefs were tried secretly. Though three were Jews, all

were charged with being in league with Hitler. All were shot.

Nicolai Yezhov had replaced Yagoda in 1937 as Commissar of State Security. To prove his zeal, he soon had the Soviet jails jammed to capacity.

"There was no way to get in," wrote one victim. "All the space was occupied to the last inch by tightly packed, half-naked men."

The purge trials frightened factory managers, engineers, and foremen. Pro-

duction slowed as panicky personnel passed the buck on decisions that might be mistaken for sabotage.

Stalin, concerned over production norms, acted. In 1938, G.P.U. chief Yezhov was deposed for arresting innocents.

Into his spot came Lavrenti P. Beria, whose first act was an order releasing thousands of baffled men from jail.

By now Stalin's power was absolute. Virtually all the old Bolsheviks who masterminded the revolution, and lesser figures whose repute antedated his apotheosis, had been wiped out. Into their places Stalin moved former non-entities, all fully aware of their benefactor's power.

## Ordeal by Gunfire

On June 22, 1941, Hitler told the German people: "The hour has come for action against the Jewish rulers of the Bolshevist center in Moscow."

Within days, the German Panzers had slashed chunks out of eastern Poland and other territories acquired by the Soviet Union in a pact of friendship which Stalin had signed with Hitler in 1939.

Large numbers of the peasantry, especially Ukrainians and other non-Russians in the Soviet "family of nations", at first regarded Hitler as a liberator. They went over to him by the millions, but the brutality of the Master Race soon stopped the wholesale surrender.

"We underrated the Russian colossus," wrote German Chief of Staff Colonel General Franz Halder after the first six weeks of war. "We reckoned with 200 enemy divisions. . . . We have already counted 360. . . . If we smash a dozen . . . the Russians simply put up another dozen."

Slowly the twisted wreckage of Stalin's tanks and the corpses of Soviet youth blunted the Panzer spearheads. And Stalin had on his side the fiercest of Russian defenders, "General Winter".

Meanwhile, millions of tons of U.S. lend-lease supplies had immeasurably strengthened the Soviet war machine. Along with American aid, which turned the tide of war on the eastern front in Stalin's favor, came Allied round-the-clock air raids on Germany, and finally the Allied invasion of Europe. Yet, after the war, as Stalin stood master of an empire stretching from the Kurile Islands to Berlin, Marshal Vasili Sokolovski declared: "The second front was opened only when it had become evident that the Soviet Union was capable alone . . . of defeating Germany."

## The Second Bolshevik Crusade

The first Bolshevik attempt to conquer the world had come to an end in 1920 when war-torn Europe refused to collapse into chaos. World War II, Stalin thought, had definitely made Europe ripe for the plucking.

As a matter of fact, Eastern Europe was overripe, thanks to Soviet occupation forces and tiny bands of indigenous Reds. Bulgaria, Romania, Hungary, Albania, Poland, East Germany, and Czechoslovakia quickly succumbed to the Soviet colossus. Only President Truman's 1947 decision to bolster Greece and Turkey blocked the Soviet bid for an outlet to the Mediterranean.

Soviet ambitions with respect to Western Europe were rudely frustrated. The Marshall Plan, which provided life-giving sustenance for the war-torn economies of that area, wrecked Communist plans to take over France, Italy, and other West European states. Apparently undismayed, the Reds blockaded Berlin in 1948.

The American airlift parried that thrust. There followed stern U.S. warnings to the U.S.S.R., reinforced in April of 1949 by the creation of the North Atlantic Treaty Organization (N.A.T.O.). The doors to Soviet aggression seemed closed—all but the back door to Asia.

In September, 1948, North Korea had been set up as a Soviet satellite. A year later, after Chinese Communist leader Mao Tse-tung had driven Nationalist Chiang Kai-shek into the sea, the People's Republic of China came into exist-

**GONE BUT NOT FORGOTTEN:**
Wreath-laying ceremony at Stalin
Monument in East Berlin climaxes
parade in honor of dead Dictator

ence. By that time the U.S. had withdrawn its armed forces from South Korea, declaring that Korea was "militarily indefensible". The temptation to the Kremlin proved irresistible. On June 25, 1950, South Korea was invaded by the Soviet puppet, North Korea.

The Soviet peoples had hoped that when World War II ended they could live in peace. Instead they got atom-scare headlines and charges that the United States was preparing a super blitzkrieg against the U.S.S.R.

In October, 1952, the Nineteenth Party Congress, the first such meeting since 1939, convened in Moscow. In effect, the congress was preparation for the aging Stalin's death. Georgi M. Malenkov, who would succeed Stalin as dictator and who was now second in command, spoke for three hours. This was the long-awaited sign to world Communism that a new boss would soon be taking over.

When in March, 1953, Stalin's bier was placed on display in the Hall of Columns, a framework half the size of the front facade accommodated a huge portrait of the deceased pharaoh. The government planned the construction of a monumental pantheon to house the bodies of Lenin and Stalin—"indefinitely".

On Nov. 17 the red and black mausoleum under the Kremlin's walls, once the resting place of Lenin alone, was thrown open to the public. On a sarcophagus identical to Lenin's lay Stalin's body. A bright spotlight illuminated his serene features. The hairs of his head and mustache, silvery white at his death, now were artfully mixed with the brown of younger years. Across his chest lay two rows of ribbons and above them lay three medals—the highest Soviet awards.

Thus Joseph Stalin was enshrined as No. 2 god on the Olympus of Bolshevism.

**AN ANSWER** to the world's query—What next?
—lies in this icy stare. Its owner: Georgi Malenkov

# MALENKOV TAKES OVER

**MONARCH** of all he surveys, Malenkov (left) symbolically salutes troops massed in Red Square

STALIN'S DEATH LEFT THE RED LEADERS fearing three bogeys: (1) an American attack; (2) discontent among the peasants and the numerous non-Russian peoples within their empire; (3) one another.

Incessantly, the Communist leaders warned of "internal and external enemies", yet they told the people to "keep calm". The Reds' jittery vigilance was proved in mid-March when MIG-15 jets over West Germany shot down an American fighter and a British bomber.

On March 14, Premier Georgi M. Malenkov sounded a new keynote to the 1200-odd members of the Supreme Soviet: "There is no question which cannot be solved by peaceful means. This is our attitude toward all states, among them the U.S.A. [Cheers] . . . Coexistence and peaceful competition of two different systems, capitalist and socialist, are possible [Applause]."

Before the Supreme Soviet adjourned its 67-minute session, it was informed of the structure of the new post-Stalin government: the Presidium of the Communist party had been cut from twenty-five to ten members. Eight of the ten had belonged to the old Politburo, abolished in 1952. Obviously, the dividends would still be divided among those on Stalin's old board of directors.

Lavrenti P. Beria resumed his old post as Minister of Internal Affairs, replacing Semyon Ignatiev as head of the secret police. Vyacheslav M. Molotov returned to the Foreign Ministry, and Marshal Nikolai A. Bulganin to the War Ministry. These men, plus Premier Malenkov and Lazar M. Kaganovich, long the guiding genius of heavy industry and transportation, comprised the Presidium of the Council of Ministers (cabinet).

Stalin had fourteen deputy premiers, Malenkov only five. Of these, four were "first deputy premiers". The order of their listing made it clear that Beria ranked first, followed by Molotov, Bulganin, and Kaganovich. The other deputy premier, Anastas I. Mikoyan, Minister of Internal and External Trade, did not rate a "first" before his title.

Malenkov was not only Premier but also Communist party's First Secretary—Stalin's perennial job. The newly organized secretariat included, besides Malenkov, Nikita S. Khrushchev, reputed to be Malenkov's brother-in-law, and Semyon D. Ignatiev, a long-time friend.

Shortly thereafter the Kremlin made many little gestures to reduce world tensions. For the first time in seven years, a Russian broadcast gave the United States credit for having helped defeat the Axis. The Soviet government apologized for the plane incidents over Germany.

Behind the Iron Curtain the dictator-ship concept was played down, at least temporarily. On March 14 the Premier turned over his second office, that of the party's First Secretary, to Khrushchev.

Soon *Pravda* was hailing "collective leadership", saying: "Where this does not exist, [leaders] conduct themselves like autocrats."

Punishment under Stalin had seldom fitted the crime. Now a sweeping amnesty was decreed. All persons under police investigation were to be set free, as well as all persons serving terms of less than five years. Longer penal terms were cut in half. Also released were all mothers of young children, pregnant women, juvenile delinquents, and all convicts suffering from incurable diseases.

The decree pledged a general re-examination of Soviet Russia's criminal laws—a clear admission of past miscarriages of justice.

Moscow was really set rocking on April 14.

Early in January, nine doctors, five of them Jews, were accused by the wife of one of the doctors of assassinating, by deliberate malpractice, Politburo members Andrei A. Zhdanov and Alexander S. Shcherbakov. These men died in 1948. Beria was then chief of the secret police. At the time of the arrest of the doctors, *Pravda* recalled the "lack of vigilance" of the security forces, which had permitted the doctors to perpetrate their crimes.

## An About-face

But on April 14 the Ministry of Internal Security did an about-face. It declared that the case against the doctors had been based on fraudulent evidence. The government also announced that Internal Security Minister Ignatiev had been taken in by his deputy, a man named Ryumin, who supposedly had organized the frame-up and had used illegal means to extort the confessions.

Here was more evidence of what the world had long suspected: the Stalin purge trials had been carefully staged, with the defendants reciting fixed parts.

Ryumin's purpose, *Pravda* charged, was to inflame "national hostilities" among the Soviet people. Again what the West had suspected was clear: the "Jewish doctors' plot" had been part of the campaign of anti-Semitism which had swept through the Soviet Union and its satellites in 1952.

Now ardent lip service was paid to national minority rights. For violating such rights, high party officials were replaced in the Baltic countries, Armenia, Azerbaidzhan, and Stalin's own homeland of Georgia. A Malenkov protégé, L. G. Melnikov, party boss of the Ukraine, was fired for Russianizing the Ukrainians.

In Georgia, Beria himself took charge. Just a year earlier, Beria had purged the Georgian party. Three "bourgeois nationalists" had been replaced by three "loyal Communists". Now these three loyal Communists were arrested as "enemies of the people", and back into favor came the "bourgeois nationalists".

Beria named Valerian Bakradze Premier of Georgia. Bakradze slapped at Malenkov by hailing Beria as "the outstanding leader of the party".

These incidents illuminated the struggle for power, probably developing since early 1952, between party boss Malenkov and police chief Beria. Sent to Georgia early in 1952, Beria was forced to humiliate and weaken himself in his homeland by purging his henchmen and appointing Malenkov's to high party and security posts there. The doctors' plot was "pinned" on Beria, but it had probably been engineered by Malenkov's good friend Ignatiev.

After Stalin's death, Beria struck back. The amnesty, the doctors' deliverance, and the stress on minority rights all added up to a Beria bid for wide popular support.

That Beria got as far as he did with his champion-of-the people act was proof that Malenkov was as yet too insecure to risk antagonizing popular opinion. From concessions made throughout the year by the government, it was apparent that public opinion was something to worry about.

## Prices Go Down

As in 1952, April of 1953 brought a slash in the price of consumer goods. Food was down 10 percent, clothing 15 percent—a promise that life in the Soviet Union would soon be richer.

There was room for improvement. Like women the world over, Soviet women wanted stylish clothes. American nylons brought $37.50 a pair on Moscow's thriving black market. City houses were so crudely constructed that they began to fall apart before they were fully built. Associated Press correspondent Tom Whitney was walking on the other side of the street one night when a third-story balcony fell off a Moscow building.

Living in one of the capital's finest apartment houses, Whitney had poor heating and no central hot-water system. Gas and water pipes were partly exposed, as was the wiring in his apartment. There were no closets. Outside the cities, newly built houses were usually log cabins.

In May *Izvestia* figured out that for Moscow's 5,000,000 residents there was housing space of 5 square yards per person. Many families occupied only one room and shared kitchen and bathroom facilities with others. By 1960, the paper

wrote, housing space would be increased by one third. Thus Russians in 1953 seemed about to enjoy their second New Economic Policy.

For a while, at least, the Soviet regime appeared to be trying in earnest to eliminate tension in three areas of the world. It got the wheels rolling toward a Korean truce. It announced the end of its military regime in Austria. And, on May 28, it dissolved the Soviet Military Control Commission in East Germany. The Reds acted as if they might be willing to get out of East Germany, permit divided

Germany's unification, and sign the long-delayed treaty to bring World War II to its official end.

Then came June 17. On that day the people of East Germany rose up against their Communist masters, and the world witnessed a proletarian rebellion being crushed by Soviet tanks and machine guns. The revolt frightened the slightly outstretched Russian hand back into its iron glove.

On June 27, just before sundown, tanks and truckloads of soldiers rumbled through northern Moscow. That same

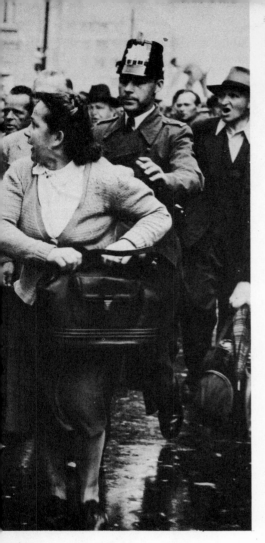

night, at the Bolshoi Theater, Malenkov and twelve top political figures attended the opening performance of the opera *The Decembrists*. Beria was not present, and his absence was noted by all Soviet papers the following day. Had something happened to him?

Something had. On July 10, in a report read by Malenkov to the Central Committee, Beria was charged with "criminal anti-party and anti-State actions . . . intended to undermine the Soviet State in the interest of foreign capital". He was expelled from the party. His case

was referred for consideration to the U.S.S.R. Supreme Court. In the Moscow Hall of Columns, 2000 people hailed the downfall of a "foul enemy".

Had the Berlin riots sealed Beria's doom? Most experts thought so. Enemies waiting for his first mistake may have sounded an alarm over the apparent laxity of East German security police. It could now be charged that Beria, chief of Eastern Europe's security network, was the wrong man to safeguard against a new revolution.

On Dec. 16 a Moscow broadcast announced Beria's confession and imminent trial. Six days later a court headed by Marshal of the Army Ivan S. Konev condemned him to be shot. The military character of the tribunal, coupled with build-ups given World War II hero Marshal Georgi K. Zhukov and other military men, indicated that the Soviet Army, in all likelihood, had tipped the Beria-Malenkov scales in the latter's favor.

After Beria's downfall, the Kremlin went all out to assure itself of the people's loyalty. The government made its bid to the peasants through a 25,000-word report written by Nikita Khrushchev, published in *Pravda* on Sept. 15.

"There is enough grain," wrote Khrushchev. ". . . now the Soviet populace wants to progress from a bread basis to a meat and milk basis, not to mention vegetables and fruit." He blamed lagging Soviet agricultural production on the "mistaken policy" of not allowing the peasant to develop his individual plot of land along with his work in the collective farm. The Kremlin ordered certain tank factories to start making tractors to increase the vegetable output.

The good life was stressed again in October. "Champagne," declared Deputy Premier Mikoyan, "has now become accessible to the working people." His speech ran on to depict a Soviet paradise based on a Sears-Roebuck catalogue. He promised 330,000 refrigerators, 500,000 vacuum cleaners, and 1,000,000 TV sets for 1955.

In other words, said *The New York Times,* one refrigerator for every 600 persons, one vacuum cleaner for every 400, and a TV set for every 200.

"It must be admitted," Mikoyan said, "that capitalist trade has some qualities that should be studied. . . ."

Goods were not packaged properly in the U.S.S.R., he went on. "To buy caviar, cream cheese, honey, jam, or marmalade, the customer has to provide his own container. Industry must supply these goods already packed."

The "butter instead of guns" policy seemed to forestall an immediate return to Stalin's program of aggression. But as the year went on the official attitude of the U.S.S.R. became suspicious, quarrelsome, and contradictory. Hopes for Big Four talks on the German question were deflated and then inflated again. The Korean truce became an endless source of irritation.

Soviet delegate Andrei Y. Vishinsky, addressing the United Nations General Assembly in November, sounded Stalin's old theme of "capitalist encirclement" of the Soviet Union. He declared that West Germany was being prepared as a "springboard for attack on the U.S.S.R."

Yet the few Americans allowed to visit the Soviet Union found its people sometimes friendly and always curious about Americans.

Nine American small-town newspaper publishers and radio-station owners spent nine days in Moscow and took many photographs.

"I am a country girl from Minnesota," write Dodee Wick, wife of one of the publishers, "and the last thing I ever expected was to be sleeping in a bed that Lenin slept in."

Zander Hollander, age 22, formerly with the University of Michigan newspaper, toured the U.S.S.R. with two United States collegians and talked to many students.

"Their questions," he wrote, "were always the same: How did we manage, living in such poverty? How did we feel about the lack of academic freedom in the United States? . . .

"Soviet students belong to the privileged class. Take the students who escorted us through Moscow's new university, a cross between the Empire State Building and a thousand pounds of French pastry. For one of them, Sergei

**TWO DOWN, ONE UP:** Beria followed Stalin to grave in 1953. Malenkov survived

Sachin, son of poor peasants . . . the new university is a dream come true.

". . . . While millions of Russians live in poverty, this is what Sergei gets as a student. . . . Almost 500 rubles [worth about $50] a month in state scholarships, free textbooks . . . hearty meals at a very low daily cost, his own room . . . daily maid service."

Hollander, however, ". . . never saw a Soviet girl I could get enthusiastic about. . . . Yet there's nothing basically wrong with Soviet girls—nothing a reducing course, a morning in a beauty parlor, or an afternoon of dress shopping couldn't fix."

Perle Mesta, noted American hostess, had a grand time gallivanting unguided through the Soviet Union. In a Moscow park, a middle-aged man started to touch the fur of her mink stole. "Don't touch that!" cried the man with him. "You'll be infected with microbes."

In the Ukraine, a cab driver warned her not to expect Ukrainians to tell her how they really felt about the Soviet system. That would mean prison. She told of watching a movie which "went into a vicious attack on the United States. A Ukrainian man, having heard me speaking English, kept leaning over to say 'Lies! All lies!'"

Mrs. Mesta was astonished to find "how Russia was divided so sharply into two broad classes . . . the rich . . . and the poor. . . . On the roof of the Moskva Hotel . . . caviar, vodka, and champagne flowed freely. . . . An excellent dinner for two . . . would run up to 120 rubles [worth about $12]. An average Russian worker, who earns about 600 rubles a month, couldn't get near the place."

But whatever else American travelers could find within the Soviet Union during 1953, they saw no evidence that the Kremlin had any intention of lifting the Iron Curtain and settling the cold war.

# The SATELLITES

THE FLAME OF FREEDOM BURNED IN THE mind of a Polish pilot named Franciszek Jarecki. On the morning of March 5, 1953, the 21-year-old lieutenant, on maneuvers over the Baltic Sea, sensed his chance. He put his MIG-15 fighter into a dive and set out for Copenhagen. Over his radio, he intercepted orders to other Polish jets from the control tower at Slupsk. He was to be chased and shot down. He dropped his spare fuel tanks to gain speed.

A hundred miles later the fuel gauge showed empty, but he was over the Roenne airstrip on the Danish island of Bornholm. Normally jets should have 3250 yards of concrete landing strip. Roenne's was grass-covered and 1300 yards long. The young Pole said a prayer and made it. He leaped from the plane and ran up to airport officials. Keeping his hands over his head, he shouted: "Communism kaput—asylum!" The Danes got the idea. Thus the first undamaged MIG-15 fell into Western hands.

Lieutenant Jarecki was only one of a number of Poles who chose freedom via unique routes. Another MIG pilot followed his lead and flew out to Danish soil. The skipper of the *Batory,* the pride of Poland's merchant fleet, jumped ship in Britain. One aide deserted from the team of Communist "neutrals" supervising the Korean truce. And Dr. Marek S. Korowicz quit the Polish delegation to the United Nations, and sought and found asylum in the United States.

Throughout the so-called "People's Democratic Republics", crashing the

**CONQUERED:** Joseph Cardinal Mindszenty, Hungarian spiritual leader jailed on treason charges, looks vainly to Moscow for freedom

Iron Curtain was a popular pursuit. Among the most ingenious fugitives were the Czechoslovaks.

A two-engined Czech air liner was on a routine flight from Prague southeast to Brno. Slowly the pilot, Miroslav Slovak, nosed the plane westward toward the U.S. zone of Germany. Two passengers entered the cockpit. One slugged the radio operator, took his place, and contacted an American control tower. He asked whether asylum would be granted to those who wished it. The answer was "yes". After hedgehopping across West Germany, the plane landed at Frankfort.

A Czech mechanic named Vaclav

Uhlik decided to get out when he learned that his shop was to be nationalized. Working nights, he used scrap iron and steel to convert his automobile into an armored car resembling a Czech army vehicle.

One midnight he piled into this crude contraption with his wife and two children, two soldiers, a gardener, and Libuse Cloud, wife of an American veteran, whom the Iron Curtain had kept from her husband. The vehicle was camouflaged with branches and leaves. As it rumbled through Pilsen, police patrols paid it scant attention.

As dawn was breaking, it lurched off

**IRONCLAD PASSPORT:** The home-made armored car in which eight Czechs fled from Red-ruled native land to freedom. Scrap-metal vehicle was built in secrecy by Vaclav Uhlik (shown holding child)

the road, past sleepy border guards, and broke through the barbed wire into West Germany. By the time the guards were ready to fire, the armored car was a scornful puff of exhaust smoke, hundreds of yards beyond reach.

Five Czechs had no difficulty crossing the border into East Germany, but then their troubles began. In Riesa they sold a cigarette case and watch to buy tickets for a westbound train. At the station the police caught up with them. Firing began. Three policemen fell, and one Czech was captured.

The other four hid out in a hay barn for seven days, eating raw potatoes and drinking milk from cans left for dairy trucks. The dragnet tightened. The Czechs dashed for the cover of nearby woods. Machine-gun fire wounded a second fugitive, who pleaded to be left behind.

After five days in the woods, the three who were left sneaked into an empty freight car heading toward Berlin. Then

they walked along the tracks until they ran into police.

Another gun battle ensued. A third Czech, Milian Baumer, was shot in the stomach. He and the brothers Maczin got away and reached a suburban train. They hung on underneath the cars. Czirad Maczin got safely through to West Berlin. His brother Jozef and the bleeding Baumer got off one station too soon. The two found themselves in a hive of Communist police. Dodging bullets, they dashed for the border. Although Baumer was wounded again, both made it. Similarly dramatic episodes occurred all along the Iron Curtain. Between 1948 and 1953, well over 1,000,-000 persons fled from Communism in Eastern Europe.

Such stories of desperate men risking their lives to escape the Kremlin's grip on its satellites belied the propaganda of the so-called World Festival of Youth and Students for Peace and Friendship. The World Festival took place in Bucharest, Romania, from Aug. 16 to 23 and was attended by 30,000 visitors who supposedly were from 102 countries.

The Romanian capital was dressed up with a new 80,000-seat stadium, two open-air theaters, and an elegant opera house. Volunteer brigades planted 40,-000 trees and shrubs. The youthful visitors danced in the streets to loud-speakers going full blast from 6 A.M. to midnight. Paul Robeson records were played frequently. So was a song entitled "Lay Your Atom Bomb Down."

During the World Festival, American journalists got their first peek at Romania in five years. The gaily white-washed main streets, the façades erected to hide dilapidated buildings, the sumptuous meals at the Hotel Athenee did not mislead them. The giveaways were the protruding bones of peasants' horses, the scrawny cats prowling around restau-

**APPRECIATIVE VIENNESE** laugh at window display of U.S. baby photos lampooning typical Communist attitudes. Incensed Soviet authorities protested in vain

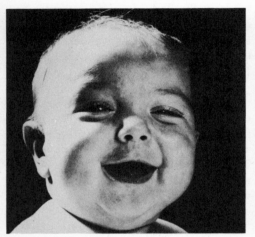

"MY DEAR SIR, YOU SIMPLY DON'T UNDERSTAND THE PRINCIPLES OF DIALECTIC MATERIALISM"

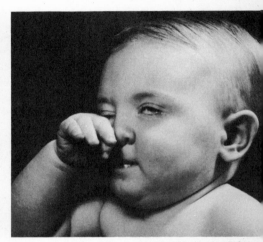

"OH! OH! NOT ANOTHER DEMONSTRATION AGAIN SO SOON"

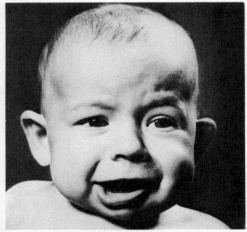

"BUT I NEVER EVEN HEARD OF A MAN NAMED TROTSKY"

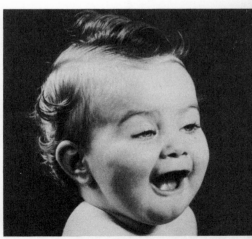

"BUT PROLETARIAN ART IS SO REALISTIC, SO . . . SO . . . JE NE SAIS QUOI"

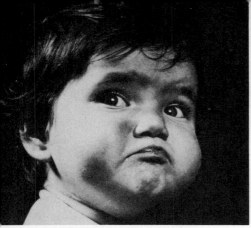

"ALL RIGHT THEN, LET'S SEE YOU TRY
TO COLLECTIVIZE THE ROMANIANS"

"WHAT IS IT? I'VE NO IDEA.
BUT I GOT THE STALIN PRIZE FOR IT"

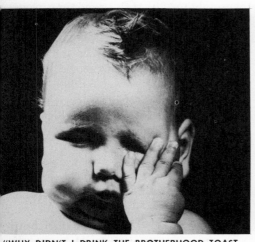

"WHY DIDN'T I DRINK THE BROTHERHOOD TOAST
WITH MALENKOV IN THOSE DAYS?"

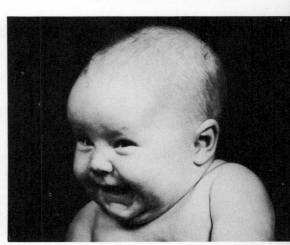

"YOU DON'T REALLY BELIEVE THE PEOPLE'S
UNITED FRONT IS PEOPLE'S DEMOCRACY?"

"MY LATEST STALIN CONCERTO SHOWS
MIDDLE-CLASS REACTIONARY TENDENCIES"

"CAN I COME OUT? HAS THE SECRET POLICE
GONE YET?"

rants. Also there were the price tags—coffee, $8 a pound.

Under the noses of the government guides, four American correspondents were handed a letter. "Don't leave with the impression that the Romanian people live as they are living during the festival," it read. "For three months preceding it, the Communist government seized all the food from the markets, and workers of all classes died of hunger in the streets."

The Soviet Union caused similar shortages in all the satellites by milking their economies for its own benefit. In Poland a pair of men's shoes retailed at $231. A customer was permitted to try on only the right shoe. It was reported that once he had both shoes on his feet, he was likely to run off.

Enduring hunger and poverty, the satellites also were subjected to religious persecution.

To the Poles, their Catholic Church is the symbol of national freedom. In 1953 the Communists speeded their campaign to destroy it. Using their pet tactics, the Communists upset the clergy by random arrests and tried to discredit it on nonreligious grounds.

In January five priests were put on trial in Cracow for black-market dealings and espionage for U.S. Intelligence. The Reverend Joseph Lalito was sentenced to death as a spy for the U.S. and the Vatican.

In September, Bishop Czeslaw Kaczmarek of Kielce, after two years in jail, stood trial in Warsaw. His confession followed the pattern of the Stalin purge-trial theater pieces.

"I led them astray," muttered the bishop, referring to his four co-defendants, "and I repent."

The bishop received a twelve-year jail term. "Legal blackmail," the Vatican's *l'Osservatore Romano* commented.

Because of its contributions to Soviet military might, the industry of Czechoslovakia is the most important in Eastern Europe. The Czech laboring man was given the greatest possible incentive—he was told, in effect, that he must work or starve.

On May 30 the currency was devalued. This action, together with the voiding of all government bonds issued since 1945, robbed the people of whatever they had saved since the war's end. The exchange ratio was 50 to 1. This meant that a bank account of $1000 dropped overnight to $20. At the same time, wages were lowered and prices were raised.

Going berserk on June 1, Czech proletarians of Pilsen smashed machinery in the Skoda armaments plant and pillaged the town hall. Pictures of Stalin and of President Klement Gottwald, who died on March 14, were ripped down. Up went photos of the last democratic President, Eduard Beneš.

"Politically unaware workers," reported the Pilsen *Pravda*, feared that "they would not be able to live on their new wages".

Having had ringside views of such unrest, the Communists in Hungary decided to ward off trouble. The Red press wept crocodile tears about "right-wing deviationist leaders" who had inhumanly "lost contact with the working classes". It showed its sympathy by printing letters to editors: Bela Szilagi's wife had been refused a holiday after her pregnancy. In the Gheorghiu-Dej shipyard, young workers ate their lunches standing up and slept on dirty straw sacks.

On July 3 Premier Matyas Rakosi was replaced by Imre Nagy, though he retained his position as No. 1 Communist. The first words of the new Premier proved that Hungary, like the Soviet Union, had embarked on a new economic policy: Emphasis, he said, must be

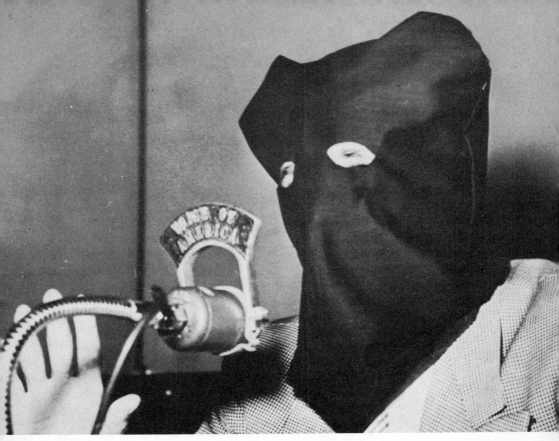

**MASKED** to hide identity, Latvian expatriate tells U.S. congressional listeners how Russia took over his little Baltic state—an early, unwilling Soviet "satellite"—during World War II

placed on production of food and consumers' goods.

"The country's economy is based on the individual farm," Nagy declared. "Exaggeration of collectivization has caused serious anxiety among the peasants. . . . Those who wish to become individual farmers once more will be freely permitted to rent land."

The Premier also gave the green light to individual retailers and artisans. To the workers he promised a higher standard of living. The brakes were to be applied to the anti-Catholic crusade. The Premier further proclaimed an amnesty for all nonpolitical prisoners.

This throwing in of the towel in Hungary was the beginning of a general

industrial retreat along most of the satellite front. By November the Czech and Polish governments had gone on record as favoring more food and a higher standard of living.

Bulgaria was an exception to this rule. Minor cuts in prices of items such as bread, flour, fats, sugar, and shoes were permitted. But by and large the Bulgarian people remained under the iron grip of a Moscow-dictated program of deprivation. The explanation lay in the strategic importance of this Kremlin puppet, which flanks the Bosporus and the Dardanelles. As a first line of defense against an anti-Soviet thrust by way of Greece and Turkey, Bulgaria was kept on a war footing.

**CHEERING REDS,** delegates to Third World Youth Congress at Bucharest, hail truce in Korea

**EVERYDAY DRAMA** at the edge of the Iron Curtain: An East Berlin youth, trying to escape to the West, is dragged back by Red police

MAN OF THE YEAR
In the councils of the great powers, a new member.

# GERMANY

THE DATE WAS JUNE 17, 1953; THE PLACE, Communist East Germany. Atop war-scarred Brandenburg Gate, at the border line between the two Berlins, the huge Soviet flag was torn to shreds. Up in its place went the red, black, and gold of West Germany.

In Potsdamer Platz the huge state store was looted and set afire. A bonfire was stoked with giant portraits of Stalin and Deputy Premier Walter Ulbricht, East Germany's hated Red boss.

At the Communist government offices on Leipziger Strasse, rocks were hurled through windows. Soviet soldiers were stoned. Voices yelled: "Freedom! Freedom! Overthrow the government!"

As Red-starred tanks clanked over the cobblestones, unarmed Berliners threw rocks at them. In Unter den Linden, a rude cross was erected at the spot where a German had been crushed by a Soviet tank.

This spontaneous revolt proved, as

never before in the Communist era, that free men could rise up against totalitarian machines. Together with Chancellor Konrad Adenauer's triumph in the Sept. 6 election in West Germany, it was as serious a setback as the Kremlin had suffered in the postwar world. And it took place in full view of the free world's outpost in West Berlin.

The June 17 uprising was touched off the day before. At 9 A.M., laborers in their wooden clogs, plasterers in their white smocks, and carpenters in their broad black hats laid down their tools. They were protesting a Red speed-up decree on the mammoth Stalinallee housing project, which had raised work norms without raising wages. By 2 P.M., Red loud-speakers proclaimed that the "mistaken" decree had been revoked.

But the news came late. A workers' strike had already broadened into a people's uprising, clamoring for free elections, German unity, and butter. It took 25,000 Soviet troops and 300 tanks to prop up Communist rule in East Berlin. The East German *Volkspolizei* (People's Police) had proved reluctant to shoot down fellow Germans.

No one knew how many persons were killed that day in simultaneous uprisings all over East Germany—in the burning of the synthetic gasoline plants at Halle, in the freeing of political prisoners from the Magdeburg jail, in the bludgeoning to death of a Red prosecutor by steel strikers in Brandenburg, in the wrecking of uranium-mining machinery near Chemnitz. It was known that seven East Berliners died, and 119 wounded were treated in West Berlin hospitals.

Drastic measures put down the uprising. Martial law was proclaimed. Mass

**PENT-UP HATRED** erupts in East Berlin as German youths hurl stones at oncoming Russian tanks during the foredoomed uprisings of June 17

meetings were banned. At least 50,000 persons were jailed. The Volkspolizei was purged. A jobless painter from West Berlin, named Willi Göttling, was the first of thirty or more so-called *agents provocateurs* to fall before a firing squad.

To his Soviet masters, the puppet Premier Otto Grotewohl, an ex-Socialist printer, bowed his thanks: "We alone would never have been able to defeat the provocateurs."

The "German Democratic Republic", as East Germany was called, had been anything but calm throughout 1953. On Jan. 16, Foreign Minister Georg Dertinger, an ex-Nazi Christian Democrat, had been arrested for "hostile activity . . . under orders from imperialist spy services". The pudgy Gerhart Eisler, who had jumped bail in the U.S. in 1949, was fired as propaganda boss.

To escape East Germany, a flood of refugees funneled into West Berlin, carrying battered suitcases or nothing, often ducking Red bullets. In January alone, 25,000 arrived. On a single February day, 3500 poured in. Chancellor Adenauer himself tried to stem the mass exodus. He broadcast: "When hundreds of thousands flee, hundreds of thousands of others take their places, and they may be Russians or Asians. Every German who remains defends a piece of Germany, a piece of the Western world."

Nonetheless, 305,737 East Germans fled to freedom in West Berlin during the year. This mass exodus, the greatest of the postwar era, drained East Germany of no less than 1.7 percent of its people.

As if aware that their power was shaky, the Reds dug a "dead zone" of roadblocks, broken transportation lines, barbed wire, and ditches around West Berlin. But they shied away from imposing a new blockade. They were warned off by James B. Conant, ex-president of Harvard University and new U.S. High Commissioner in West Germany.

Reassuring the 2,000,000 West Berliners, Conant promised that the U.S. would "see to it that this city continues as an unshakable outpost of the free world. . . . As the strength of a new Europe develops . . . the frontiers of freedom will peacefully expand, and Berlin will no longer be an isolated citadel."

As if afraid to provoke a showdown, the tough-as-nails Soviet Control Commissioner, General Vasili Chuikov, was almost polite in apologizing for "regrettable" air incidents in the trigger-happy days after Stalin's death.

General Chuikov's Control Commission was abolished in May. As the West had done in 1949, the Soviets belatedly replaced military with civilian control. They named ex-Ambassador Vladimir Semenov, a paunchy onetime professor of philosophy, as Supreme Commissar of the U.S.S.R. in Germany.

Simultaneously, Red propaganda was toned down, in keeping with the post-Stalin peace offensive. The London *Sunday Times* reported the outlawing of 178 favorite forms of abusing the West. Among them: "capitalist slaveowners . . . boogie-woogie gangsters . . . imperialist bloodsuckers".

Just before the June 17 uprising, Premier Grotewohl had even confessed a "series of mistakes" and announced the reversal of the eight-year-old effort at communization.

His regime now urged the return, with full civil and property rights, of the 1,800,000 East Germans who had fled. It eased curbs on travel to West Germany. It amnestied political prisoners. It restored ration cards to 2,000,000 bourgeois "nonproducers". It offered credits to boost "private industry". It lowered the detested quotas of produce collected by the government from the farmers. It even stopped collectivizing the farms.

The Reds also appeased the Protestant Evangelical Church. They offered to end persecution, restore confiscated properties, reinstitute religious classes in the schools, even subsidize the church.

This Communist about-face failed to forestall the June 17 uprising. But to prevent another such revolt, the Reds promised to raise living standards, ease farm quotas further, and put some socialized factories back into private hands.

Searching for scapegoats, they fired Wilhelm Zaisser, whose Volkspolizei had failed so miserably. Thus they turned on a German-born Soviet citizen and Russian Army colonel, whom they had once glorified as "General Gomez", the commander of the International Brigade during the Spanish civil war. They also replaced Max Fechner, the "too lenient" Minister of Justice, with Hilde Benjamin, a cruel-eyed and sadistic woman who became known as "The Red Guillotine". To help prop up their rule, they sent to East Germany Field Marshal Friedrich Paulus, the German commander who had surrendered at Stalingrad in 1943.

## The Eisenhower Parcels

But the nightmare of June 17 could not be forgotten. To keep the pot boiling, President Eisenhower, on Chancellor Adenauer's advice, offered $15 million worth of food to East Germany. "Imperialist provocation," the Communists stormed. The project was put into effect anyway.

By early August, these Eisenhower parcels had proven the most popular American move since the Berlin airlift. By then 2,000,000 food packets had been passed out free to East Germans. Each contained 10 pounds of food: lard, flour, condensed milk, and dried beans or peas. Each was worth only $1.15. But to pick up the parcels, one tenth of the East German population flocked into West Berlin from as far as 125 miles away, often risking both life and liberty to do so.

"For once we can do something besides just talk," Socialist Mayor Ernst Reuter of West Berlin exulted. His motto was: "We must stop acting like rabbits in the presence of a snake." *Herr Berlin*, as he was nicknamed, knew how to stand up to the Communists. Himself once a Communist commissar for the German Volga Republic in the Soviet Union, he was thus described by Lenin: "Young Reuter has a brilliant and lucid mind but is a little too independent."

## Reuter Dies

On Sept. 29, Mayor Reuter, 64, died of a heart attack. At his hero's funeral, his coffin was covered with the flag of Berlin. On it lay the Reuter trademark—a black beret.

To replace Reuter—if anyone could—Dr. Walther Schreiber was promoted from deputy mayor. Erect and humorless, Schreiber, 69, was the Berlin leader of the Christian Democrats, Chancellor Adenauer's party. Bombed out five times during World War II, he philosophized: "Material possessions are only borrowed from God."

Mayor Schreiber had been standing up to Russians since 1945. He had told off Marshal Georgi Zhukov: "What you and your government are doing is wrong." In 1951 he had welcomed Jesse Owens, the four-time winner in the Berlin Olympic games of 1936, whom Hitler had snubbed because he was a Negro. "Hitler would not give you his hand," Schreiber told Owens. "I give you both of mine."

If Reuter's death was disheartening, Adenauer's defeat in the Sept. 6 elections would have been "disastrous". Secretary of State John Foster Dulles said just that. For Chancellor Adenauer personified

West Germany's emergence into full partnership with the free world. In March he had forced the European Defense Community and the companion peace contract through crucial votes in the Bundestag (lower house of Parliament). In April he had become the first German chancellor ever to visit the U.S.

At 77, *Der Alte* (The Old Man) insisted on a coast-to-coast flying tour. "I want to see it all," he said. He brought President Eisenhower fifty bottles of a dry Moselle and an Old Master "Adoration of Three Kings". At Arlington Cemetery, he laid a wreath on the Unknown Soldier's tomb as a U.S. Army band played both "The Star-Spangled Banner" and "Deutschlandlied", the democratized version of "Deutschland über alles".

A U.S.-German communiqué on the Adenauer visit reported "a far-reaching identity of views and objectives". It looked forward to Germany's eventual reunification. Yet no concrete progress toward this end was produced by a whole series of notes between the Western Big Three and the Kremlin.

A document reviving the 1923 Treaty of Friendship, Commerce, and Consular Rights was signed by Adenauer and Conant in June. It was the first back-to-normalcy pact to be negotiated by postwar Germany.

Overshadowing such pieces of paper in importance was the Sept. 6 outpouring of 28,000,000 voters in the so-called German Federal Republic. That night the Chancellor went to sleep peacefully in his home on the Rhine. When he woke up, he was told that he had won the greatest victory ever won by any German in a free election.

The Chancellor's Christian Democrats polled 45.2 percent of the popular vote. They won an absolute though bare majority of 244 out of the 487 seats in the Bundestag. By adding the Rightist All-German Bloc (Refugee party) to his old partners, the Free Democrats and the German party, Adenauer tallied a two-thirds majority over the Socialists for his conservative coalition. The Communist party skidded to a mere 2.2 percent of the popular vote and lost all of its 14 seats. The neo-Nazi German Reich party also was shut out.

In October, by a 304-to-148 vote of the Bundestag, Adenauer was officially given another four-year term. He had won his first term in 1949 by a single vote—his own.

When Chancellor Adenauer formed his new Cabinet, he kept the cigar-smoking, evangelistic Ludwig Erhard as economics minister, and the pfennig-pinching, schoolmasterish Fritz Schaeffer as finance minister. In the final analysis it was Erhard's free-enterprising policies, backed to the hilt by Adenauer, which had spark-plugged West Germany to a remarkable economic boom.

Three times in his 77 years, the Catholic Adenauer had escaped sudden death. In 1917 his auto had crashed into a streetcar and left his face a mass of scars. In 1933, as mayor of Cologne, he had been fired by the Nazis for ordering all swastikas torn down in advance of a Hitler visit. In 1945, while living the life of a gardener under the Gestapo's watchful eye, he had been narrowly missed by three shells from an American tank. He had survived to become the most pro-American and pro-European of all Continental statesmen.

His electoral triumph put new life into the moribund crusade for European unity. "Europe," Adenauer predicted, "will now come into being."

**FRATRICIDAL STRIFE:** A West Berlin policeman arrests an East Berlin Red trying to halt distribution of food to other East Berliners

# DIPLOMACY

NEVER IN THE POSTWAR ERA HAD THE WORLD'S hopes for a real thaw in the cold war soared so high as they did during 1953. These hopes were not fulfilled by a genuine peace. Nonetheless, there developed a deep-seated conviction, on both sides of the Atlantic, that a third world war was now less imminent and less inevitable than at any time during the cold conflict. The hopes soared suddenly with the news of Joseph Stalin's death on March 5.

**VISHINSKY** (above), Soviet U.N. delegate, shouts as world listens. Selwyn Lloyd, U.K. (left); J. J. Wadsworth, U.S. (center); and (bottom) Charles Malik, Lebanon; N. C. Lodge Jr., U.S. Sir Gladwyn Jebb, U.K.; Dag Hammarskjöld, U.N. Sec. Gen.; Mme. Vijaya Pandit, India

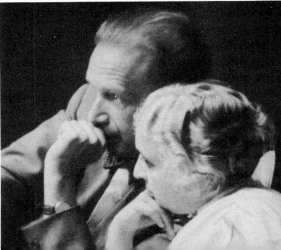

**AWESOME NEW WEAPON,** U.S. Army's 280-mm. atomic cannon, may be needed if diplomacy breaks down. During year U.S. forces in Germany were equipped with six

They helped to bog down the build-up of the North Atlantic Treaty Organization, to stall the proposed European Defense Community, to promote a top-level meeting with Georgi M. Malenkov or, at least, a second-level session with Vyacheslav M. Molotov. The biggest single step toward peace: the signing of the Korean armistice on July 27.

But the basic clash between West and East, whether with Stalin or without, was still unmistakable. It was dramatized by the East German uprising of June 17, by the purge of Lavrenti P. Beria, revealed on July 10, and by the Soviet's hydrogen-bomb explosion on Aug. 12.

Still Western diplomacy was able, by the end of 1953, to entice the Russians into agreeing to high-level talks on two issues of overriding import—Germany and the atom. As the West thus moved to test the Russians' real intentions, Premier Malenkov came forth on Dec. 31 with as enigmatic a statement as ever issued from the Kremlin: "I believe that there are no objective obstacles to an improvement of relations between the U.S.S.R. and the U.S.A. in the new year . . . and I hope that it will be so."

Even before Stalin's death, the drive to stiffen N.A.T.O.'s defenses was flagging. No longer defenseless or bankrupt, our allies in Europe were growing reluctant to follow American leadership.

The European Defense Community treaty, signed in Paris on May 27, 1952, had not yet been ratified. It remained only a blueprint for a single European army, led by one commander, financed by one budget, firing one series of weapons, wearing one uniform. Still on paper were its 43 divisions—14 French, 5 Benelux (Belgium-Netherlands-Luxembourg), 12 Italian, 12 from a rearmed West Germany.

Secretary of State John Foster Dulles toured Western European capitals in early February. Unless the E.D.C. members stopped procrastinating, he warned, the U.S. would have to do "a little rethinking" about its own policies.

E.D.C. was "not dead but only sleeping", he telecast on his return to Washington. "There is a good chance that [it] will be brought into being."

But this chance, basically, depended on France. There, time and again, E.D.C. was sidetracked by petty politicking and pedantic debates, by genuine fears of Germany and by siren songs from inside Soviet Russia.

Only in three of the six E.D.C. members did the treaty even reach crucial votes in lower houses of parliaments during 1953. The West Germans ratified, 224 to 165, in March; the Dutch, 75 to 11, in July; the Belgians, 148 to 49, in November.

On April 23, when the N.A.T.O. Council met around a green baize table in the Palais de Chaillot in Paris, Secretary Dulles declared: "The missing element in making Europe defensible at this time is the lack of any German forces." Proposals that, as an alternative to E.D.C., West Germany be admitted to N.A.T.O. with its own national army, brought from Dulles the reminder: "The French have a veto."

"Don't mind me—just go right on talking."

From
THE HERBLOCK BOOK
(The Beacon Press)

"The era of the handout is over," Dulles warned. "The Europeans should be the pacemakers." The new N.A.T.O. pace was the stretchout—as N.A.T.O. proposed to improve its defenses in 1953 by raising the quality rather than the quantity of its fifty divisions in Western Europe.

Said the Secretary of State to our European allies: "I do not believe that we are warranted . . . in increasing so rapidly the military expenditures that it throws budgets really out of balance . . . We believe that it is important to operate N.A.T.O. for the long pull."

For the long pull, General Matthew B. Ridgway, the former grenade-toting paratrooper who was to be the new U.S. Army Chief of Staff, was replaced as N.A.T.O.'s Supreme Allied Commander, Europe, by General Alfred M. Gruenther. In his valedictory, Ridgway expressed doubt that "the military danger from the East has lessened . . . As a soldier, I cannot afford to deal with conjecture." He added: "A full-scale Soviet attack within the near future would find N.A.T.O. critically weak", especially in tactical air power. He complained that a German "contribution" was still lacking.

His successor, who had served both Eisenhower and Ridgway in Paris as chief of staff, was 152 pounds of brilliant intellect. General Gruenther was a genius at the bridge table. Now he laid out his cards: "I do not think war is ever going to come [in Europe]. We are going to stop it from starting. [But] if ever there was a time for relaxation, this is not it."

N.A.T.O. increasingly relied on atomic materiel to offset Soviet manpower. For example, in June, from its base in Maine, a full wing of B-47 swept-wing jet bombers was flown to Britain carrying dummy

**WEEPING WOMEN** identify bodies of South Koreans captured, then killed by North Koreans

A-bombs, in as short a time as 5 hours and 22 minutes. Furthermore, the 848th Field Artillery Battalion landed in Bremerhaven in October with six 280-millimeter cannon, weighing 85 tons each and capable of firing atomic shells. It was to be followed by five more atomic artillery battalions within a year.

## Soviet H-Bomb

The British joined the U.S. in building up N.A.T.O.'s atomic potential, even as the Russians were touching off their first hydrogen-bomb explosion on Aug. 12. At dawn on Oct. 15, British scientists under Sir William Penney sent a man-made sun swirling up from the red desert sands at the Woomera rocket range in far-off Australia. This atomic weapon, nicknamed the "Penney utility", was adaptable to a wide variety of tactical purposes — bomb, shell, torpedo, guided missile.

Yet N.A.T.O.'s progress was still stalled and E.D.C. was still a dream when the N.A.T.O. Council met again in Paris in December. The Atlantic allies pronounced themselves "generally satisfied" at having attained 95 percent of their 1953 objectives. They aimed to boost their air power by 1300 planes, to a total of 5600, as their chief 1954 goal.

Their complacency was jarred when Secretary Dulles bluntly warned that if France did not ratify E.D.C. within a few months, the U.S. would have to make an "agonizing reappraisal" of its basic policies. But France, far from being cured of its indecision by this shock treatment, reacted with hurt pride at this "clumsy" and "brutal" advice.

Only in economic life did Europe really move toward unity. On Feb. 10 the High Authority of the European Coal and Steel Community (E.C.S.C.), the nine-man supranational cabinet created in 1952 by the Schuman Plan, got going. It took over the coal and iron-ore industries of the same six nations that were to be E.D.C. partners. Soon thereafter, it took over their steel industries.

"We have the power," rejoiced Jean Monnet of France, chief of the High Authority. "We do not have to consult anybody." He began to chop down a "jungle of restrictions" which hamstrung free enterprise—subsidies, tariffs, quotas, fixed prices, and discriminatory freight rates.

From this economic unity came progress, at least in idealistic theory, toward political unity. This occurred in March within the horsehide panels of the Palais de l'Europe at Strasbourg, France. There a six-nation Constitutional Assembly voted 50 to 0 for a 116-article constitution for a United States of Europe (U.S.E.).

Within its blue leather binding, this constitution called for a president of the U.S.E., an executive council (cabinet), an 87-man senate selected by the national parliaments, and a 268-man "people's chamber" elected by popular vote.

As chairman of the drafting committee, ex-Premier Paul-Henri Spaak of Belgium declared: "Not ten years ago, the countries represented here . . . had but one thought: to destroy each other . . . This draft treaty is not only a moving message of reconciliation; it is an act of confidence in the future."

Europe's economic renaissance had been sparked largely by the Marshall Plan. It was fitting that the Nobel Peace Prize for 1953 should be awarded to the plan's author, General of the Army George C. Marshall. He was the first professional soldier to win the (tax-free) prize of $33,954.

Simultaneously, the Nobel Peace Prize for 1952 was given belatedly to Dr. Albert Schweitzer, 78, medical missionary to

French Equatorial Africa, for discharging "the greatest unpaid debt of Western civilization"—presumably to the Western powers' less civilized colonies.

There was one great obstacle to progress in the diplomatic sphere equal to that in the economic sphere—the Kremlin. In the spring of 1953 the West split sharply on how to handle the Kremlin diplomatically. President Eisenhower insisted on "concrete evidence of the Soviet Union's concern for peace". Britain's Prime Minister Sir Winston Churchill called for "a conference on the highest level . . . without delay".

Was there any way of reconciling the two positions? To find out, the Western Big Three announced that Eisenhower, Churchill, and the French Premier would meet in Bermuda on June 17. But the Bermuda meeting was delayed when the French government fell, and was again postponed when Churchill had a slight stroke.

## Big Three Meet

Instead, a "Poor Man's Bermuda", beginning July 10, brought together in Washington Secretary Dulles, Lord Salisbury (pinch-hitting for Britain's Foreign Secretary Anthony Eden), and French Foreign Minister Georges Bidault. They discussed Churchill's dream of a top-level meeting with Malenkov. The London *Times* said: "Never has so much cold water been poured by so many on something so little."

The foreign ministers approved Eisenhower's precept of deeds, not words. They decided to test Soviet intentions on the main issue and prize of Europe—Germany. On July 15 the Western Big Three invited the Soviet Union to a four-power meeting of foreign ministers to discuss "free elections" for all Germany and "a free all-German government".

A whole series of notes went to the Kremlin, which sent evasive replies. The West got more and more specific. On Sept. 12 it proposed a meeting place—Lugano, Switzerland—and a date—Oct. 15.

That date came and went. Convening again, this time in London, the Western foreign ministers sent a new set of identical notes to the Soviet Union. This time they proposed that the Lugano meeting begin on Nov. 9.

But the West was losing hope. Churchill himself admitted that, while a meeting with Malenkov might be "useful", it might result "in a still worse deadlock".

An icy diplomatic note from the Kremlin on Nov. 3 appeared to clinch the failure of the Western effort to set up a diplomatic parley. In President Eisenhower's words, the note's eighteen pages manifested "an intention to create as many difficulties as possible".

Said Secretary Dulles: "The Soviet leaders bluntly demand that the European and Asian nations not now subject to Soviet domination, shall first unconditionally surrender their protective principles and practices and present themselves, divided and thus weakened, in order to gain the privilege of conference with the rulers of the Soviet and Chinese Communist world."

For as Dulles pointed out, the Soviets had demanded "immediate suspension" of E.D.C. and European unity plans, prohibition of German "sovereignty or unity", and "abandonment" of N.A.T.O. Undaunted, the Western Big Three replied by reviving Churchill's plan to meet in Bermuda with President Eisenhower and France's Premier Joseph Laniel.

At that, the Kremlin, on Nov. 26, made an astonishing about-face. In a mere eight pages it abandoned its impossible demands and mildly suggested that the

Big Four foreign ministers meet in Berlin to discuss "security in Europe" and "the German problem".

The Kremlin's new diplomatic tactics made the Bermuda meeting almost unnecessary. However, it was held. The first meeting of a Big Three—Eisenhower, Churchill, and Laniel—since wartime had few decisions to make except to suggest that the Berlin conference begin on Jan. 4, 1954. Churchill theorized that there was "a new look" in Moscow, and Eisenhower, that there was merely "a made-over garment". Both put renewed pressure on the French to approve E.D.C.

## Bermuda Conference

The four-day sessions, from Dec. 4 to 7, seemed to be overshadowed by trivia: Eisenhower wore a bandage on one hand, nicked when he was examining a pistol; Churchill never missed a chance to caress the immaculately groomed goat, mascot of the Royal Welch Fusiliers; Laniel had little to say in French, could not speak English, and spent most of his time in bed with a lung infection.

Only a Big Three agreement on Eisenhower's proposal for an international pool of atomic energy for peaceful pursuits, and the President's dramatic flight from Bermuda to the United Nations to propound his plan, kept the Mid-Ocean Club sessions in Bermuda from seeming like a diplomatic dud.

Whatever the Russians really thought of the atom-pool proposal, they finally agreed, on Dec. 21, to discuss it. And on Dec. 26 they similarly agreed to begin in Berlin, on Jan. 25, 1954, the first meeting of the Big Four foreign ministers since 1949.

Against the diplomatic background of the cold war, it was no surprise that the United Nations could not unite the nations during 1953. The two most notable agreements between East and West in the U.N. concerned not diplomatic issues but personalities.

On April 7 the U.N. General Assembly elected Dag Hammarskjöld of Sweden as the U.N.'s $40,000-a-year (tax-free) Secretary General, to succeed Trygve Lie of Norway. "Call me Hammershield," he advised. "It's exactly what my name means in English." For purists, he pointed out that "skjöld" should rhyme with "pulled".

An aristocratic bachelor of 47, Hammarskjöld was the son of the Swedish prime minister during World War I. He likes *avant-garde* and T. S. Eliot's poetry, Picasso paintings, and Swedish ceramics. His favorite sport is mountain climbing. As he entered his new post, he said: "The safest climber is the one who never questions his ability to get to the top of the mountain."

The other personality was an Indian. On Sept. 15 the Assembly elected Mme. Vijaya Lakshmi Pandit, the sister of Prime Minister Jawaharlal Nehru, as its first woman President. Tiny and silver-haired, she floated to the rostrum in a flowing, mist-gray sari.

At 53, a widow and a grandmother, Mme. Pandit looks upon herself primarily as an individual. "I don't care for this emphasis on women as women," she said. At birth she was named Swarup Karumi ("Beautiful Princess"). On her marriage, her husband substituted the name Vijaya Lakshmi ("Goddess of Victory").

As India's ex-Ambassador to both the U.S.S.R. and the United States, Mme. Pandit insisted on maintaining "a certain aloofness" toward the cold war. She declared: "My purpose is to find ways and means to make the U.N. successful." One couldn't quarrel with her ambition, but the cold war made real success impossible for the U.N. in 1953.

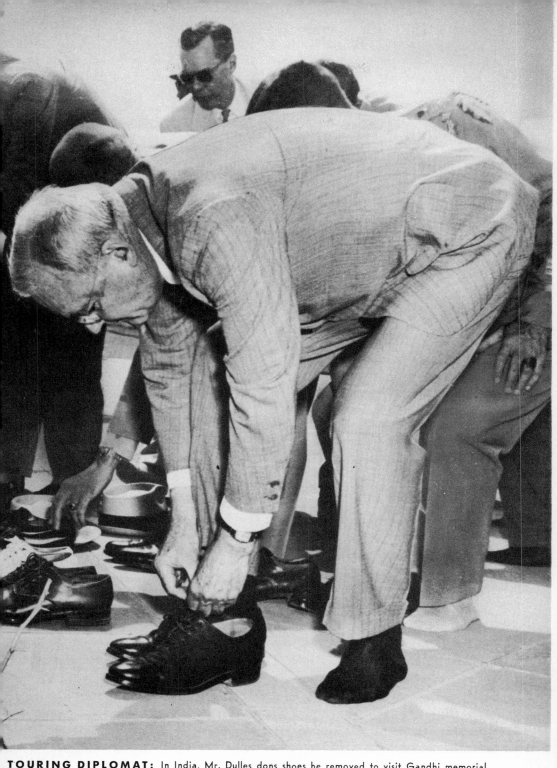

**TOURING DIPLOMAT:** In India, Mr. Dulles dons shoes he removed to visit Gandhi memorial

**GAIETY:** At $100,000 ball in France, host Marquis de Cuevas kisses dancer Jeanmaire, one of 2000 guests. This was Europe in 1953

# WESTERN EUROPE

FRANCE WAS "THE SICK MAN OF EUROPE" during 1953—in the opinion of chipper Paul Reynaud, who as Premier had presided over its collapse in 1940.

The French system was an "evil regime"—in the opinion of General Charles de Gaulle, who had led its wartime rebirth.

The French Parliament had "the means of imposing its will on everything, provided it had a will"—in the opinion of monkish Robert Schuman, the foreign-affairs specialist who had personified the dream of a united Europe.

Yet it wasn't only France that underwent a slackening of will and a crisis of complacency during 1953. As the Soviet threat eased and the N.A.T.O. defenses stiffened, a tendency to relax plagued the bulk of Western Europe. This tendency was reflected in France's failure to ratify its own brain child—the E.D.C. treaty; in Italy's ditching of Premier Alcide De Gasperi, in Yugoslavia's feuding with its Italian neighbor, in Scandinavia's refusal to face the military facts of life.

As 1953 opened, France was leaderless. Premier Antoine Pinay had quit just

**TROUBLE IN TRIESTE:** In the Allied occupied zone, one man defies (above), then attacks a policeman during bloody riots protesting delays in returning zone to Italy

before the New Year. Then, on Jan. 7, René Mayer won the unusually large majority of 389 to 205 in the National Assembly; he would preside over France's eighteenth postwar government.

At 57, puffy-eyed Premier Mayer smokes a pipe, plays Chopin on the piano, and drinks milk for a queasy stomach. A rabbi's grandson, he is a cousin by marriage of the Rothschild banking clan. As finance minister, he had prescribed austerity for France's ailing economy. "A good finance minister is always unpopular," he said.

"A good European", Mayer called himself. But he won his striking majority by promising not to press too fast for a European Defense Community. In the Foreign Ministry, he replaced Robert Schuman—an idealistic internationalist who had given his name to the European Coal and Steel Community—with clever Georges Bidault, who was acceptable to General de Gaulle's right-wing nationalists.

But, himself a middle-roading Radical Socialist, Mayer refused to admit the Gaullists to his Cabinet. "They must pass

through Purgatory," he said, "before they get to Paradise."

"When the time comes," Mayer predicted, "the French Parliament will accept its responsibilities" in E.D.C. The time was slow in coming. In March, Mayer and Bidault flew to Washington for four days of top-level talks. They were pressed for progress on E.D.C. They could promise little.

Soon the political scales tipped against Mayer. In the April municipal elections, the Gaullist Rassemblement du Peuple Français (Rally of the French People) slipped from 21 to 10 percent of the popular vote. Thus repudiated, General de Gaulle freed his 85-man block in the National Assembly to act as individuals "in the games, the poisons, and the delights of the system".

Promptly the R.P.F. bloc dumped the Mayer regime from power. On May 21, just after the Premier had proudly disclosed his plan to meet with Eisenhower and Churchill, he was toppled by a vote of 328 to 244.

Now France was plunged into the longest Cabinet crisis in its history. Four men tried and failed to win the 314 votes needed to become Premier.

(1) Paul Reynaud, Independent, proposed to clip the Assembly's wings by

dissolving it if it defeated a government within eighteen months. His vote: 276.

(2) Pierre Mendes-France, Radical Socialist, proposed to lighten the "crushing burden" of the Indochina war. His vote: 301.

(3) Georges Bidault, Popular Republican Movement, proposed to impose needed reforms by decree. His vote: 313 —one shy.

(4) André Marie, Radical Socialist, proposed only a timid "minimum program". His vote: 272.

France finally found a Premier on June 26. He was Joseph Laniel, 63, a conservative Independent, a linen magnate from Normandy. He had been an artillery captain during World War I and a Resistance leader during World War II. Still a crack shot, he once bagged sixty-two rabbits in one outing.

Laniel promised little, but won a 398-to-206 vote of confidence. He took the Gaullists into his Cabinet and relied heavily on Paul Reynaud as deputy premier. He kept Bidault as foreign minister.

But when his regime tried to pare its budget a little, it was plagued by France's most paralyzing strike since 1936. All Laniel wanted was to lower some pensions a little, raise some rents a bit, drop some employees from the government payroll. But the Socialist Force Ouvrière (Workers' Force) called a general work stoppage. The Catholic and Communist labor outfits joined in to battle for prestige.

Soon 4,000,000 Frenchmen, half of them government employees, were refusing to work. Telephones went dead. Trains stopped. The Paris subway halted. Garbage littered the streets. Births went unregistered. The dead went unburied.

Doggedly, Laniel proclaimed on the radio: "I say 'no' to a strike which seeks to paralyze everything." But after three weeks of paralysis, his regime said "yes"

to some of the strikers' demands. It revoked some of its economy decrees and agreed to consider hiking wage minimums. The strike ceased.

Now the Premier tried to bring down the soaring cost of living. He told butchers to slash meat prices 10 percent. With flour, coffee, and soap to follow, it was the time for *la baisse* (the lowering). Laniel also cracked down on tax dodgers. Example: One Frenchman owned three cars, kept three servants, but declared no income; he was ordered to pay taxes on $43,000 a year.

Above all, the Laniel government got the U.S. to boost its aid for the Indochina

war from $400 million to $785 million. Its hope: to force the Reds to give up the war that was sapping France's strength. Still it could not do anything about the overriding E.D.C. issue. All it could do was win a timid vote of confidence on Nov. 27 by 275 to 244. This merely expressed the National Assembly's hope that "the continuity of building a united Europe be assured".

Never was France's paralysis so well proved as in the election for the seven-year sinecure as President of the Republic to succeed retiring Vincent Auriol. It took the French Parliament seven days and thirteen ballots to elect, on Dec. 23, a dark horse named René Coty, 77, by a bare 477 votes out of the 871 cast. Such better-known hopefuls as Premier Laniel had too many enemies to win. Like Laniel an Independent, Coty was an obscure senator from Le Havre who was known for having taken no stand on E.D.C., and for not being related to the Coty perfume family. His opinion of France's political system: "It's a pity to shoot the pianist when the piano is out of tune."

As France suffered from a lack of leadership, Italy, during the confused election on June 7 and 8, dropped its leader—Alcide De Gasperi. At least 18 political

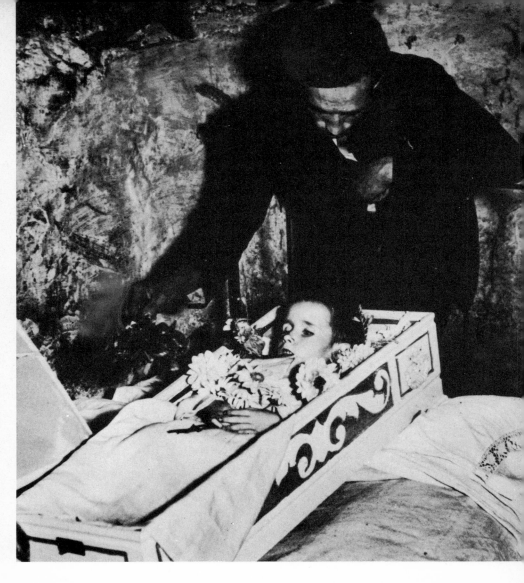

parties placarded every *piazza* with election posters. Three Leftist splinter parties used rival hammer-and-sickle symbols. One party showed a rising sun, a second a noonday sun, a third a setting sun.

The Catholic Church called it "a grave sin" to vote for Leftist or Rightist extremists. Clare Boothe Luce, the first woman ambassador ever sent to Rome by the U.S., was undiplomatically blunt. If Italy should go Right or Left, she said, there would be "grave consequences for this

warm cooperation we now enjoy"

These warnings either went unheeded or else backfired. In the original vote count, the middle-of-the-road De Gasperi coalition slid from its 62 percent of the popular vote in 1948 to 49.8 percent. It fell barely short of the 50.01 percent popular majority which, under a tricky new law, would have given it a solid 64.5 percent majority in the Chamber of Deputies. A recount of challenged ballots later indicated that the De Gasperi

**DEATH IN SPAIN:** Child mortality still runs high under the Franco regime. This girl, attended by grieving but helpless relatives, was only 4 years old

coalition really had won the needed majority. But since the coalition had prematurely conceded defeat, it was then too late to redistribute the seats in Parliament.

Thus the Democristiani (Christian Democrats) of De Gasperi, together with their anticlerical allies, slipped from 370 to 303 deputies and retained only a hairbreadth margin. The Communists and left-wing Socialists jumped from 183 to 218 seats. More spectacularly, the right-wingers sprouted from 20 to 69 seats.

Of these, 29 were held by neo-Fascists in the Movimento Sociale Italiano; 40 by Monarchists led by Mayor of Naples Achille Lauro, noted for his handouts of free spaghetti.

At 72, De Gasperi was out, after eight years as Premier. Cold and cloistered, he had been the European-minded counterpart of Robert Schuman of France and Konrad Adenauer of West Germany. He had led a postwar revival of Italy with its

**TOP-DOG YUGOSLAV:** President Tito, an able pianist, relaxes at the keyboard. His credo is that Yugoslav music should reflect native, not foreign, ideas

grimly realistic movies, its putt-putting motor scooters, its fashion-setting styles, its hard-money lire. Now the onetime filing clerk in the Vatican Library took a breather in the mountains to reread Virgil's *Aeneid*.

In mid-August, his successor, Giuseppe Pella, was comfortably confirmed by 315 to 215. A Piedmont sharecropper's son, he had a florid face and unruly reddish hair. He was an expert economist and, as finance minister for the previous six years, had kept Italy's currency sound.

Premier Pella, a Christian Democrat like De Gasperi, formed a one-party government of "technicians". "Our future is temporary," he predicted. Yet he was

soon being hailed as a *uomo di equilibrio* (man of balance). To save money, he refused to use the Premier's personal railroad car.

But just before the end of 1953, Premier Pella's regime was doomed by a revolt of the more liberal wing of his party. "It is important for a politician to know how to tiptoe into public life and also how to tiptoe out of it when necessary," he admitted. "I am prepared to do just that."

As slow as the French to push E.D.C. through to ratification, Pella had been warning Italy's allies that the Trieste question is "the testing bench of our friendships".

**BOTTOM-DOG YUGOSLAV,** all in rags, clenches fist to show his defiant faith in Communism

Thus prodded, Washington and London, on Oct. 8, announced that, "as soon as practicable", they would withdraw their 7000 occupation troops from the Free Territory of Trieste and turn over their zone to Italian control.

## Yugoslavia Riot Over Trieste

The Free Territory, G.I.'s jested, was divided into "Upper and Lower Slobbovia", after Al Capp's mythical country in his comic strip "Li'l Abner". The Anglo-American Zone A of 86 square miles contained perhaps 245,000 Italians and 65,000 Yugoslavs, plus the city of Trieste itself, with its bustling docks, shipyards, and oil refineries. The Yugoslav Zone B of 199 square miles contained perhaps 50,000 Yugoslavs and 25,000 Italians.

The hope of the U.S. and Britain was that their Trieste plan would break an eight-year stalemate between Italy and Yugoslavia. The Italians were delighted at this "act of justice". But Yugoslav mobs shouted "Trieste is ours!" and they stoned both the American and British offices.

Marshal Tito blustered that he would order his troops into Zone A if the Italians marched in. Premier Pella warned the West against backing down. Six Italians were killed in Trieste when they rioted in favor of Rome's rule.

Damned if they did and damned if they didn't, the Western Big Three foreign ministers in late October agreed "to persevere in their joint efforts to bring about a lasting settlement". Although these efforts brought no success during 1953, at least the Italians and Yugoslavs withdrew their troops from their embittered border.

Within Yugoslavia, Marshal Tito, in January, had been nominated to become the nation's first President. The Skupshtina (Assembly) was asked if there were other nominations. Everyone laughed. The ballots were cast. On 568 of them, the name Tito was underlined. On a single ballot—rumored to be Tito's own—the name was crossed out.

In March, President Tito became the first Red chief of state to visit Britain. The anti-Kremlin Communist brought a keg of *slivovitz* (plum brandy) to Churchill, Montenegrin costumes to Queen Elizabeth and the Duke of Edinburgh, and six dolls for their children. He saw the Magna Carta, lunched at Buckingham Palace, and took home two English setters—plus "full agreement" with Churchill that, "in the event of aggression in Europe, the resulting conflict could hardly remain local in character".

More formally, Yugoslavia, in February, had allied itself with two N.A.T.O. members, Greece and Turkey. This new Balkan treaty bound its signers, mustering 865,000 troops in seventy divisions, to "common defense measures" and, in effect, gave Yugoslavia a N.A.T.O. guarantee.

The Kremlin betrayed its worry by assuming a pose of appeasement. The Soviets offered to withdraw their claims on Turkish territory near the Caucasus and their demands for a share in controlling the Turkish straits around Istanbul. Romania, the U.S.S.R. satellite, agreed with Yugoslavia to reopen to shipping the "Iron Gate" gorge on the Danube River. And the Russians again exchanged ambassadors with the Yugoslavs.

But Tito distrusted Malenkov as much as he had Stalin. "On the frontier, their rifles are still shooting our guards," he warned.

The Kremlin tried similar tactics to appease Austria, now divided between Soviet and Allied control. It replaced its military high commissioner in Austria with a civilian ambassador. It closed down its check points and stopped censoring mail, telegrams, and telephone calls in Austria, as the Western Allies had prodded it to do thirty-eight times.

But on the 64-schilling question, the Russians, at the 260th meeting with the West since 1947 concerning an Austrian peace pact, did nothing to break the deadlock.

While the Malenkov regime was trying appeasement tactics in the Balkan area, it did not even pretend to appease Franco Spain. There, American Ambassador James C. Dunn, on Sept. 26, signed a twenty-year Spanish-American defense agreement that had taken two years of hard bargaining. This alliance was bound in ribbons of red and gold—the Spanish colors. It gave the U.S. the right to develop and use certain unspecified air and naval bases in Spain in return for $226 million in military and economic aid.

Thus the impoverished nation behind the Pyrenees barrier, which had not joined the Western Allies in either of two world wars, joined in the newest effort to develop the "defensive strength of the free world".

## N.A.T.O. in Scandinavia

Ironically, the two N.A.T.O. members in Scandinavia, although more exposed than Spain to the Soviet threat, still refused to admit their Allies' troops. Laborite Norway was preoccupied, as Premier Oscar Torp put it, with "transforming the Norwegian commonwealth along Socialist precepts". Laborite Denmark was busy raising Greenland to partnership, under King Frederik; and entitling 13-year-old Princess Margrethe to be the first Danish woman ever to inherit the crown.

In February the Danes were plagued by their first mutiny in history. It was provoked by the N.A.T.O.-requested extension of the draft from twelve to eighteen months. One hundred conscripts in the King's Own Foot Guards marched on Copenhagen. Burly Major General Richard Allerup intercepted them and commanded: "Attention! Get on these trucks and get home." They did. Defense Minister Harald Petersen jailed twenty-four mutineers. He blamed Red agents, "obviously directed from abroad".

The Netherlands and Belgium had cause to fear an invader even more awesome than Red agents—the sea. At 4 A.M. on Feb. 1, air-raid sirens screamed and church bells tolled. It was too late. The worst flood in centuries, pushed by a 115-mile-an-hour hurricane and a full-moon tide, took some 2000 lives in the Low Countries and in the English lowlands. It poisoned 500,000 fertile Dutch acres with salt water. But to the suggestion that some islands be surrendered permanently to the watery invader, the Dutch government replied: "We do not abandon our land."

As Dutch Queen Juliana was touring the flooded areas, her car stuck in the mud. "Come on, let's get out and push," she said, and did. At 72, Queen Mother Wilhelmina toured the disaster zone for two days. So did Queen Elizabeth in England. But 22-year-old King Baudouin quit Belgium in mid-disaster. He joined his deposed father, King Leopold, and his commoner stepmother, the Princess de Réthy, on the sunny Riviera.

Heeding a public outcry, Baudouin rushed back to Belgium—only to catch cold and return to the Riviera.

The Socialist newspaper Le Peuple, assailing the Princess de Réthy's "provocative" blouses and slacks and her "indiscreet" behavior, declared: "Madame de Réthy, we are sure, was primarily responsible for this detestable incident. She is exercising a palace influence to which she has no right."

**YEAR'S WORST DISASTER** hits Greece as earthquakes and tidal waves devastate three thriving Ionian islands. Death toll: over 400; buildings destroyed: 20,000; persons left homeless: almost 93,000

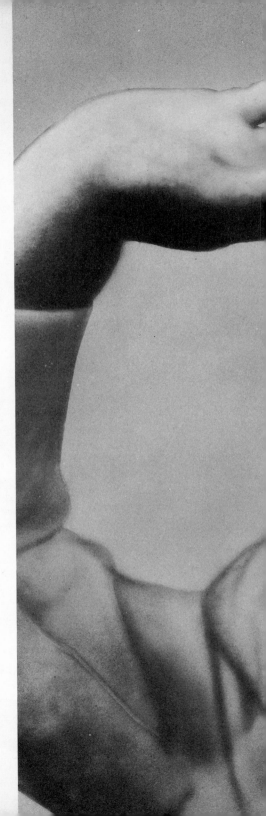

# GREAT BRITAIN

AT WINDSOR CASTLE ONE APRIL AFTERNOON in 1953, Prime Minister Winston Churchill, at 78, knelt before his 27-year-old Queen, Elizabeth II. Taking a ceremonial sword from the Duke of Edinburgh, the Queen touched her First Minister on both shoulders. "Arise, Sir Winston," she said.

Thus the Queen bestowed on Britain's leader the Most Noble Order of the Garter, highest and oldest order of knighthood, together with its eight-pointed silver star and gold pendant showing St. George and the dragon. Any higher honor would have raised the Prime Minister out of the House of Commons into the House of Lords.

Far from craving an honorable retirement during 1953, the Prime Minister dreamed of crowning his career by leading the world to a "generation of peace". On May 11 he won his loudest cheers in Commons since wartime by calling for "a conference on the highest level" among "the smallest number of powers and persons possible".

In proposing, in effect, to meet with

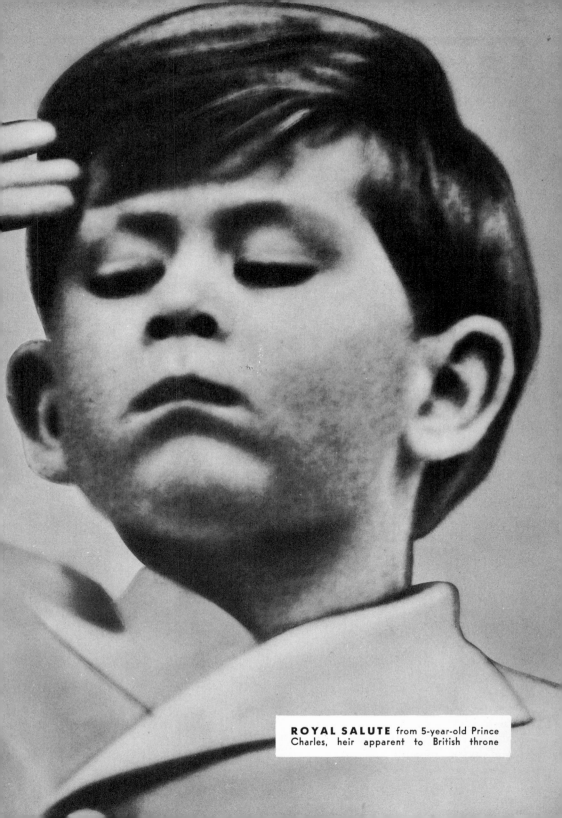

**ROYAL SALUTE** from 5-year-old Prince Charles, heir apparent to British throne

**CORONATION CLIMAX:** Before hushed members of her court, Queen Elizabeth II bows to receive the Crown of St. Edward from the Archbishop of Canterbury

Malenkov and Eisenhower over a bottle of vodka, Sir Winston aroused American. fears of losing the diplomatic initiative to Moscow, and French fears of being left out. But he pleaded that Stalin's death had produced "a change of attitude and, we all hope, of mind" in Moscow. "It would, I think, be a mistake to assume that nothing can be settled with the Soviet Union unless or until everything is settled . . .

"It might be that no hard and fast agreement would be reached . . . But there might be a general feeling among those gathered together that they might do something better than tear the human race, including themselves, into bits . . . At the best, we might have a generation of peace."

## New Locarno Pact Suggested

Sir Winston recognized Russia's "right to feel assured" against a rearmed Germany. He suggested: "The Locarno Treaty of 1925 . . . was based upon the simple provision that if Germany attacked France we should stand with the French, and if France attacked Germany we should stand with the Germans . . .

"I have a feeling that the master thought which animated Locarno might well play its part between Germany and Russia."

Aside from the royal family, the story of Sir Winston's ambition was the story of Britain in 1953. The Old Man could not wait until President Eisenhower's inauguration on Jan. 20 before steaming into New York harbor aboard the *Queen Mary.* Artfully he said he was just going to Jamaica to "soak up some sun", and "looked in to pay my respects". His real aim was to restore his relationship with the President-elect to the friendly basis of wartime.

More officially, the Prime Minister in March sent his nephew-in-law, Foreign Secretary Anthony Eden, and his Chancellor of the Exchequer, R. A. ("Rab") Butler, to Washington for four days. The Chancellor put his "trade, not aid" position this way: "It takes two to make love and it takes two partners to make trade . . . Unrequited love or unrequited exports are equally unsatisfactory."

That same month, Commons voted 304 to 271 to denationalize Britain's steel industry and thus to fulfill the Tory party's biggest political pledge. Supply Minister Duncan Sandys, Churchill's son-in-law, boasted that steel was being returned to "the invaluable stimulus and driving force of private enterprise".

On Budget Day, in April, Rab Butler unlocked Britain's best economic news from his battered red dispatch box and set Tory back-benchers to tossing their silk toppers into the Commons air. New taxes were avoided and old taxes were reduced—for the first time since 1929.

The income tax was cut by sixpence (7¢) per pound ($2.80) of income. Thus the tax burden of a married person with two children, earning $5600, was slashed from $1346 to $1264. The sales tax was scissored by 25 percent. The excess-profits tax was doomed. Even the entertainment tax on cricket matches was ended. Sugar rationing was to follow egg rationing into history.

Now, said Butler, "we step out from the confines of restrictions to the almost forgotten but beckoning prospects of freer endeavor and greater reward for effort." As the coronation festivities loomed, Londoners sang gleefully: "I've got sixpence, jolly, jolly sixpence."

But once the coronation was over, and just as Sir Winston was leading a reinvigorated Britain into a new Elizabethan age, a terse medical report from No. 10 Downing Street struck a sobering note: "The Prime Minister has had no respite for a long time from his very arduous duties, and is in need of a complete rest."

Actually Churchill had had a slight stroke on June 24. He had to cancel the Bermuda meeting, scheduled for July 8, at which he had hoped to get President Eisenhower and Premier Joseph Laniel of France to agree to confer with Malenkov.

Even "a complete rest" at his Chartwell country home did not make Sir Winston any the less Churchillian. Asking his doctors if he could drink cointreau, he said: "I neither want it nor need it, but I should think it pretty hazardous to interfere with an ineradicable habit of a lifetime." When he drove to Chequers, the prime ministerial country residence, a box of his inevitable cigars was spotted on the seat alongside him.

During Churchill's convalescence, his 56-year-old heir apparent, Anthony Eden, was recuperating from three operations on gall bladder and bile duct. Sir Winston therefore lent his reins to Rab Butler, the Tories' No. 3 man. At 50, Butler, a former Cambridge don, was brilliant but chilly. Like Churchill, he enjoyed painting—mostly Cornish coastal scenes. He was married to the heiress to the Courtauld silk-and-rayon fortune.

## One Man "Brain Trust"

A one-man Tory "brain trust", Butler stood for "wresting the initiative . . . from the Left". Already living at No. 11 Downing Street as Chancellor of the Exchequer, he became a good bet to move next door some day.

Eden's stand-in at the Foreign Office, nicknamed "Bobbety", was Robert Arthur James Gascoyne-Cecil, 5th Marquis of Salisbury, Earl of Salisbury, Viscount Cranborne, Baron Cecil of Essendon. His Cecil ancestors had served both Queen Elizabeth I and Queen Victoria as prime ministers. A frail, lisping, six-footer of 59, Lord Salisbury helped keep up his family's historic Hatfield House by admitting sight-seers for 35¢. He had been an aggressive foe of appeasement from Munich on, and he dared argue with Sir Winston, claiming that to meet Malenkov would be silly.

Could the Tories carry on with their No. 1 and 2 men ailing? Aneurin Bevan, fiery Welshman and left-wing Socialist, challenged: "If you cannot get leaders who are capable of leading . . . clear out!"

Paradoxically, Nye Bevan was incapable of leading his own party. On the Isle of Man in September, the Trades Union Congress, the Labour party's backbone, voted 2 to 1 to go slow on new Bevanite schemes for nationalization. The T.U.C. vice-chairman, Arthur Deakin, silenced the Bevanites with: "What you're demanding, brothers, is the economics of bedlam." The Labourites' 52nd annual conference at the Channel resort of Margate confirmed that cautious Clement Attlee, the 70-year-old ex-Prime Minister, and not Bevan, was still in the Socialist saddle.

In September Churchill did a tidying-up job on his government; among other changes, he brought Minister of Education Florence Horsbrugh into the Cabinet; she thus became the first woman to achieve this distinction in a Conservative government. On Oct. 5 Eden reported himself "back and fit and ready to work".

Despite Lady Churchill's pleadings, despite his growing deafness and crotchetiness, despite his approaching 79th birthday on Nov. 30, Churchill was not ready to pass on the burdens of his office.

As the Tories' turn came for their annual meeting at Margate, Sir Winston rebutted rumors of his early retirement. To 4000 Tories assembled in Margate's Winter Gardens on Oct. 10, he harked

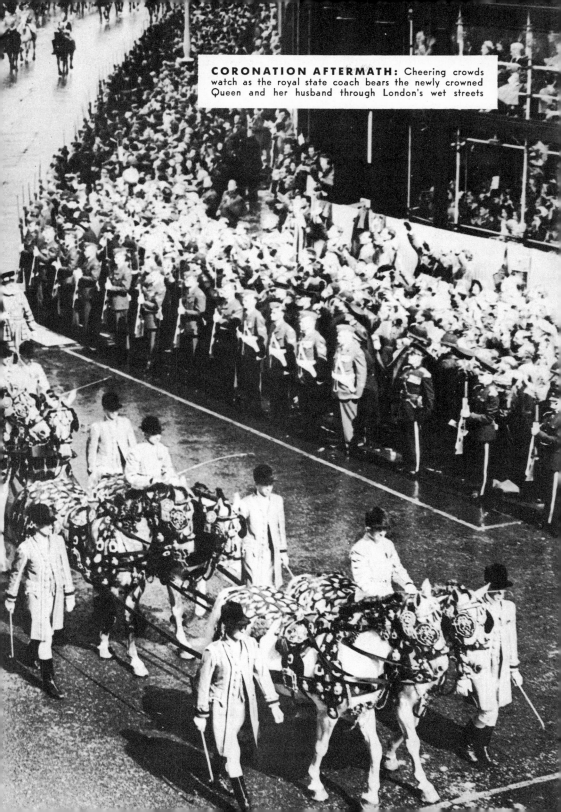

**CORONATION AFTERMATH:** Cheering crowds watch as the royal state coach bears the newly crowned Queen and her husband through London's wet streets

back to the theme of May 11 about Russia. "I thought that friendly, informal, personal talks between the leading figures . . . might do good."

To the Russians, he repeated his faith in the "master thought of Locarno". To the French he warned that should they not ratify the European Defense Community, "we shall have no choice in prudence but to . . . join the strength of Germany to the Western allies through some rearrangement of what is called N.A.T.O." Praising Rab Butler, he rejoiced: "Now, at least, we may claim solvency."

Sir Winston paused for a glass of water. Renowned for his Falstaffian taste for brandy and champagne, he panicked his listeners by remarking: "I don't often do that."

"A word about myself," the Old Man concluded, looking exhausted from his oratorical efforts. "If I stay on for the time being, bearing the burden at my age, it is not because of love for power or office. I have had an ample feast of both. If I stay, it is because . . . I may . . . have an influence on what I care about above all else—the building of a sure and lasting peace."

But once again his hopes of crowning his career as a peacemaker were delayed if not dashed. On Oct. 18 a session of the foreign ministers of the Western Big Three in London produced a noncommittal communiqué that did not even mention a face-to-face meeting with Malenkov. Churchill himself told Commons that such a session might produce "a still worse deadlock".

As if in consolation, Sir Winston crowned his literary career by winning the $35,000 Nobel Prize for Literature. Also in consolation, more stooped than ever and limping noticeably, he finally brought off the Bermuda meeting at the beginning of December—only to have his four days with Eisenhower and Laniel prove singularly unproductive. In Bermuda Sir Winston was spotted sitting alone by the water's edge for forty-five minutes, using his cane to trace figures in the sands of history.

## Strangler of Notting Hill

"Well, at least I've pushed that fellow Christie off the front page," Churchill had joshed after his stroke in June. In the Old Bailey in London, John Reginald Halliday Christie, a $23-a-week clerk of 55, was pouring out his ghastly confessions.

The balding, bespectacled "Strangler of Notting Hill" told how he had murdered seven women: An Austrian girl, a radio factory hand, a neighbor upstairs, his own wife, a woman who wanted money for gratifying his desires, a woman who was due to give birth in three months, and a Scottish mother of two children. He had hidden their bodies in his closet, under his floor, in his garbage cans. The name for this strange breed of criminal deviate was "necrophile".

Justice Sir Donald Finnemore ruled: "The abnormal are not necessarily insane."

He covered his wig with the traditional black cap and sentenced Christie to "suffer death by hanging".

As the Christie case was Britain's crime of 1953, the Maclean case was its mystery. Donald Maclean and Guy Burgess, two Foreign Office experts with unconventional habits and Communist interests, had disappeared on May 25, 1951. They were often rumored but never proved to have gone behind the Iron Curtain—or to have been shot by British agents.

On Sept. 11, 1953, American-born Melinda Maclean packed their two sons and one daughter into a black Chevrolet and drove off from her apartment in Geneva, Switzerland, supposedly to meet an old friend at a hotel in Montreux. Mrs. Maclean never arrived.

To her mother, Mrs. Melinda Dunbar, went a telegram from the outskirts of Montreux: "Unforeseen circumstances have arisen. Am staying here longer." It was not written in Mrs. Maclean's handwriting. It was sent by someone much stouter and more heavily made up.

At a Lausanne garage the Maclean Chevvy was found parked, supposedly left for eight days. On its front seat was a children's book, *Little Lost Lamb*.

The trail led toward Vienna and vanished. The British Foreign Office surmised that Mrs. Maclean had disappeared with her children behind the Iron Curtain. But Moscow insisted the whole Maclean-Burgess case was "without the slightest connection with the Soviet Union".

## Coronation

THE CORONATION OF QUEEN ELIZABETH II on June 2, 1953, quickened the Western world's jaded spirits.

It was all things to all men. It was a pageant of fairy-tale characters come alive. It was a deeply religious ceremony, mingling Christian ritual with echoes of pagan rites. It was an evocation of British history. It was a fabulous family party to which 200,000 paying guests from overseas were welcomed. And it was the subject of a modern communication miracle—television.

The reign of the first Good Queen Bess almost four centuries earlier had brought England undreamed-of wealth, power, and glory. Now the new Queen's subjects almost superstitiously believed that the second Elizabethan Age would restore the wealth, power, and glory lost in World War II. Poet Laureate John Mase-

field spoke his countrymen's feelings in his "Coronation Ode":

> *May this old land revive and be*
> *Again a star set in the sea,*
> *A kingdom fit for such as She*
> *With glories yet undreamt.*

The day upon which these hopes were focused dawned cold and rainy. Some 2,000,000 men, women, and children lined London's streets. Thousands had camped on the sidewalks since dawn the day before. They came with blankets, camp stoves, vacuum bottles of tea, and flags. The 10,000 ambulance workers on duty treated scores for exposure.

Peers, peeresses, and the rest of the 7500 dignitaries assigned seats within the Abbey Church of St. Peter—as Westminster Abbey is officially named—arose at 2 A.M. to dress. Wearing their state robes, many ventured into the unfamiliar underground to avoid traffic jams. Special subway trains carried them to within a few hundred yards of the abbey's great west door. Their pages carried their coronets in plain cardboard boxes. Most had sandwiches tucked beneath their robes, for, once within the abbey, there was no chance of slipping out for lunch. All had to be in their places by 8:30.

By then, the 27-year-old Queen had been up for an hour in the royal apartments overlooking the garden at the rear of Buckingham Palace. She prayed alone. On her tea tray she found a vase of fresh flowers and a note reading: "With every possible good wish today and always. From Mac and Smith"—her personal maids.

Then it was time to don her coronation dress of white satin, encrusted with pearls and diamonds in the emblems of England, Scotland, and the Commonwealth countries. Over it went her crimson robe of state.

With her husband, the Duke of Edinburgh, clad in his uniform as Admiral of

**FORMAL OR NOT,** Queen Elizabeth suits the average Briton. Here she acknowledges the obvious affection of a race-track crowd

the Fleet, the young Queen entered the 192-year-old, gilt state coach. The high, gold-tipped gates of Buckingham Palace swung open. Eight Windsor grays drew the coach ponderously forward. The lead horse was named "Eisenhower".

Cheers rose from the massed throngs until sound filled the wet air like a solid substance. It drowned the jingling of trappings, the clatter of hoofs, the rumbling of the four-ton coach.

Through the great windows of the coach, the crowds could see their Queen by the light of specially installed fluorescent lamps. She nodded from side to side and smiled graciously. Her lips moved as she recited the phrases designed to give her something to say throughout the slow procession. She was saying, "So kind, so nice, so very, very loyal."

## Arrival at Westminster

As Big Ben tolled 11 A.M., the state coach halted in Parliament Square outside the modernistic glass-and-plastic Abbey annex built for the occasion. The Queen descended and entered.

A fanfare of silver trumpets shivered through the lofty nave of the 900-year-old church. The Queen passed through the west door. Six maids of honor, all titled, carried her train.

A 400-voice choir swelled in the joyous words of Sir Charles Hubert Parry's anthem: "I was glad when they said unto me: We will go into the House of the Lord." Through them cut the high boyish voices of the Queen's scholars of Westminster School, chanting, "Vivat regina! (Long live the Queen!) Vivat Regina Elizabetha!"

The Queen passed into the coronation theater within the sanctuary and knelt in prayer. Then she came forward to stand beside King Edward's chair. Beneath its carved oak seat rested the Stone of Scone

(pronounced *scoon*). Legend said the stone was Jacob's pillow when he dreamed of a ladder ascending into heaven. This stone had been the coronation throne of ancient Scottish kings until Edward I carried it to England in 1296. Since then, every English monarch had been crowned on it. Scottish nationalists had stolen the stone on Christmas Day of 1950, but it had been recovered.

Now, as Queen Elizabeth stood before her nobles, the Archbishop of Canterbury, Dr. Geoffrey Fisher, strode to the four corners of the sanctuary. At each, he proclaimed: "Sirs, I here present unto you Queen Elizabeth, your undoubted queen." Four times the answer rolled back: "God save Queen Elizabeth."

This ritual of the recognition was a reminder of the days when rebellious barons might refuse to acknowledge an undoubted monarch. Next the archbishop administered the coronation oath to the Queen. She promised to govern her peoples "according to their respective laws and customs" and "to maintain . . . the Protestant reformed religion".

Within the communion service, the ceremony moved to its climax with the most holy ritual of the anointing. The Queen laid aside her robe, her diadem, and the collar of the Order of the Garter. She was buttoned into a humble garment of white linen. Four Garter knights lifted a silk canopy over her.

Carefully, the Dean of Westminster, Dr. Alan Campbell Don, poured the holy oil into a golden spoon. The archbishop dipped his finger and anointed the Queen on the palms of both hands, on the breast, and on the head.

Now, as a consecrated sovereign, the Queen received her emblems of majesty. Among them:

The sword of state: symbol of her duty to "punish and reform what is amiss, and confirm what is in good order".

The armills (bracelets): "tokens of the Lord's protection embracing you on every side, and . . . pledges of that bond which unites you with your peoples".

The orb with the cross: symbol of "the whole world . . . subject to the power and empire of Christ".

The scepter with the cross: "the ensign of kingly power and justice".

The rod with the dove: symbol of "equity and mercy".

Into the royal gallery at the Queen's right slipped a blond-haired four-year-old boy. He wore a white satin suit. Wide-eyed, he stood beside his grandmother, Queen Mother Elizabeth, and watched. He was Prince Charles, heir apparent to the throne. His sister, Princess Anne, not yet three, remained in the nursery at Buckingham Palace.

## The Crowning

The dean lifted St. Edward's crown from the altar and handed it to the archbishop. Reverently, the archbishop placed it upon the Queen's head.

With one breath, the assembled multitude cried: "God save the Queen!"

Peers and peeresses put on their coronets. Trumpets sounded.

Even the heavens opened. A flash downpour drenched the millions in the streets. But they picked up and carried on the "loud and repeated shouts" specified in the order of the service: "God save the Queen!"

Within the abbey, Elizabeth seemed a doll-like figure beneath the five-pound crown. This next half hour was the only time she would ever wear it.

Elizabeth II took her place on the throne. Kneeling on the steps of the dais, the Archbishop of Canterbury was the first to pay homage. Next came the Duke of Edinburgh to pledge to his wife: "I,

Philip, do become your liege man of life and limb, and of earthly worship."

Together Elizabeth and Philip knelt at the altar to take the sacrament. Then, to the *Te Deum*, the Queen passed behind the altar into St. Edward's Chapel. There she exchanged her heavy crown for the lighter imperial crown. "The solemnity of the Queen's coronation" was ended.

Elizabeth reappeared to the triumphal strains of the national anthem. Back through the nave and out the west door to the annex, the Queen departed in state.

After a pause for lunch, the procession wound back through the streets to Buckingham Palace. This was the big show for the public. The line of troops stretched for nearly two miles as it passed along the five-mile, 250-yard route. Twenty-seven bands played; 9400 soldiers marched at a stately 112 paces a minute. Another 15,000 lined the route.

Not a single automobile was there to mar the pageantry. Some 450 horses carried officers or pulled dignitaries' carriages. Among those cheered most loudly: the six-foot, three-inch Queen Salote of Tonga, who braved the rain in an open carriage despite having caught a cold in the chill climate far from her native South Pacific; and Prime Minister Sir Winston Churchill, in a blue cloak with an enormous diamond-studded star of the Order of the Garter.

Few went to bed that night. Hundreds of thousands gathered before Buckingham Palace to watch the Queen press a switch on the balcony floodlighting London's buildings. A $40,000 fireworks display blazed above the Thames. By special dispensation, all pubs stayed open until midnight. Long after that, the crowds remained, staring at the silent palace.

Behind the spectacle lay months of

**IN THE ROYAL BOX:** Queen Elizabeth (right foreground), Princess Margaret, and Captain Peter Townsend (standing left), Margaret's commoner suitor

preparation. The procession was ordered by a red-bound, 128-page book. It went into such details as allowing troops twenty minutes for their box lunches.

One man was in supreme command. He was 44-year-old Sir Bernard Marmaduke FitzAlan-Howard, the Duke of Norfolk. As Earl Marshal of England, his duties include arranging coronations, royal weddings and funerals, and state openings of Parliament. His only pay for this job, which has been in his family since the seventeenth century, is $56 a year.

Norfolk's most controversial decision was to ban television from the abbey ceremony. A clamor of protest arose, and the decision was reversed. Only the most sacred parts of the ceremony—the anoint-

**PRINCESS MARGARET** (right) is the trim young lady whose romance with Townsend fascinated American and British press (below)

ing and the administering of communion —were kept from the cameras. Some 50,-000,000 persons eventually saw the spectacle on TV. Among them was the Duke of Windsor, Elizabeth's uncle, who abdicated as King Edward VIII to marry "the woman I love". He and his duchess watched in Paris.

Norfolk's chief assistant was David Eccles, handsome, 49-year-old Minister of Works. He was knighted for his efforts. To the public, Eccles' main contribution was the construction of stands for 110,000 along the coronation route. They glittered like medieval jousting pavilions. Prices for seats ranged from $11.20 to $84. Private speculators built twice as many and charged up to $150—or whatever the traffic would bear.

London was a city transformed. Giant replicas of guardsmen's helmets towered over Whitehall. Selfridge's department store featured a four-ton, fourteen-foot-high statue of the Queen riding her horse "Winston". Fiji Island soldiers in soulu skirts, and Indian ranis in flowing saris lent an exotic touch to the crowds. African chieftains with huge ceremonial umbrellas appeared at the Queen's garden parties. The familiar red-coated sentries outside Buckingham Palace disappeared as bronze-turbaned Pakistanis, slouch-hatted Australians, and other Commonwealth troops took over guard duty.

The show cost the government $7,204,-400. Seat sales and the disposal of used timber and decorations cut the final bill to perhaps $5,600,000. But millions of dollars in precious foreign exchange were garnered from tourists. And British brewers calculated that the taxes on the extra beer drunk during festivities more than made up the balance.

The British public joined in the spending spree. Personal savings decreased by $14 million during the excitement.

The great upsurge of national morale was given a boost by news that reached London on coronation eve. Halfway across the world, in Nepal, a British expedition had conquered the seemingly unconquerable summit of Mount Everest. Its 29,141-foot peak is the highest in the world. It was scaled by Edmond Hillary, a New Zealand beekeeper, and Tensing Norkay, a Sherpa tribesman from Nepal.

The Queen was wakened to hear the news. On Coronation Day itself, she paused to cable her "warmest congratulations".

The Queen's coronation honors list, issued on May 31, delighted sports-loving Britons. It granted knighthoods to retired cricket star Jack Hobbs, 70, and to top jockey Gordon Richards, 49.

Sir Gordon returned the royal favor by riding his horse, Pinza, to victory by four lengths against the Queen's own colt, Aureole, in the Epsom Derby four days after the coronation. The queen lost a token wager of two shillings (28¢).

Elizabeth had her revenge at the Royal Ascot meet. There her four-year-old, Choir Boy, beat Sir Gordon's mount to win the Royal Hunt Cup.

The coronation year closed with the Queen and her 32-year-old husband away on a grueling round-the-world Commonwealth tour. Its almost constant round of public appearances and state occasions was to last five and a half months. No other reigning sovereign had ever undertaken such a trip. The purpose: strengthening the bonds that hold the independent Commonwealth nations together.

The royal couple left London on the raw, damp night of Nov. 23, aboard a British Overseas Airways Corporation Stratocruiser named "Canopus". Next day they were in sunny Bermuda. At Jamaica they transferred to the 15,902-ton liner *Gothic*, of the Shaw Savill line, which had been converted to a royal yacht for the major portion of the trip.

**LOYAL OPPOSITION:** Left-wing Laborite Aneurin Bevan appears aggressive even at cricket

Townsend, 38, a Battle-of-Britain hero and an equerry at Buckingham Palace. He was slated to become controller of the Queen Mother's household when she and Margaret moved from the palace to Clarence House after the coronation. Townsend was the father of two young sons. He had divorced his wife, Rosemary, in December, 1952, for adultery.

Since the Church of England does not recognize divorce, there seemed no way for Margaret—as sister of the Defender of the Faith—to marry Townsend. But the tabloid London *Daily Mirror* polled its readers and, of 70,000 replies, 96.8 percent said Margaret should be permitted to marry whom she chose.

Margaret went off to Africa with her mother on a state tour of Rhodesia. In her absence, Townsend was shipped off to Brussels, as air attaché at the British Embassy in Belgium.

Some Britons had respectfully criticized Margaret for her low-cut gowns, her night-clubbing with Danny Kaye, her dancing the cancan at a private party. Since King George VI's death in 1952, however, she had seemed more grave. Now she was taken ill. She returned from Rhodesia looking wan and miserable.

Perhaps there was a way for Margaret to achieve happiness. It involved a change in the Regency Act of 1937.

The law provides for the selection of a regent to act in the Queen's place if she should die or be incapacitated before Prince Charles is 18. Under the old law, the choice automatically fell upon the adult first in the line of succession—Margaret.

In November, however, Parliament amended the act to nominate Philip as regent. The change removed Margaret farther from the regency, and possibly would make it easier for her to marry the man of her choice.

In the Pacific Ocean, they put in at the Fiji Islands, and returned Queen Salote's visit in Tonga. On Dec. 23 they began nearly six weeks in New Zealand, at Auckland.

There was other royal excitement during the year. It centered about the Queen's sister, Princess Margaret, 23. American newspaper stories that quickly filtered back to Britain declared that Margaret had fallen in love with a divorced commoner.

He was R.A.F. Group Captain Peter

**NATIVE** "Sir Walter Raleigh" spreads cloak for Queen Elizabeth as she visits Jamaica on Empire tour

THERE WASN'T MUCH LEFT, IN 1953, OF
the once legendary British Empire on
which the sun never set. One by one,
colonies and dominions had grown up
and broken away from London's apron
strings.

But two dominions, on the other side
of the world, Australia and New Zealand,
remained sturdily loyal. In Australia and
New Zealand, Queen Elizabeth II and
the Duke of Edinburgh decided to spend
half of their six-month, 30,000-mile tour
of the Commonwealth.

To most outsiders, Australia is the fabulous Down Under, land of sheep, kan-
garoos, koalas, and the duck-billed platy-
pus, home of a race of tough, brawling
soldiers. But this island-continent, almost
as large as the United States, is also one
of the most forward-looking members of
the Commonwealth.

During 1953, Australia was fighting obstacles to its growth. Eight years of Socialist government had ended in 1949
when Robert Gordon Menzies, a thickset,
fast-talking corporation lawyer, had become Prime Minister, heading a conservative coalition of the Liberal and Country parties. Menzies had promised an end
to gasoline rationing and other annoying
shortages and government controls. But

# The COMMONWEALTH

he found it easier to promise than to deliver.

The country was also suffering from inflation. Prices went up more steeply than wages and salaries. But the drastic steps Menzies took to end the inflation made matters temporarily worse. Cutting down on free-spending public works, for example, meant more unemployment.

Menzies' government had a very slim majority at best in the federal Parliament at Canberra. And most of the state governments—Australia has the same federal-state setup as the United States— were still controlled by the Labour (Socialist) party. In one local election after another during 1953, the Socialists gained ground. Apparently Australia's man in the street, from the tropical sugar lands of Queensland in the far north to the snowy southern mountains of Tasmania, blamed the party in power for unemployment, high prices, and general economic tightness.

The conservative coalition and the Labour opposition were bitter toward each other, for Australians take their politics hard. And the political bad feelings were reflected in labor discord, which periodically threatened to strangle Australian industry. The loud and active Communists, who only a couple of years before had run the most important unions, were under control for the time being. But there was no assurance that they would not pop up again.

## New Zealand

Even less known in the U.S. than Australia is the beautiful, prosperous, and socially advanced Dominion of New Zealand. Slightly smaller than the United Kingdom, the Dominion was called to the attention of the American housewife during the year. The reason: cheap beef from New Zealand herds.

An outbreak of hoof-and-mouth disease had shut Canadian beef out of the United States. Rather than lose their U.S. market, Canadian dealers bought frozen beef in New Zealand and shipped 60,-000,000 pounds of it across the border. American cattlemen complained at the competition. But the argument ended on March 1, when the Canadian embargo was lifted and Canadian beef began to come in again.

New Zealand's ability to meet this sudden demand for beef in a new market was a good illustration of why the Dominion was flourishing. Grass grows freely all the year round in New Zealand. There are no disastrous droughts. The climate is so good that livestock can live out of doors. Barns are unnecessary. As a result, it doesn't cost much to raise sheep and cattle. So when prices are high for wool, meat, and dairy products, as they were in 1953, the country is quietly prosperous.

The big event of the year in New Zealand was the preparation for the visit of Queen Elizabeth and Prince Philip, who arrived on Dec. 23. But their gala reception was saddened by one of the worst railroad disasters in history.

The rail line between Wellington and Auckland skirts the base of Mt. Ruapehu, a 9175-foot active volcano. At the top of the snow-capped mountain is a curious natural phenomenon called a crater lake—a huge bowl of solid ice filled with hot, sometimes boiling, water. Apparently the outlet through which the water normally flows had been blocked up. On Christmas Eve, just before the night train was due to pass, the water broke through another point in the icy wall, poured in a raging torrent down the Wanganui River, and washed out a railroad bridge.

The seven-car train, unwarned, hit the demolished bridge. The locomotive and five cars plunged into the river. One car was carried two and one-half miles downstream. Only 114 passengers were saved; at least 150 drowned.

## India

To the west of Australia and New Zealand lies that part of the British Empire which was falling away most spectacularly.

Once India had been the proudest jewel in the imperial crown. Now it was divided into two quarreling segments. India proper was already a republic. Moslem Pakistan was about to become one, under a new constitution. Both were still members of the Commonwealth. But republican India recognized Elizabeth not as queen but as the Commonwealth's head.

Until 1947 there had been no such thing as Pakistan; the whole subcontinent had been India. But two of its pieces, one in the northwest, the other, nearly 1000 miles away in the northeast, had been different from the rest. The difference was primarily not one of race, language, or way of life, but of religion. Nine-tenths of the people who live in what is now Pakistan are Moslems, most other Indians are Hindus. By and large the Hindu and Moslem villagers live peacefully together. But their religious and political leaders stirred up trouble between them.

When India broke away from Britain, Pakistan broke away from India. A new nation was born, the world's sixth largest in population. The bitterness which brought about the division never died out; in 1953 India and Pakistan were still quarreling.

Their newest feud broke out when the Indians began monkeying with the headwaters of the rivers that rise in India, flow into Pakistan. The Pakistani depend on these rivers to irrigate their fields; they complained that the Indians were diverting the water. India, Pakistan charged, was "depriving 76,000,000 persons of the waters of the Indus basin, by which they live". It complained to the United Nations that it faced "starvation by slow strangulation".

But the bitterest rivalry between India and Pakistan was still, as it had been from the beginning, over the beautiful Vale of Kashmir in the high Himalayas. Most of its 4,000,000 people were Moslems, and therefore attached to Pakistan. But it was governed by Hindus, who wanted to unite it with India. Unable to reach a compromise, the men who drew the twisting boundary between the two countries left Kashmir as a no man's land. For six years Pakistan and India had both been grabbing at Kashmir, trying to take it over by diplomacy if possible, by force if necessary. The United Nations made feeble attempts to make both sides see reason, but in 1953 a solution seemed as far off as ever. "The bitterness between India and Pakistan is a frightening thing which grows from day to day, sometimes from hour to hour," a correspondent reported.

Pakistan, which had started from scratch, with no government machinery, no trained officials, was still having trouble attaining stature as an Asiatic power. India, using the government machinery left behind by the British, was doing better. It still had its hands full of the economic and social problems of a poverty-stricken population. However, it was busy building up its position meanwhile as the leading "third force" in world affairs, midway between the Eastern and Western coalitions.

This ancient, colorful country—where bullock carts with gaily colored awnings trundle through hot clouds of dust, monkeys play by the road, and shaggy black pigs root beside ponds in which water

**RELIGION** still solaces most Indians. Here devoted Jains pour milk over the 57-foot granite statue of St. Gomateshavara in a rite celebrated every 12 years

buffalo cool themselves—does not impress the tourist as a modern world power. But its million square miles and its nearly 360,000,000 people make it hard to overlook.

Its Prime Minister, proud and energetic Jawaharlal Nehru, conceals an iron will under a deceptively mild manner. He is a man of learning, an aristocrat, a spellbinder on the platform, and his is the hand which leads India. Nehru has no use for Communism, which he keeps under control in his country. But he is not enthusiastic about the Western world, either—he remembers the years he spent in British prisons. So in 1953 he was trying to steer India down the middle of the road between Communism and Western democracy, without committing himself completely to either side.

His powerful influence was reflected when his sister, Mme. Vijaya Lakshmi Pandit, was elected President of the U.N. General Assembly and when India was chosen to head the commission of neutrals in post-armistice Korea.

In October India got its twenty-ninth state, when Andhra, a rich rice land carved out of the old state of Madras, was created. The new state was custom-built for the 20,000,000 Dravidian people who speak Telugu, one of India's fifteen languages. Five other language groups were demanding states of their own. Nehru accepted the new state but worried lest it start a movement to break India up into small, unfriendly bits. Another point that worried him: Andhra is the strongest Communist area in India; some day it might have a Communist government.

In 1953, Canada, greatest of the Queen's overseas domains, was so busy building up its economic muscles that it had little time for other pursuits.

Great projects were nearing completion. A mighty hydroelectric plant at Niagara Falls was almost finished. Near the sleepy little Indian village of Kitimat, in the bear-infested northern wilds of British Columbia, the Aluminum Company of Canada was spending $1 million a week to build seaports, airports, townsites, powerhouses, roads, and dams. As soon as the construction was complete, the world's largest aluminum smelter would go into business.

In Quebec a railroad inched its way almost into the wasteland along the Labrador-Quebec border, where 480,000,000 tons of iron ore were waiting to be shipped to the steel mills of Pennsylvania and Europe.

New mineral deposits, including precious uranium, were being discovered in Canada every day. New highways, bridges, dams, factories, and grain elevators were springing up everywhere. More goods were being produced, more money was being invested, more money earned than in any previous year in Canada's history.

Canadians had little energy left for politics, even for a general election.

In Canada, instead of electing a president, the voters choose members of the House of Commons. As in Britain, the leader of the party winning the most seats becomes Prime Minister.

The issue in Canada in 1953 resembled that in the United States in 1952. Like the American Democrats, the Canadian Liberals had been in office a long time—eighteen years. Like the American Republicans, the Canadian Progressive Conservatives thought it was time for a change. But Canada was booming, and a majority of the voters seemed content with things as they were.

The Conservatives were hard up for an issue. In January they thought they had one: scandal in the Defense Department. When Parliament dug into the story, it became a three-ring circus, complete

**"NEUTRALIST"** leader of India, Prime Minister Nehru, eyes the split between Russia and West, ponders his country's course

with horses. A report charged chiseling and thievery at the Petawawa army camp. One specific charge was that horses had been listed on army rolls and had drawn army pay. Actually, laborers had been put on the payroll at the rate usually paid only to teamsters with their own horses. Cartoonists and columnists had a field day. But by election day, Aug. 10, the furor had died down.

This dénouement left the Conservatives with nothing to offer but general promises to end "waste, inefficiency, and extravagance".

The ten-week campaign was listless. The Conservatives kept demanding a change; the Liberals insisted everything was all right.

On Aug. 10, Canadian voters elected almost a carbon copy of the old Parliament, top-heavy with Liberals. Benign, scholarly French-Canadian Louis S. St. Laurent continued as Prime Minister.

One of his problems was the friction between Canada and the United States, normally the best of friends. A visit to Canada by President Eisenhower in November didn't help much.

Canadians were sore about a number of things.

The St. Lawrence Seaway was a cause for irritation. For years Canada had been trying to persuade the United States to help it deepen the St. Lawrence River, which flows between them, so that ocean-going ships could sail up to the Great Lakes. American businessmen who thought it would hurt their business always managed to block it in Congress. Disgusted, the Canadians decided to go ahead and build the seaway on their own. But President Eisenhower, who was strongly in favor of it, made one last effort to push the bill through Congress.

American tariff policies also annoyed Canada. Lead and zinc miners in far-western British Columbia were grumbling. On the wide-spreading grain farms of the prairies there was uneasiness. The cheese makers of Ontario saw hard times ahead, and Nova Scotia fishermen were unhappy: all of their pocketbooks were being, or might be, pinched by U.S. tariffs.

All these things bothered Canadians. Then American congressmen dragged Canada into their investigations of Communism. This story began when *The Chicago Tribune* published an interview with Igor Gouzenko, the cipher clerk who deserted the Soviet Embassy in Ottawa in 1945 and disclosed the secrets of a Russian spy ring in Canada. In the interview, Gouzenko, now living in Canada under an assumed name and constantly guarded by the Mounties, was quoted as saying that it might be "worth while" for him to talk to the American investigators.

Twice the U.S. Senate Internal Security Subcommittee asked Ottawa to arrange an interview. The Canadians turned down the first request, saying Gouzenko had nothing to add to his original story. The second time they agreed to an interview, but on condition that they censor anything Gouzenko said before it was made public. This annoyed the committee.

Then some American writers accused Canadian Foreign Minister Lester B. (Mike) Pearson of helping the Communists. Secretary of State John Foster Dulles said the charge was nonsense, but the Canadians were still annoyed. The committeemen finally accepted the Canadian terms.

Now they had only to persuade Gouzenko, who kept changing his mind, to see them. He finally agreed to an interview early in January, 1954. Canadians hoped this would clear the air and remove the most serious issue between a Commonwealth country and the United States.

**AT THE SUMMIT** of Mount Everest, Tensing, the Sherpa, holds aloft four flags — British, Nepalese, Indian, U.N.—for Hillary to photograph

**THE OLD AFRICA** is symbolized by this gorgeously painted Turu tribesman of Tanganyika

# AFRICA

FOUR MAU MAUS, FLASHING LONG PANGA knives, broke into the living room of an isolated cattle ranch in Kenya. One grabbed Kitty Hesselburger's throat. The others rushed at Dorothy Raynes-Simson. Mrs. Simson snatched a pistol from her pocketbook. Although she recognized one of her attackers as her male cook, she shot him and another man dead. Then she killed Mrs. Hesselburger's assailant. The fourth Mau Mau fled to a bathroom. She followed and killed him.

Another Mau Mau mob attacked Roger Ruck, a British planter, and his doctor-wife Esme as they strolled in pajamas in their rose garden. Ruck was hacked to death on his woodpile. His blond wife fell by his side. Bursting into a padlocked bedroom, the Mau Maus slashed six-year-old Michael Ruck to death while he slept with his teddy bear.

Such atrocities bore out the vows of the Mau Mau secret society to drive every white from the British Crown Col-

**THE NEW AFRICA** emerges as Egyptian diplomat Salah Salem, striving to promote good will in Anglo-Egyptian Sudan, capers in war dance with Dinka tribesmen

ony of Kenya, straddling the equator in East Africa.

In the moonlight of March 26, 1953, as loyal "Kukes" (Kikuyu tribesmen) slept in beehive mud huts at Lari, Mau Maus knifed sentries, barred doors, fired grass roofs, and cut down fleeing victims. Children's heads were chopped off with axes.

A boy's throat was cut with a panga and his blood drunk before his mother's eyes. At least 125 were slaughtered.

The British rushed new orders from their Nairobi capital: "If you see any numbers of Negroes assembling and get no quick satisfactory reply to your first challenge, shoot immediately and to

**BARBED WIRE** encloses Kikuyu tribesmen rounded up in drive to halt Mau Mau terrorism in Kenya, East Africa. Gallows (left) is a sobering influence as they await questioning or removal to native reservations

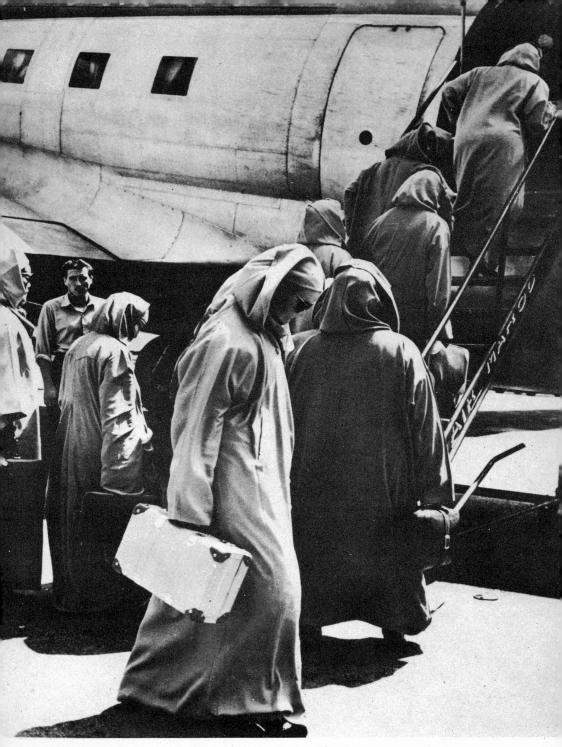

**CHANGE IN MOROCCO:** Shrouded concubines board Corsica-bound plane to join former Sultan Sidi Mohammed ben Youssef, deposed by French for nationalist leanings

kill." A small army of 6750 British infantrymen (many airlifted from Suez), 3000 African riflemen, 10,000 Kikuyu home guardsmen, and 6500 Indian settlers was mobilized.

As the Mau Mau switched to company-sized operations, Major General William Hinde rejoiced: "We like them to attack in large numbers, because then we can mow them down."

By the end of 1953 the Mau Mau's back seemed broken. Some 2900 terrorists had been killed, 27,000 imprisoned, and 89 hanged. But 730 Negroes, 16 whites, and 11 Indians had been murdered.

The Mau Mau's field commander—a scarred ex-teacher of 30 who called himself "General Russia"—appealed: "It is only peace we want. We cannot live without food. If the police and soldiers are withdrawn, the fighting will stop." The Royal Air Force replied with leaflets: "Only starvation and death await you if you continue the fight. To arrange surrender, come out of the bush in daylight, waving green branches." Many did.

But Sir George Erskine, who had been rushed from Suez to take over, expected the war to last to mid-1954.

The story of West Africa in 1953 was less violent than that of East Africa. Sir Charles Arden-Clarke, British Governor of the Gold Coast, boasted: "We are showing the way. The African, given a chance, is capable of managing his own affairs with such advice as he himself seeks from his European friends."

Of the 4,000,000 natives in the swamps, jungles, and 20-foot-tall cocoa groves in that Crown Colony, one half still believed in witches. Seven out of ten could not read or write. Yet from an air-conditioned office in Accra, Prime Minister Kwame Nkrumah (pronounced *qah-croom'-ah*), a 43-year-old bachelor, was asking "the status of a Dominion within the Commonwealth".

When catapulted to power, Nkrumah was residing in a British jail. Now he proudly wore on his cap the letters P.G. (Prison Graduate). He was sobered by

**NEW SULTAN,** Sidi Mohammed ben Moulay Arafa, handpicked by French, salutes his subjects as he arrives to assume Moroccan throne

responsibility, and threw Communist leaders out of the Gold Coast's trade unions. "About self-government," he said, "they must not make me go too fast—and I must not go too slow. My job is to keep things level and steady." But by the end of 1953 the Nkrumah regime was unsteadied by a spate of stories that Cabinet members and the Prime Minister himself had been profiteering from bribery and graft.

In neighboring Nigeria there was also internal conflict. Dr. Nnamdi ("Zik") Azikiwe, a U.S.-educated newspaper publisher, was pressing for home rule of Britain's most populous (30,000,000) colony by 1956. But his people were divided between blue-eyed Moslems in the northern highlands and pagan or Christianized Negroes in the southern delta lands.

The strife between these two groups dyed with blood the yellow dirt streets in the mud metropolis of Kano. In three May days, fifty-two persons were killed and 200 injured. The cause: The Moslems did not want to give up their British guardians, only to be subjected to pagan and Christian overlords.

To Prime Minister Daniel F. Malan of the Union of South Africa, the West African trend toward Negro home rule was "a disastrous step. . . . How can illiterate people with so little civilization govern themselves? It can't be done."

An old-time *predikant* (minister) in the Dutch Reformed Church, Malan preached to his flock of Nationalist voters: "This is South Africa's last chance to remain a white man's country. . . . Every vote cast against the Nationalists is a vote for the Russians, Indians, United Nations, British Labour party."

Boer hoodlums broke up election rallies of the more pro-British, less fanatical United party by throwing eggs and tomatoes and wielding *sjamboks* (rhinoceros-hide whips). Calvinist predikants warned of "God-fearing white girls" marrying "niggers".

An Afrikaans newspaper cartoon showed a panga knife, labeled "Mau Mau", hanging over a family of whites. Its caption: VOTE NATIONALIST TO AVERT THIS.

On April 15 the South Africans gave a 7-to-6 edge in popular votes to Malan's opponents. But because the electoral system was biased in favor of the Boer rural areas, the Nationalists boosted their parliamentary majority from 86 to 94 of the 159 seats in the House of Assembly. At 78, Malan thus won a new mandate for his white-supremacy program of *apàrtheid* (racial segregation).

Africans and Indians in South Africa turned to passive resistance. At 60, Manilal Gandhi, chubby son of India's martyred Mohandas K. Gandhi, switched his South African residence to a jail cell for thirty-eight days for violating apartheid laws. "By my voluntary sufferings," he said, "I seek to melt the heart of the government."

Amid a world-wide barrage against the Nationalist racist policies, the Prime Minister flew to London for Queen Elizabeth's coronation, only to hear that a New Orleans Negro named Marie Bryant was singing this show-stopping ditty at London's Hippodrome:

*Don't malign Malan because he dis-*
*likes our tan.*
*We know that it's wrong to have skin*
*that's all brown,*
*And wrong to be born on the wrong*
*side of town.*
*It is quite right that our filthy old*
*homes be burned down.*
*Malan is a wonderful man—don't ma-*
*lign Malan.*
*He's doing the best he can.*

Was any compromise possible between the whites and blacks of Africa? Across the Limpopo River from South

Africa, Sir Godfrey Huggins, a dapper little surgeon, dreamed of a "virile British state" to "preserve Africa for the Empire and the British way of life". Huggins, Prime Minister of the self-governing colony of Southern Rhodesia,

**NATIVE POLICE** drive off some of a group of 500 Kikuyu women who stormed a police station near Nairobi, Kenya, hoping to release Mau Maus

had come out from London in 1911 for a rest, and had not rested since. To protect himself from bores, he switches off his hearing aid.

The Huggins plan called for an hourglass-shaped Central African Federation of 475,000 square miles, twice the size of Texas. It would become the Commonwealth's eighth dominion. Politically, it would unite 175,000 "Europeans" and 6,000,000 Africans. Economically, it would marry Southern Rhodesia's coal mines, Northern Rhodesia's copper belt, and Nyasaland's Negro labor.

"A Black Front is advancing from the Gold Coast; a White Front is moving from the South," Huggins warned. Unless federated, "the Rhodesias will become the clashing point".

In March his plan was approved by the British Commons, 304 to 260, with some special safeguards for Negroes. It was approved by Southern Rhodesia's settlers in April by a 5-to-3 edge. No fair test was made of Negro sentiment. Only 429 natives had the $1400 in assets or $700 annual income needed to vote.

In September, at 70, Sir Godfrey was sworn in as the first Prime, Defense, Finance, and External Affairs Minister of his Central African Federation.

Far away, north of the Sahara, French North Africa on the night of July 1 was awakened by two shots from the pistol of an ex-convict paid by Moslem nationalists. One bullet missed. The other killed Prince Azzedine Bey in his luxuriant garden in Tunisia.

Thus died the heir presumptive to Tunisia's French-protected throne. He was the most pro-French and the eldest of the reigning Bey's 220 princely relations. As so often before in Tunisia, this new nationalist outbreak made the French shy away from granting real home rule.

On the Moslem Sabbath of Friday, Sept. 11, in Rabat, French Morocco, a 28-year-old house painter roared his 1930 Ford convertible at 50 miles an hour at Sultan Sidi Moulay Mohammed ben Arafa. The Model-A attempt at assassination failed. The Ford glanced off the horse the Sultan was riding and merely bruised the 64-year-old ruler. The would-be assassin flashed a knife. He was shot dead. The wealthy, weak-kneed Sultan gasped: "*Sibismaken*" ("No harm done").

As recently as Aug. 20, another sultan,

Sidi Mohammed ben Youssef, had lived in Rabat's stucco palace, complete with private zoo and harem. But he was anti-French. So the French Resident General, General Augustin Guillaume, ringed the palace with tanks and artillery. Ben Youssef was flown off to Corsica along with his two wives, best-beloved concubine, and five tons of baggage. He was later joined by thirteen more of his forty other concubines. The French foreign ministry explained: "He is in exile with all the honors due his rank."

Ben Youssef's ouster resulted from his having lent his prestige as *Imam* (Commander of the Faithful) to Communist-backed Arab extremists in the outlawed Istiqlal (Independence) party. Also, his daughters horrified devout Moslems by being photographed in scanty bathing suits, and his sons by attending cocktail parties.

In replacing Ben Youssef, the French put their faith not so much in the Arabs, but in the more puritanical Moslem Berbers, who lived in the rugged Atlas Mountains before the Arabs arrived twelve centuries ago. Indeed, the Berber leader, His Highness Hadj Thami el Mezouari el Glaoui, Pasha of Marrakech, an 84-year-old ex-bandit boasting concubines by the hundreds, had forced the French hand by ordering his warlike tribesmen to saddle their stallions as the first step toward Berber-Arab civil war. It was when thus prodded that the French applied their old divide-and-rule policy, switched to the new pro-French sultan, arrested 1000 Istiqlal partisans, and incidentally safeguarded the new American bomber bases in Morocco.

"Now I can die," el Glaoui gloried. "Morocco is saved."

**THE UNKNOWN:** A malaria fighter, robed and masked against his own insecticide, gets the customary reaction from this Liberian village child

ON AUG. 22, 1953, MOHAMMED RIZA Pahlevi, Shahinshah (King of Kings) of Iran, taxied his twin-engined Beechcraft to the Teheran airport's apron. Wearing an air marshal's uniform, he stepped out into the 105° noonday heat. The Shah tried to hold back his tears as he embraced his new Premier, Major General Fazollah Zahedi.

He was obviously embarrassed as top-hatted Iranians prostrated themselves and kissed his feet. To American Ambassador Loy W. Henderson he offered a warm handshake. At Soviet Ambassador Anatoli I. Lavrentiev he aimed a frigid stare.

Thus the 34-year-old Shah returned to his throne after a six-day exile. He had been lunching with his half-German second wife, Queen Soraya, at the Hotel

# The MIDDLE EAST

Excelsior in Rome when told of a popular uprising against Iran's fainting fanatic, Premier Mohammed Mossadegh.

"I knew it; I knew it; they love me," the Shah rejoiced.

Once the Shah had been called a spineless figurehead with a fancy for fast Cadillacs and concubines, a man with admirable dreams for his people but no stomach for his responsibilities. Now he boasted: "While returning from Rome I had a feeling that I was a completely new man."

And Iran was a new nation. It was saved at the brink of a Red abyss which might have engulfed the whole Moslem Middle East. For Premier Mossadegh had rejected every Western proposal to settle a 29-month-old dispute over Iran's nationalization of the Anglo-Iranian Oil

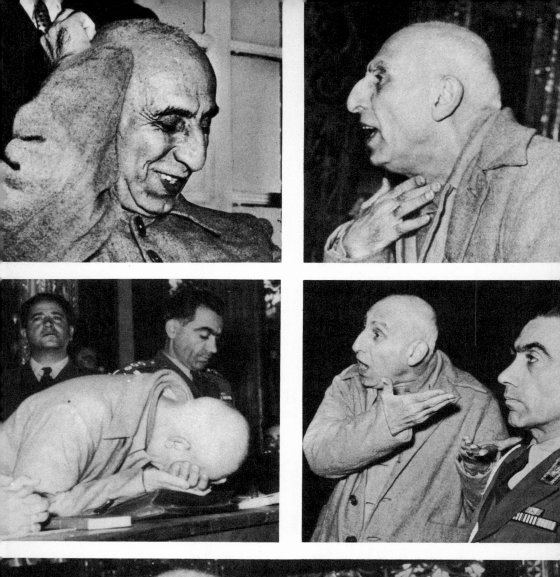

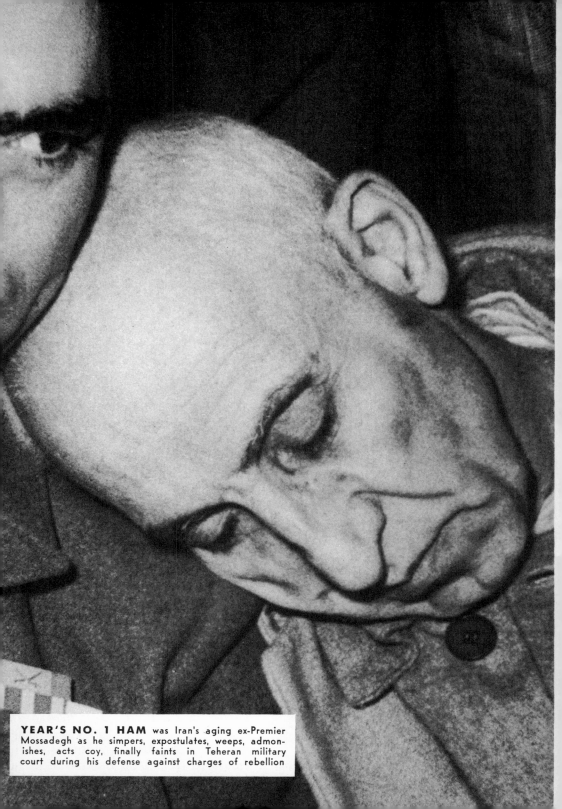

**YEAR'S NO. 1 HAM** was Iran's aging ex-Premier Mossadegh as he simpers, expostulates, weeps, admonishes, acts coy, finally faints in Teheran military court during his defense against charges of rebellion

**SHAH DOWN:** With Iran's ruler in exile, pro-Mossadegh rioters knock over statue of Shah's father

Company. Though he also nationalized the Soviet's caviar concession, he had come to rely on the Communist Tudeh (Masses) party as his chief prop.

"Could anyone with a car and air coolers and a good bed like mine be a Communist?" Mossadegh challenged. "The people know he won't steal from them," a close adviser added. But personal honesty would not replace $180 million in lost oil revenue and $61 million in operating deficits in the nationalized oil fields.

On Jan. 17, 1953, by a vote of 59 to 1, "Old Mossy" had pushed through the Majlis (lower house of Parliament) a one-year extension of his power to rule by decree. The Majlis Speaker, Ayatollah ("God's symbol"—equivalent to a Moslem reverend) Kashani, broke with him over this issue and warned: "You'll be sorry."

Known as "Iran's Black Eminence", Kashani saved the Shah's throne at the end of February. Learning that Old Mossy had talked the young Shah into planning to leave Iran for his "health", Kashani's thugs swept into Teheran's streets. "Our Shah or death!" they shouted. A Kashani fanatic nicknamed "The Brainless One" crashed a jeep through iron gates into the Premier's garden. Mossadegh fled in pajamas to the U.S. Point Four offices and on to claim *bast* (sanctuary) in the Majlis. The Shah agreed to stay.

Old Mossy's thugs then took their turn at shouting: "Mossadegh or death!" The Premier also agreed to stay.

Now Mossadegh made a threatening appeal for American aid. In reply, President Eisenhower bluntly voiced his "hope that, before it is too late, the government of Iran will take steps . . . to prevent a further deterioration."

Old Mossy's only steps were to have Kashani deposed as the Majlis Speaker, to dissolve the Majlis, and to take a plebiscite approving this unconstitutional act. He boasted a 166,550-to-116 vote in

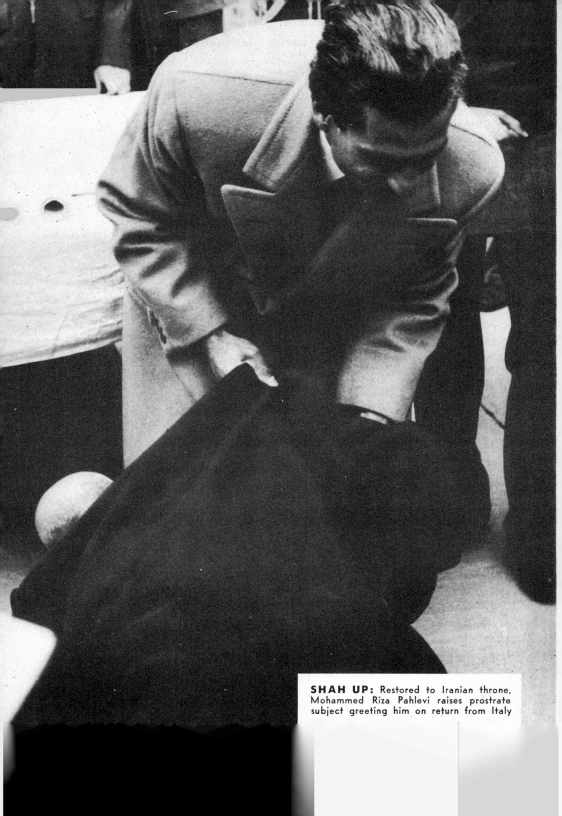

**SHAH UP:** Restored to Iranian throne, Mohammed Riza Pahlevi raises prostrate subject greeting him on return from Italy

Teheran, or 99.93 percent—purer than Ivory soap. "The will of the people is above law," he gloried.

The Premier's downfall followed. On Aug. 16 he blatantly ignored legal decrees by which the Shah had dismissed him in favor of General Zahedi. The Shah flew off to Rome. Zahedi, who not many months earlier had been living in the Majlis for sanctuary, skipped to the hills.

Yet the Iranian Army remained true to its oath to defend "God, Shah, and country." The Iranian people still revered their Shah as "viceregent of God", "shadow of the Almighty", and "center of the universe".

What especially enraged the people was the way Communist and nationalist extremists alike raced through the Teheran bazaars screaming: "Death to the Shah!"

Suddenly Old Mossy himself woke up and realized that the Reds might turn against him. He ordered his troops to put down the riots. The soldiers did so with bayonets, rifle butts, and tear gas. They clubbed the rioters into shouting: "Long live the Shah!"

At that display, the Shah's supporters took heart. General Zahedi, from his hiding place, ordered the Army to disobey the "illegal Mossadegh government".

At 8 A.M. on Aug. 19, a gang of wrestlers, weight lifters, and tumblers rallied at the railroad station. Brandishing knives and iron bars, they smashed their way to Teheran's central squares to enforce the Shah's cause. Police and Army forces disobeyed Mossadegh's orders to crush these royalist rallies. Red bully-boys no longer acted as Mossadegh's prop. They sulked. "No more aid to Mossadegh," the Tudeh ordered.

Eight government buildings were burned by the Shah's men. Pro-Mossadegh and Red newspaper plants were wrecked. Radio Teheran and police headquarters were captured. The death toll was sixty-three.

After a pitched battle, the mob sacked Mossadegh's house, tore apart his famed iron cot, auctioned off his new electric refrigerator on the spot—for $36. Old Mossy had fled.

Within hours, wearing pink pajamas, he gave himself up to Zahedi at the plush Officers' Club. As Mossadegh stumbled in leaning on a yellow cane, Zahedi offered his hand and said: "Salaam aleykom" ("Peace be with you"). Mossadegh replied: "Aleykom salaam" ("And with you be peace").

Tossed into an army barracks, Old Mossy threatened: "I will fast to death." After going without breakfast and lunch, he changed his mind and asked for "three roast chickens every day".

He threatened to jump out of the window. When a guard opened it for him, he chose to live.

He was full of antics like these, when, still in pajamas, he was court-martialed for plotting to overthrow the constitutional government. He wept; he fainted; he cat-napped; he tried to bolt the courtroom; he punched his defense attorney. "I will not speak again," he threatened—but he always did. His prosecutor called him "funnier than Charlie Chaplin".

Not so funny was a pro-Mossadegh coup which the nationalist-Communist alliance tried to pull off in the bazaar's labyrinths on Nov. 12. Tipped off in advance, the Shah's soldiers and police slugged the rioters into surrender.

Nonetheless, the Shah asked for mercy for his foe to keep from making him a martyr. Accordingly the court-martial, although finding Mossadegh guilty on all thirteen charges, sentenced him in December to a mere three years of solitary confinement.

General Zahedi meanwhile had been

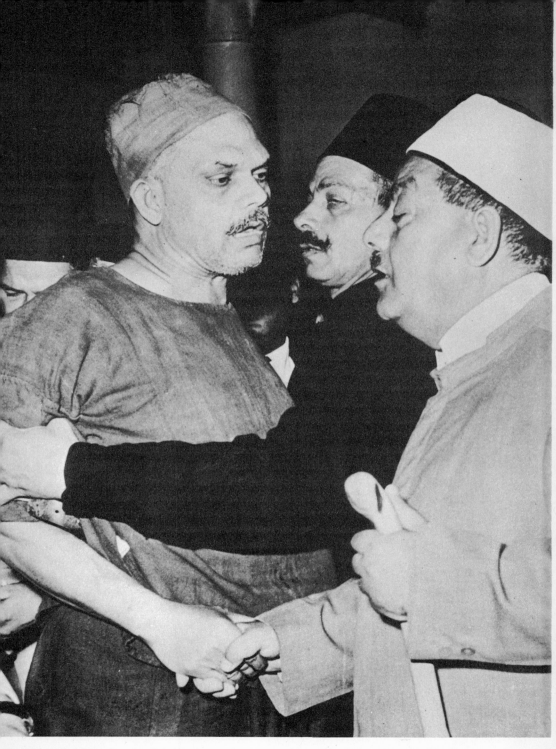

**LAST WORDS:** Sentenced in Egypt to die as spy for a "foreign power", Mahmoud Sabry (left) gets religious comfort from a Moslem sheik just four minutes before execution

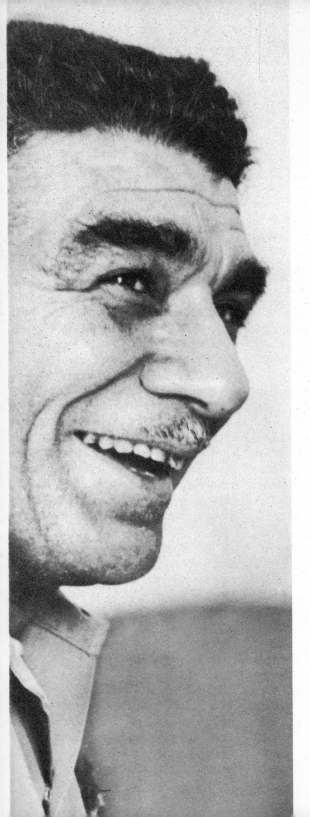

working from 6 A.M. to midnight. In two weeks he lost 19 pounds.

Graying at 56, the new Premier stood his full 6 ft. 2 in., although he suffered from arthritis and was missing four ribs from a fight with Red revolutionists in 1921. More recently he had been interned by the British for being pro-German during World War II.

Once in power, Zahedi went as far as any Iranian could in the oil dispute with his old captors. As if promising to settle with the British, he wrote President Eisenhower on Aug. 26: "The new government . . . will pursue a policy of eliminating such differences as may exist between other countries and itself."

On Sept. 5 the Summer White House in Denver replied by granting Iran $45 million in emergency economic aid. President Eisenhower's hope: to tide over the new pro-Western regime pending a renewed flow of oil revenue. While Herbert Hoover Jr., the former President's son, sought an international grouping of big oil companies to get Iranian oil back into the world markets, the Zahedi regime on Dec. 5 ended the diplomatic break with Britain.

In 1953 the Shah's ex-brother-in-law, ex-King Faruk of Egypt, was not as lucky as the Iranian monarch. Faruk had nothing to do but to philander and read comic books while living in exile in his rented thirty-room villa, "Grotto Ferrata", outside Rome. He gambled so much that the 10,000-franc note, France's largest (worth $28.62), was nicknamed the *faruk.*

Faruk's commoner second wife, Narriman, 19, drove off in her red Mercedes-Benz with her poodle, Jou-Jou, and flew by plane to Cairo to sue him for divorce. Faruk blamed Premier Mohammed Naguib (pronounced *nah-geeb'*), the Army

**DEFIANCE** of Britain lies behind the smiling eyes of Egypt's "strong man", General Naguib

strong man who dethroned him in July, 1952: "[He] has broken up our happy marriage by using that most powerful of all weapons, the mother-in-law."

Narriman left Faruk's 18-month-old son, King Ahmed Fuad II, in his father's custody. Soon the boy king lost the throne on which he had never sat. "We proclaim today, in the name of the people, abolition of the monarchy," Naguib broadcast in June. The Premier also became Egypt's first President. Lieutenant Colonel Gamal Abdel Nasser, a six-footer of 35 known as "Jimmy", became deputy premier.

## Sudan Pact Signed

On Jan. 23, in Liberation Square in Cairo, Naguib proclaimed his Hayat el Tahreer (Liberation Movement). Disbanding twenty-two old political parties and earmarking their leaders for trial, he led a hero-worshiping throng in the Liberation Oath: "We swear by Thee to strive with all our might to fashion a free future for our country."

Naguib wished to liberate the whole Nile valley, ousting "British imperialism" from the Anglo-Egyptian Sudan and the Suez Canal zone.

Himself one quarter Sudanese, he attained his first goal on Feb. 12. Along with British Ambassador Sir Ralph Stevenson, he signed a sheaf of blue papers to end half a century of wrangling over the Sudan, a cotton-rich area one third the size of the United States. :

The Sudan pact empowered the 8,000,-000 Arab and Negro Sudanese to elect their own parliament, form their own government, and in three years decide whether to join Egypt or be independent. As if foreshadowing the future, the pro-Egyptian National Unionist party swept the Sudan's first parliamentary election.

To win the Sudanese to his aid, Major Salah Salem, Egyptian Minister of National Guidance, indulged in "strip-lomacy". He stripped to his shorts to join with naked Sudanese chiefs in a tribal dance.

Turning toward his other goal—Suez —Naguib warned in May: "Hot bloodshed is the only way of attaining independence. We are not afraid of death." More incidents involving hot blood-shed speckled the calendar of Suez history.

Amid that crisis, John Foster Dulles landed in Cairo to begin a twenty-day, 20,000-mile flying tour of the Middle East. He handed Naguib a Colt automatic pistol with a silver plate reading: "To General Mohammed Naguib—from his friend, Dwight D. Eisenhower."

Dulles cautioned: "It's not for use." Naguib grinned: "I know. It's for defense, not aggression."

By the end of September the Egyptians and British were within whispering distance of a Suez settlement. Within eighteen months, the 80,000 British troops were to leave their sun-baked, $1.5 billion Suez base, which had taken years to construct. They would be permitted to return if any Arab nation were attacked. They would be allowed to keep 4000 technicians at Suez to maintain the base. Despite this agreement in principle, however, a Suez settlement still was not signed by the end of 1953.

Throughout the rest of the Moslem world, as Secretary Dulles phrased it on his return from his Middle Eastern trip, the Arabs in 1953 remained "more fearful of Zionism than of Communism". In his opinion, "the Western powers can gain, rather than lose, from an orderly development of self-government."

In pursuit of such self-government, Brigadier Adib Shishekly decreed a new American-inspired constitution for his 3,000,000 Syrians and, in July, got it O.K.'d by a plebiscite. The people, cast-

ing nonsecret ballots under the eyes of Syrian soldiers and policemen, gave 99.6 percent of their votes to the only presidential candidate: Brigadier Shishekly.

Also in pursuit of self-government, King Ibn-Saud, ruling Saudi Arabia from his wheel chair, set up the first Cabinet for the oil-gushing deserts which brought him $200 million a year. Half blind at 73, he named as Premier Crown Prince Saud al Saud, eldest of his forty-four sons. A puritanical Wahabi Moslem, Ibn Saud had married between one hundred and two hundred wives, but never had more than the legal four at one time. On Nov. 9 the old desert warrior died and was succeeded by the Crown Prince.

The democratic idea also was voiced in regal oaths by the Middle East's two youngest monarchs. On May 2, two 18-year-old jazz addicts, second cousins in the Hashemite family, were enthroned—rather than crowned—in accordance with Moslem custom.

In the gold-braided white blouse of a field marshal, King Feisal II took his oath in Baghdad, Iraq: "I swear by God to safeguard the constitution and independence of the country." In the gilded blue blouse of an Arab Legion general, King Hussein took a similar oath in Amman, Jordan. Both monarchs were hailed with 101-gun salutes.

As if to awaken his sleepy country, Hussein toured his government's offices and warned: "I saw coffee, newspapers, piled official papers, and dirt, but I did not see work and efficient officials, and I shall not allow this thing to go on."

The Arabs' long-standing feud with Israel, featuring many border raids by both sides, broke out bloodily on the night of Oct. 14-15. What the U.N. Truce Commission called an "Israeli army bat-talion" shot up the Jordan frontier village of Kibya. It killed fifty-three Arabs and blew up forty homes and a mosque. The U.N. Security Council voted, 9 to 0, the "strongest censure" against Israel. Israel retorted that Jordanese had killed or wounded 421 Israelis during 866 armed raids since 1950.

Because of this feud, Eric Johnston, President Eisenhower's special envoy, had no luck in selling the Arabs on a $121 million plan, prepared by the Tennessee Valley Authority, to set up a T.V.A. system on the Jordan River without regard for national frontiers. The Israelis liked the plan, but in the face of Arab intransigence, speeded a plan of their own to divert river waters for hydroelectric power. Thereupon the U.S. halted $26 million in economic aid to Israel. At that, Israel bowed and suspended its plan, and on Oct. 28 the U.S. restored its aid.

On Feb. 9, Israel's other problem—Russian Communism—had exploded with a homemade bomb at the Soviet Legation in Tel Aviv. The wife of Soviet Minister Pavlov Yershov was injured. Premier David Ben-Gurion denounced this "abomination committed by hooligans".

The "abomination" gave the Soviets a pretext to curry the Arabs' friendship by breaking off diplomatic relations with the Israelis. The Israeli leaders were "a pack of mad dogs", the Communist organ *Pravda* shrieked. But after Joseph Stalin's death, Moscow swallowed these words and resumed diplomatic relations with Israel on July 20.

"I cannot continue," Premier Ben-Gurion wrote in November. "I cannot bear up any more against the mental strain that I suffer in government." At 67 he decided to retire to study philosophy in a three-room hut in the Negeb desert. The new Premier: Moshe Sharett, formerly foreign minister.

**READY** to the last cartridge, a young Israeli stands guard at border of his even younger nation

**REALITY:** A tiny Salvadoran child exemplifies the malnutrition still prevalent in Latin America

# LATIN AMERICA

SOUTH AMERICA'S STEAMY NORTHEASTERN coast, the only part of the continent which is not self-governing, is a largely forgotten area. It is normally forgotten even by the European governments which own British, French, and Dutch Guiana. In 1953 they were rudely reminded of its existence.

For the British, their Guiana is a valuable source of sugar, rum, gold, diamonds, and bauxite (aluminum ore). Most of the colony's 450,000 people live along the flat, swampy coast. Half of them are East Indians, 40 percent are

Negroes, the rest Europeans, Chinese, mixed bloods, and, back in the jungle and savanna, primitive American Indians.

Many are illiterate. Practically all are underpaid and undernourished. They share their thatched huts or rotted wooden shanties with pigs and chickens. None of the races gets along with the others. They all dislike the "Water Street imperialists" who run the country.

This setup was made to order for the Communists. For a few October days, it looked as if British Guiana might be-

**BULL-RING RIOT** raises havoc when 16,000 Guatemalans, gathered for opening of luxurious new Guatemala City arena, learn show is postponed two days

come the first Communist government in the Western Hemisphere.

The man behind the Red move was 35-year-old Cheddi Jagan, whose parents came from India as sugar workers. A classmate says Cheddi earned his way through Howard University in Washington, D.C., by running blackjack games. He operated a laundry while studying at Northwestern University's dental school.

## Jagan Organizes P.P.P.

In Chicago he met a strawberry-blond student nurse named Janet Rosenberg, a member of the Young Communist League. In 1943 he married her and took her home to British Guiana. They set up a dental clinic for sugar workers, then organized their patients into the People's Progressive Party (P.P.P.). The P.P.P. called itself nationalistic and socialistic, but it seemed to have connections with Moscow.

The P.P.P.'s slogan was: "We Want to Run Our Country; Limeys, Go Home." It won everything in sight in the April elections, British Guiana's first. Cheddi Jagan became Chief Minister. Janet was made Deputy Speaker of the House.

At once the Jagans and the P.P.P. called troublesome strikes, tried to replace the police with their own militia, and whittled away at the powers of the governor. The British Colonial Office sat on its hands until Governor Sir Alfred Savage reported the P.P.P. was getting ready to proclaim an independent People's Republic. Then, scared, it went into action.

On Oct. 8, 500 Royal Welsh Fusiliers landed in Georgetown, the capital city. Other soldiers came in by plane. The Governor was given emergency powers. He suspended the new constitution and ousted Jagan and other P.P.P. ministers.

The country quieted down as soldiers patrolled the capital and the sugar plantations. Jagan flew to England in search of support, but even the Labour party socialists brushed him off. So he went on to India. Truckloads of flag-waving, chanting Communists met him at the New Delhi airport, then launched a series of fund-raising rallies in scores of towns and villages. Prime Minister Jawaharlal Nehru invited Jagan to dinner and introduced him to members of Parliament. But Nehru carefully sidestepped Jagan's plea that he bring up the issue in the United Nations.

Janet, meanwhile, was keeping things stirred up at home. On the night of Dec. 13 she climbed out of a car at a sugar plantation fifteen miles from Georgetown and joined a group of some forty East Indian field hands in a tent. Wearing a white Hindu sari, she told the workers: "They have taken away our constitution and bring soldiers on us. We must not be downhearted."

Half an hour later police arrested Janet and nine of her companions for holding a public meeting without a permit. She protested that the meeting was actually a Hindu religious ceremony. The judge called it an "unholy farce". On Dec. 28 she was convicted and given the choice of paying a $147.50 fine or going to jail for three months. She appealed the verdict. With Janet under sentence and Cheddi off in India, British Guiana stayed quiet.

At the other end of the Caribbean Sea, in Guatemala, the Communists were also growing in power. Actually the government was not Communist. There were only about 1200 real Reds in the whole country. But they were shrewd and tireless, and they had worked their way into key jobs. The government was afraid of them and usually did what they told it to.

Among other things, the Communists had taken control of the agency which enforced a new agrarian law. They were busy dividing up large estates, including the landholdings of the U.S.-owned United Fruit Company, among the landless Indians. The poverty-stricken, illiterate Indians knew nothing of Communism, but they did know the value of land, and so followed the Red leaders. In many cases they did not wait for the law, but seized the land themselves. There were ugly incidents of killing and burning. The anti-Communist majority in the country wrung its hands, but let the Reds get away with the seizures.

In addition to digging in at home, the Guatemalan Communists during 1953 tried to wriggle into the neighboring nations of Central America. They did not make much headway.

## Cuba

In Cuba, the political honeymoon of President Fulgencio Batista ended. Many Cubans had shrugged when the smiling, hard-boiled Batista took over the island without benefit of elections in 1952. The old regime had been corrupt, disorderly, and inefficient.

To be efficient Batista had to be tough. The tougher he got, the more the highly individualistic *Cubanos* complained. By the middle of 1953, the President was slugging it out with a screaming press. Opposition politicians were plotting. Exiles were trying to raise expeditionary forces in Mexico, Canada, and the United States.

The lid blew off on a lazy Sunday morning in July. As Batista was handing out regatta prizes at Varadero Beach outside Havana, word reached him that 200 armed daredevils had attacked the barracks at Santiago de Cuba. Eventually they were scattered. Now Batista suspended constitutional rights, set up an open press censorship, and started a roundup of his enemies. But by the end of the year he had relaxed most restrictions. So long as the well-fed, well-paid Army stood by him, he had little to fear.

His most dangerous rival, the well-heeled Carlos Prío Socarrás, whom Batista had thrown out of the presidency, was not in Cuba but in the United States, trying to organize a comeback. In December, 1952, a police raid on a garage in Mamaroneck, N.Y., had turned up a cache of grenades, bazooka shells, and explosives, said to have been bought by Prío's henchmen. The State Department quietly warned Prío to watch his step. He paid no attention. So, in December, 1953, a U.S. marshal arrested him on the charge of conspiring to smuggle arms out of this country. Arraigned in a federal court in New York, Prío insisted he was innocent. He was released on $50,000 bail, awaiting trial.

In oil- and iron-rich Venezuela, Colonel Marcos Perez Jimenez, named President by a stooge Congress, bludgeoned his way into a firmer position. The top leadership of Acción Democrática (A.D.), the largest political party but now outlawed, was in exile. But some of its chiefs had managed to remain in the country. They carried on underground war against the government, while the security police hunted them down.

At the beginning of the year Dr. Alberto Carnevali was the ranking A.D. leader on the scene, and hence Public Enemy No. 1 to Perez Jimenez. On the morning of Jan. 18, police located him in a house in downtown Caracas. Under a screen of protective gunfire they stormed the building and arrested Carnevali and thirteen of his followers. Five others climbed to freedom from an upstairs balcony. Carnevali remained in prison until April. Then the authorities reported to a skeptical public that he had undergone an emergency operation for cancer but was doing well. His death was announced in May.

Antonio Pinto Salinas, Secretary General of A.D., was left as the top rebel chief. In the middle of June he was shot to death by the police. He was the fourth A.D. leader to die within nine months.

While Perez Jimenez built himself up, the dictatorship of the ailing, fascist-minded Laureano Gómez in neighboring Colombia collapsed. On the morning of June 13, troops backed by ten tanks moved into Bogotá, Colombia's high-perched capital. By 10 P.M., without firing a shot, the Army Chief of Staff, Lieutenant General Gustavo Rojas Pinilla, had taken over the presidential palace, deposed Gómez, and assumed control.

Gómez had himself to blame for his downfall. He had been using guns to fight Liberals on the eastern plains, and maneuvering politically against the moderates within his own Conservative party. He had been forced by illness to give up the active presidency. But his grip remained firm until he became suspicious of General Rojas, moderate Conservative who was loyal to the President, in the best nonpolitical tradition of the Colombian Army. On June 13, Gómez suddenly demanded that Rojas be fired. When the Acting President refused, Gómez reassumed the presidency and ordered Rojas' dismissal.

Top military men stood by their general and sent a plane to bring him to Bogotá. When he arrived, his troops had already seized public buildings and transportation. That night the national radio announced that he had the support of the armed forces, the police, and both political parties. Gómez, unharmed, was put under house arrest and later exiled.

The quick-smiling and quick-thinking Rojas got a great kick out of being President. He toured the booming country making speeches to crowds in banner-decked plazas and trying to soothe political passions. He did not yet dare to re-establish Colombia's proud democracy, but bit by bit he gave the people back their rights. Most Colombians accepted Rojas' promise of eventual elections and complete freedom. Liberal guerrillas trudged in from the plains to surrender their arms. Even skeptics commented: *"Mejor que antes* (better than before)."

To the south, Ecuador and Peru again shook fists across their long-disputed boundary. At home, Peru was prosperously quiet under the mild and intelligent dictatorship of President General Manuel Odria. In Ecuador, the fiery-tempered José María Velasco Ibarra tried for the third time to get through a term as President without being thrown out by an irritated people. But for the third time he got himself into hot water.

The trouble started when the newspapers *El Telégrafo* of Guayaquil and *El Comercio* of Quito speculated in print about impending cabinet changes. The President accused them of trying to stir up political strife, and he ordered every newspaper in Ecuador to print his criticism. Jorge Mantilla, publisher of *El Comercio,* refused. On the night of Nov. 13, Velasco closed *El Comercio* and its radio station.

For the next week heavily armed troops and police roamed the streets of Quito, using tear gas to break up demonstrations in support of Mantilla. "Tempers are short," a correspondent reported. But things quieted down when Velasco finally permitted *El Comercio* to publish again.

In Argentina, President Juan D. Perón was on a spot. The workers were his strongest supporters, and the workers were suffering. More and more were los-

**TRAGIC FACES** evoke sympathy from Bolivia's President Victor Paz Estenssoro. They belong to widows of two of hundreds killed in revolts in his Andean land

ing their jobs. The cost of living was going up. The last straw was another beef shortage, as ranchers, dissatisfied with prices, held up shipments. The Argentines, once the world's greatest meat eaters, queued up for pot-roast scraps at black-market prices.

In an apparent effort to show that Perón had not lost his grip, Peronista labor leaders called a mass meeting on April 15. Perón appeared on a fourth-story balcony of the Casa Rosada and began to explain the economic situation.

In the middle of his speech two bombs went off, one in a restaurant and one in a subway. Six persons were killed and a hundred injured. The bombs exploded several hundred yards from the President and could not possibly have hurt him, but they turned his sober speech into a rabble-rousing outburst.

"Our enemies must not get away with this," he shouted. "We must walk with nooses of baling wire in our pockets, prepared to hang them wherever they are found."

CAUTION, South American style: "Popular guards" in mufti protect staircase of Bolivia's Government Palace in La Paz

"Beat them up, beat them up!" the crowd shouted back.

"Why don't *you* beat them up?" Perón asked.

The mob took him at his word and went on a ten-hour rampage. It tore apart the headquarters of the opposition parties. Then it went to work on the world-famous Jockey Club in the swank shopping street, Calle Florida.

This palatial five-story stone building, constructed in 1897, housed a superb collection of Goya paintings and other art treasures. Its fine library featured rare maps. Its wine cellar was the best in the hemisphere.

But to the Peronistas it was just a hangout of hated aristocrats. What treasures were not looted or thrown into the streets were destroyed by fire. The magnificent building was left a total smoldering loss.

This night of bombs, pillage, and arson showed Argentina and the world that Perón was very much top man.

Encouraged, Perón cracked down harder than ever on his domestic enemies, and opened up on the United States again. He seemed determined to distract his people's attention from their living costs.

But in July, Dr. Milton S. Eisenhower flew into Buenos Aires on a 36-day, 20,000-mile trip around South America to size up the situation for his brother, the President. He was in Argentina only for a week end. Most of his time was spent at parties and sports events. But he and Perón got along fine.

After he left, Perón changed his tune. For the rest of the year he had nothing but kind words for the United States, compliments for President Eisenhower, and helpful hints for North American businessmen. It looked as if he were trying wheedling rather than blustering to get help for his ailing economy. The State Department, eager to end the long Argentine-U.S. feud, kept its fingers crossed.

While waving at the U.S., Perón promoted a trading bloc in which Argentina, rather than the U.S., would be senior partner. He easily made an economic deal with Paraguay, the poverty-stricken, landlocked republic up-river from Buenos Aires. He found President Carlos Ibáñez, of Chile, his old friend, willing —but not the independent-minded Chilean people. After an exchange of state visits, he could arrive only at a vague face-saving arrangement with the Chilean President. As for Bolivia, it would work with any country which would buy its tin, and the U.S. was the best customer.

## Brazil

Brazil, the largest country in Latin America, was preoccupied with financial troubles in 1953. Spiraling prices pinched people's pocketbooks. Unemployment grew. A severe drought dried up the country's northeastern bulge and sent hundreds of thousands of Brazilian "Okies" straggling dustily into overcrowded southern cities. And imports fell because Brazilian importers lacked $400 million in exchange to pay for goods already bought in the U.S.

This dollar shortage was pretty well cleared by a $300 million loan from the United States. But Brazilians thought the terms of the loan were harsh. Hard feelings against the United States grew in that country, usually the most friendly in Latin America.

Brazilian Communists encouraged the ill will, of course. During the fall they concentrated on a dispute over oil. Brazil spends nearly a third of its dollar exchange to import oil, although about 6 percent of all the world's oil lies untouched beneath Brazilian soil. President Getulio Vargas proposed to set up a company to get out the oil, and called on United States money and know-how to help. Communists and nationalists raged against the proposal, insisting that the Brazilians do the job themselves. Parades and demonstrations demanded that foreign "imperialists" be kept out.

The Brazilian Congress finally passed a bill setting up a strictly Brazilian company—just what the Communists and nationalists wanted. The decision to go it alone meant that it would be years before the Brazilians could supply any large part of their oil needs at home.

During the summer there had been foreshadowings of more economic trouble. Over the July 4 week end a heavy frost hit the great coffee-producing areas of Paraná and São Paulo. The exact amount of damage would not be known until the harvest in 1954. But it was certain that the crop of coffee, Brazil's largest export, would be much smaller than usual—and that coffee prices would spiral in the United States.

## Mexico

In sharp contrast to the commotion in South America was the quiet revolution in Mexico. Accustomed to the *mordida* (graft or bribe; literally, "bite"), Mexicans rubbed their eyes as they watched their new President live up to his promise to clean house.

Adolfo Ruiz Cortines was that rare bird in Mexican politics: a completely honest man. What distinguished him from other honest but ineffective men was that thirty years' experience had taught him all the tricks of the trade. "There is no use trying to get around el Señor Presidente," one veteran operator complained. "He knows all our tricks."

Foreigners found they could no longer get working papers by stiff payments to immigration attorneys who knew where to pay off in the government. "You can't buy papers now for a million or even a billion pesos," one lawyer said, "but if you are entitled to them, you can get them faster than ever before."

Orders went out to all government officers to enforce the law without fear or favor. Politicians' cars were hauled away when found in no-parking zones. Army generals were refused diplomatic passports unless they were on diplomatic missions. Contractors found out that the Construction Code meant what it said. The jaws of U.S. businessmen dropped when they discovered that the *mordida* no longer helped get them juicy contracts.

Ruiz cleaned up Mexico City, too. The police hustled beggars off the streets. Broken sidewalks were repaired. Squatter shopkeepers were thrown out of the Zócalo, the main square.

The President also went to work on the high cost of living. He bought eggs and grain in the U.S. and dumped them on the Mexican market. He forced movie theaters to cut prices. Even bullfight tickets were reduced by a ban on scalping. Proclaimed one tabloid: "Don Adolfo Has Produced a Miracle!"

All this activity seemed to add up to a good deal of excitement—as usual—in Latin America during 1953. But from the long view, most of the troubles would probably turn out not to be too serious. Washington's greatest worry was over the growing strength of Communism in the Caribbean area within striking distance of the Panama Canal. That worry, and all the other family problems of the Americas, would be taken up at the Inter-American Conference, held every five years, which was set to meet in Caracas, Venezuela, in March, 1954.

# WAR in ASIA

**THE INNOCENT** suffered with the guilty in Korean War. Here, laden South Korean women flee past a dead compatriot from a battle zone guarded by U.S. troops

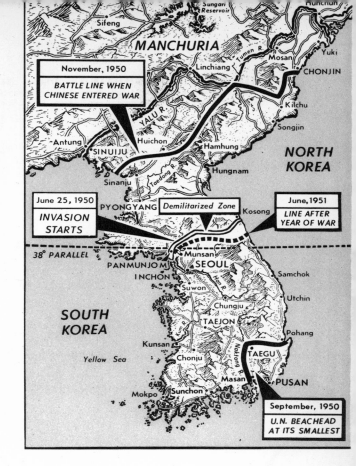

# KOREA

A G.I. WATCHED THE LUMINOUS SECOND hand sweep the dial of his watch. At 60 —10 P.M., July 27, 1953—a flare burst over the battlefield. He slumped and heaved a sigh.

"That's it," he said. "It's all over."

"I hope so," said his buddy. "I sure hope so."

There was great relief in the front lines. But there was no rejoicing, no backslapping, no mutual congratulation. It was merely a cease fire, not a victory.

The battle had ended, but not the war.

After three long years and thirty-two days, shooting was to stop while representatives of both sides met to arrange a peace conference. But at year's end— five months and many meetings later— there was still no peace in Korea. There was not even agreement on the actual time and place for a peace conference.

Some progress had been made, however. Truce negotiations had begun back in July, 1951. After long, wearisome hag-

**THIS WAS THE FIGHTING:** Artillery battering an enemy position, a moment's lull, then a short advance by weary men (these are U.S. Marines) — and later, too often, a retreat

gling, agreement had been reached on every issue except one: The United Nations insisted that P.O.W.'s who refused to accept repatriation must not be forced to do so. The Communists were just as adamant that P.O.W.'s must be returned, whether they liked it or not.

Our motives stemmed from a shocking experience at the end of World War II, when we forcibly repatriated the million Russian P.O.W.'s liberated from the Germans. Many of the repatriates threw themselves from train windows or chose some other form of suicide rather than return to Communist Russia, where a "traitor's" execution awaited them. The Communists, on the other hand, would not admit that a Communist might want to be anything but a Communist.

## Negotiations Deadlocked

On March 25, 1952, the U.N. announced that its decision was "irrevocable". The Communists said their decision was equally "irrevocable". Negotiations were deadlocked.

For the U.N. the issue was basic. Americans were prepared to die for it, and many did so. Between April, 1952, and the signing of the truce almost sixteen months later, 7000 Americans were killed and 28,000 wounded in defense of this principle.

The deadlock was broken dramatically on March 28, 1953, twenty-three days after the death of Stalin. In an unexpected reply to a month-old letter from America's General Mark Clark, North Korean and Chinese Communist leaders accepted his offer to exchange seriously sick and wounded P.O.W.'s. The Reds went even further. They suggested that the exchange could "lead to the smooth settlement of the entire question of prisoners of war, thereby achieving an armistice in Korea".

Two days later, Red China's Premier Chou En-lai broadcast from Peiping a statement that both sides should repatriate only those P.O.W.'s who insisted on going home, and deliver the rest to a neutral state "to insure a just solution". This was indeed a full retreat from the "irrevocable" Communist position, for it accepted the U.N.'s insistence that no P.O.W. be repatriated against his will.

Fighting fell off sharply, while almost overnight Marine engineers threw up a tent city near Munsan, complete with processing center, mobile hospital, and a well-stocked kitchen, ready to receive disabled P.O.W.'s from North Korea. The sign at the head of the village read: "Freedom Village—The End of the Rainbow". Every available helicopter stood by to rush the most serious cases to hospitals in the rear.

On April 6, U.N. and Communist negotiators sat down in a little Red-built wooden shack at Panmunjom to arrange what had already been dubbed "Operation Little Switch". Later, it was hoped, a "Big Switch" might be arranged, involving all P.O.W.'s on both sides.

The first wounded prisoner to be returned did not come through official hands at Panmunjom. Some 350 yards from the neutral perimeter, a Chinese commander called over his loud-speaker to the Americans in an outpost opposite him. "We have one of your wounded here. Send two men as soon as possible. . . . We will allow you to come as far as the defilade area without firing."

Through binoculars the Americans watched the wounded man stagger out of the Chinese lines and drop among some Korean gravestones in No Man's Land. As a squad of Marines moved cautiously toward him, one of their number recognized the man as Pfc. Francisco González Matías, 21, of San Sebastián, Puerto Rico.

The Marine shouted encouragement to his friend, who rose and stumbled forward holding a rosary in an uplifted hand. Twice he fell, and when he didn't get up again, 2nd Lt. Kenneth Clifford exploded: "Hell, let's go get him." In full view of the enemy he stood up, calmly cut the barbed wire, and with four men walked out boldly to get Matías. The Chinese didn't fire a shot.

Operation Little Switch, which began on April 20, yielded only 684 disabled P.O.W.'s for the United Nations—including 149 Americans—in exchange for 6670 Communists.

Private Carl W. Kirchenhausen of New York, was the first American to be released. As he hobbled across on frostbitten feet, he murmured: "I'm glad it came true." A soldier on a stretcher said: "It's good to be free again." A Turkish trooper sobbed unashamedly.

## Red Returnees Defiant

While the United Nations P.O.W.'s were quiet and orderly en route to exchange points, many of the Red returnees were defiant, rowdy, and abusive. They had been given new G.I. uniforms and packets of toiletries, as well as haircuts and inoculations. But as they approached Panmunjom they threw away their toilet bags, tore their clothes, ripped belts and shoelaces, and wrapped soiled rags about their heads and feet to give the appearance of having been badly treated. At the exchange point they were photographed by Red cameramen. The pictures were later circulated widely in Asia, with captions referring to the P.O.W.'s as "mutilated, emaciated wrecks".

One hundred and forty U.N. correspondents were on hand to interview prisoners turned over by the Communists. The men told harrowing tales of atrocity and neglect that had caused the deaths of many thousands of captured U.N. troops.

According to Sergeant James F. Daniel of Alameda, Calif., who had kept a detailed diary, malnutrition and lack of medical care alone had killed 2538 prisoners—mostly Americans—in two of the Red camps. "It was just starvation and disease," he said. "We could feel the lice crawling over us."

Another released American told a grisly story of what happened when the Communists captured an American truck convoy with 800 wounded men on Dec. 2, 1950. "The Chinese," he said, "sprayed burp guns into the wounded, then bayoneted them. They were screaming. They couldn't do anything."

A "Freedom Airlift" rushed the P.O.W.'s back to their homes in America. Twenty of the men, officials said, "showed signs of having succumbed to Communist indoctrination". These were flown to Valley Forge Army Hospital near Philadelphia, for special "psychiatric and medical care".

There, sudden conversion took place. After a good meal and a sound night's sleep, the men were brought before reporters. Each denied he had accepted any of the Communists' indoctrination. Each told in great detail how the Reds had subjected him to an ordeal of "brainwashing" with endless ideological harangues.

"A guy can only take so much," said one of them. "But once you get back home, it don't take long to get patched up as good as new."

Almost as soon as Little Switch was completed, negotiators sat down to work out an agreement for Big Switch. But optimism turned quickly to pessimism as the Reds began to haggle and stall over where and how to handle the exchange of reluctant P.O.W.'s. Eventually, on

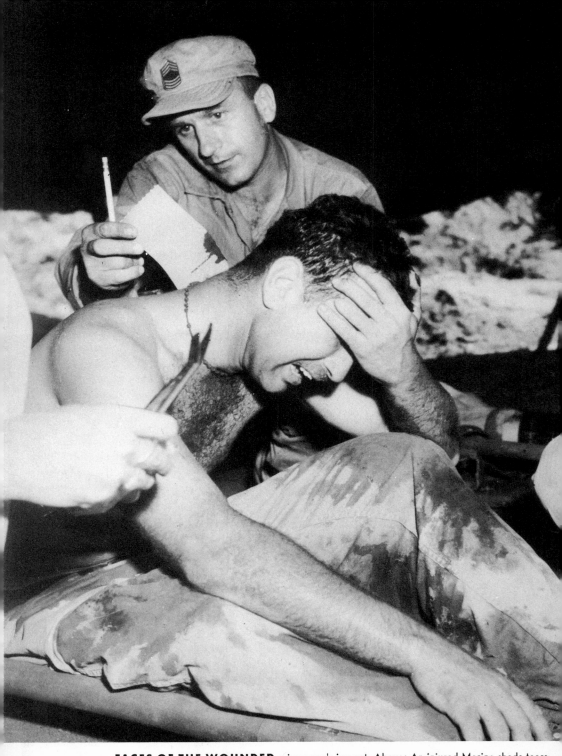

**FACES OF THE WOUNDED** mirror war's impact. Above: An injured Marine sheds tears of exhaustion. Right: Hit during battle, infantryman is helped to the rear by two buddies

**COMMUNIST PRISONERS** often gave trouble. These Koreans had to be stripped as a precaution against concealed weapons—and to guard against their trying to escape on way to U.N. prison camp

June 8, they agreed to turn the whole problem over to a five-nation custodial commission composed of Sweden, Switzerland, Poland, Czechoslovakia, and India.

All P.O.W.'s willing to go home would be returned within sixty days after for-

mal signing of the armistice. Reluctant P.O.W.'s would remain in the commission's custody for another ninety days, while "explainers" from each side tried to persuade them to return to their homelands. The problem of P.O.W.'s still unwilling to be repatriated would be dealt

was reached, they were to be released within thirty days after the "persuasion period" ended, and freed as civilian refugees.

In Seoul, South Korea's American-educated, 78-year-old President Syngman Rhee informed the U.N. negotiators that the truce terms were "completely unsatisfactory". Inasmuch as an armistice left Korea still divided, he would recognize no cease-fire agreement that did not provide for withdrawal of all Chinese Communist troops from Korea. Threatening to fight on alone, he stormed, "While they remain, we cannot survive."

"Spontaneous" demonstrations flared in the streets of the city. Thousands marched bearing inflammatory banners and shouting: "Puk Chin! Teng 'l'" ("March north for unification!"). In wild frenzy they threw themselves against U.N. roadblocks and fought sympathetic South Korean police, who tried to handle them as gently as possible.

Whether or not Rhee was bluffing when he threatened to order his sixteen R.O.K. divisions against the Reds, it was clear they could not possibly last more than a few days without American supplies and air and naval support.

Although the Communists said nothing, it was apparent they were waiting to see if the U.N. could control the fiery old statesman. With an armistice so near, the United Nations brought increasing pressure upon Rhee to accept what was admittedly the best of a bad bargain in Korea. Indeed, it was made clear to him that the U.N. intended to go ahead with a truce—with his assent if possible, without it if necessary.

Then, just when they thought they had his reluctant agreement, Rhee exploded a bombshell. Soon after midnight on June 18, 1953, thousands of North Korean prisoners began streaming through gaps in the barbed wire, cut from the

with at the political conference to be called under the armistice.

So that these reluctants might not be held in limbo indefinitely, should the political conference be unable to agree on their disposition, a time limit was set. Regardless of whether or not a decision

outside, while South Korean guards stood by to let them pass. Once out, the P.O.W.'s were met by organized South Korean civilians who supplied them with clothes and passed them along until they faded into the countryside. Some 27,000 —all but about 7000 of the North Korean anti-Communist P.O.W.'s—escaped.

Next morning, Syngman Rhee boldly announced that he had planned and ordered the entire operation.

There was consternation in U.N. capitals. In Washington, Secretary of State Dulles told a conference of congressional leaders: "This is as critical as June 25, 1950" (the first day of the Korean War). From London, Prime Minister Winston Churchill sent a note to Rhee denouncing his "treachery". President Eisenhower called together a group of senators from both parties, pointing out that American forces would inevitably be drawn into any renewal of conflict in Korea.

The President rushed trouble-shooting Assistant Secretary of State Walter Robertson to Korea to explain the facts of life to Dr. Rhee. After weeks of exasperating discussions, Robertson announced that an understanding had been reached.

Rhee agreed not to take any further action on his own for approximately six months—that is, until three months after the beginning of the political conference which was to follow the signing of the armistice. In return, the United States promised South Korea sizeable economic aid ($200 million to start) and a security pact which would guarantee full-scale American military aid, should the South Koreans be attacked again.

A curious side light to all this was the relative silence on the part of the Communists. They grumbled a bit and half-heartedly demanded that we round up the escapees, but they knew this was impossible.

Whatever else might be said about

Syngman Rhee's highhanded recklessness, it proved one thing: the Communists did want a cease fire. Whether they wanted more—a full peace in Korea—remained to be seen.

Some of the bloodiest fighting of the

entire war took place in the fortnight preceding the actual signing of the armistice. In driving rain on the night of July 13, hordes of screaming Chinese stormed across No Man's Land against a hill held by the crack R.O.K. Capitol Division. The R.O.K.'s wavered and broke, and the command posts of supporting American artillery units were overrun— one battalion losing 300 killed and captured.

Reds penetrated U.N. lines for at least

seven miles and were pouring across the swollen Kumsong River when the weather cleared. Immediately U.N. planes came roaring out to attack the Chinese, whose drive then petered out. When the battle ended, the Reds were in possession of the hills above the river, and firmly entrenched against a counterattack.

The signing of the armistice in a "Peace Pagoda" at Panmunjom on July 27 had nothing of the dramatic impact of other armistices, such as the surrender of the German generals in the little schoolhouse at Rheims, France, in May, 1945, or the Japanese capitulation on the bristling deck of the battleship *Missouri* in September, 1945. At Panmunjom neither side could claim total victory.

The meeting in the stifling-hot truce building was stiffly formal. U.N. and Communist guards stood motionless as attendants buzzed about arranging papers on three large tables. Promptly at 10 A.M. the two principal signers appeared. Tieless, with only the insignia of rank on his collar tabs, Lieutenant General William K. Harrison, senior U.N. delegate, sat down and began signing documents with his ten-year-old fountain pen. At another table, North Korea's chief negotiator, Nam Il, wearing jack boots and a uniform emblazoned with ribbons and medals, signed for the Reds. The signing over, each rose and left without so much as a look at the other. It was a deliberately underplayed ceremony, as if neither side were pleased or proud of what it had achieved.

Specifically, the armistice terms called for a cease fire, withdrawal of all troops from a 2½-mile neutral zone along what had been the front line, the exchange of war prisoners, and a political confer-

ence to be held within ninety days after the signing.

For the United States it had been a frustrating, unpopular war. It had been the third costliest in American history (142,118 casualties, $22 billion), and the first one we had not won outright. It had also been history's first jet war. The Air Force had destroyed 984 Communist

planes and added 159 as probably destroyed, nearly all of them Soviet-made MIG jet fighters. The Air Force had lost a total of 971 planes, two thirds of them to ground fire. Only 94 had fallen in aerial combat, a ratio of about 14 MIGs shot down for every U.N. plane lost in battle. The United Nations counted approximately 1,466,419 casualties, including at least 415,004 South Koreans and 30,350 Americans killed in action. According to official estimates, Communist casualties included at least 2,000,000 dead and wounded.

Civilian casualties had been even heavier. It could only be guessed how many North Korean noncombatants had been killed or wounded during three years of bombing and shooting. In South Korea, according to President Eisenhower in his message to Congress, 1,000,000 South Koreans had died, and 2,500,000 had become homeless refugees in what he called "a colossal disaster". An additional 5,000,000 South Koreans were dependent in whole or part on American relief to keep alive. Property destruction amounted to more than $1 billion.

As loud-speakers announced the final cease-fire order in nine languages, an eerie silence fell over battlefields brilliantly illuminated by the light of a full moon. On the U.N. side there was little celebration. "What the hell's there to celebrate," said a British captain. "Nobody *won* this war."

The Chinese, however, worked hard to convince U.N. soldiers that there should be no hard feelings between them. At T-bone Hill they built a span of spruce boughs during the night, and in the morning invited the G.I.'s to "come over and we will walk through the arch as brothers". At other points they came out of their trenches and danced a harvest dance while they banged pans and beat drums. An American-accented voice boomed across the valley: "The war is over. Let's sing 'My Old Kentucky Home'. Begin when I give the downbeat." No one joined him.

Later in the day there was some mingling of troops, when burial parties from both sides gingerly picked their way through a No Man's Land littered with exploded grenades and shells, to recover their dead.

## Operation Big Switch

Operation Big Switch began on August 5. As Soviet-built, P.O.W.-laden trucks rolled into Panmunjom from the north, the men appeared to be in better spirits than the sick and wounded P.O.W.'s who were traded three months earlier. They laughed, cheered, and consumed huge quantities of ice cream, milk, and cookies.

Thumbing through a batch of picture magazines, one exclaimed: "Yipe! Get a load of this Marilyn Monroe!" A graying American warrant officer stretched luxuriously on an air mattress in a Red Cross lounge and drawled: "I just love to sit here and look at those capitalistic lamps built by you American warmongers." Some moments later he was crying over a photograph of his wife, which he found in a waiting letter.

There were others, of course, who still couldn't believe they were free. They spoke little and said "sir" even to enlisted men assigned to attend them.

Later came the tales of privation and torture similar to those told by the sick and wounded exchanged in Operation Little Switch. The general opinion was that the Chinese were less brutal than the North Koreans, although they did their utmost to convert the P.O.W.'s to Communism.

The Chinese were toughest toward American Air Force officers. They accused the fliers of germ-bombing, and sometimes went to extremes in an effort to prove it. Sergeant Edward Hewlett, of Detroit, told how a Red lecturer, angered by skeptical G.I.'s, showed them the "proof"—a vial containing a little bug which, he said, was impregnated with virulent germs. As the G.I.'s filed by, one of them grabbed the vial and swallowed the bug. He lived.

One of the last to be exchanged by the Reds was their prize P.O.W., Major General William Dean, the highest-ranking American to be captured in Korea. Scarcely a month after fighting began, he and a few comrades were cut off in desperate combat, and General Dean was last seen in a one-man battle against a

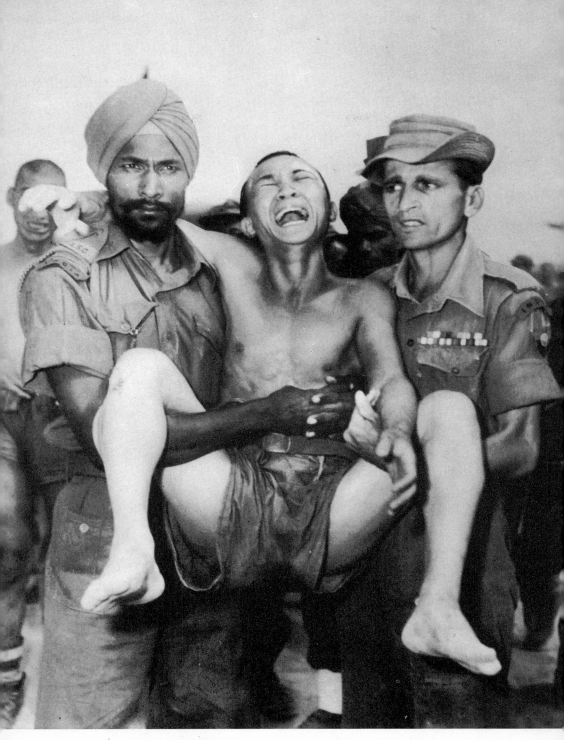

**HYSTERICAL RED** war prisoner, who changed his mind and agreed to re-patriation, is carried to exchange point at Panmunjom by two Indian soldiers.

Red tank. For a month he wandered about the Korean hills, until he was betrayed by a South Korean civilian. For three years he languished in prison while his sandy hair turned white and his health almost broke.

"It is a wonderful thing, like a dream," he said to his welcomers. "You look better to me than I look to you, I'm sure."

The U.N. had originally held 125,000 Communist prisoners, including the 27,-000 who were liberated by Syngman Rhee's R.O.K.'s. Approximately 75,000 were repatriated during Big Switch, leaving some 23,000 who did not want to return to their Red homelands.

On their side, the Communists returned about 13,000 P.O.W.'s, including 3313 Americans. The Pentagon, however, had listed 8705 American soldiers as missing, and complained that the Reds were returning only a handful of these. There was, of course, no way of telling how many of the men had died on the battlefields or in captivity. Among the 359 U.N. soldiers who announced their decision to remain with the Communists were twenty-three Americans and one Englishman.

The P.O.W.'s from both sides who refused to be repatriated were turned over to the neutral custodial commission. India, as chairman of the commission, sent 5000 troops to Korea to guard the reluctant P.O.W.'s until their ultimate fate was decided.

**SOME HATED THE TRUCE.** This South Korean schoolgirl shows her violent resentment by lying on a Korean flag during a protest demonstration in Seoul

## Operation Convincer

Operation Big Switch ended on Sept. 6. Now began the second phase of the prisoner-of-war problem—"Operation Convincer"—the battle for the "unrepatriates". The first group of Chinese reluctants was to have appeared before Red persuaders at 8 A.M. on Oct. 15. When the P.O.W.'s refused to show up, the custodial Indian troops coaxed, argued, finally threatened to beat them with staves. After seven hours the Chinese finally marched into tents, where each man in turn faced a Communist "explainer". The Reds had confidently expected to persuade a high percentage of the reluctants to return to Communism. They were dismayed as one after another cursed, spat, and banged on tables.

"Don't you want to go home to your family?" a young Chinese was asked by his interrogators.

"You Communists have killed all my family," he screamed back.

Of the first 500 interviewed, only ten changed their minds. Of the next 450, nine more were persuaded. The 2 percent average was about the same for the North Koreans interviewed. To neutral observers—and neutrals throughout the world—it seemed a whacking propaganda defeat for the Communists throughout Asia.

To cover their chagrin and confusion, the Reds began to drag out the interviews—some lasted for hours—and to make impossible demands on the Indian custodians. In mid-November the Communists called off the persuasion sessions altogether.

When U.N. officials began their interviews, their batting average was not

**PRIZE P.O.W.:** Korean War hero Maj. Gen. William F. Dean, one of last Americans released in "Operation Big Switch". Photo made in Red P.O.W. camp

much better than that of the Reds. Only seven of the 327 South Koreans and a single American changed their minds. When the American, Corporal Edward S. Dickenson, a 23-year-old mountaineer from Cracker's Neck, Va., was asked why he had originally decided to remain with the Reds, he explained that it was because he had been jilted by a girl back home. "She sent me a 'Dear John' letter, if you know what that is."

## Americans Indict America

The other twenty-two Americans flatly refused to meet U.N. persuaders. In a formal statement which was handed to newsmen they said: "Our staying behind does not change the fact that we are Americans; we love our country and our people."

In America, they charged, "the voices of those who speak out for peace and freedom are rapidly being silenced". The statement concluded: "We will return some day . . . when the American people have in fact achieved that freedom which [General] Mark Clark boasts you now have. We hope to play our part in achieving this, and we know the American people will receive us back on that day with open arms."

For a brief period it was hoped another of the Americans might change his mind, when Mrs. Portia Howe, mother of Pfc. Richard R. Tenneson, flew 6500 miles to Tokyo from Alden, Minn., only to learn that U.N. officials would not permit her to see her son. The Communists, they said, might demand the same visiting rights for mothers of thousands of anti-Communist P.O.W.'s.

A letter from Tenneson, however, was delivered to his mother. He would be glad to see her, he said, but he was sure nothing would be accomplished by the meeting. He wrote: "I love peace. I love

mankind. I love them enough to fight for them. . . . Now I have a goal and a reason for life."

"If Communism can break up a family, it can break up a nation," sobbed the heartbroken mother. "Where did I fail? Oh, where did I fail?"

With letters and loud-speakers, the Allied officials continued their efforts to get the reluctant G.I.'s to change their minds. When the Dec. 23 deadline for persuasion sessions passed, the U.N. Command classified them as "absent without leave" until midnight, Jan. 22, 1954, when neutral custody was to end and all remaining P.O.W.'s were to be released. After that date they would be listed as deserters.

Meanwhile, almost within shouting distance of the persuasion tents, special delegates from both sides were meeting to arrange time and place for a political conference. The American representative was Arthur H. Dean, a white-haired Wall Street lawyer. The meetings began Oct. 26. Dean held his temper through thirty-nine of them, while the Communists called him "Warmonger!" "Liar!" "Rogue!" Then, on Dec. 12, came a charge that the "perfidious" United States had masterminded Syngman Rhee's liberation of the anti-Communist North Koreans. "What utter nonsense!" Dean exploded. "How silly can you get?"

He demanded a retraction. When, instead, the Reds repeated the slur, Dean announced he assumed that they wanted the talks recessed indefinitely. He rose and stalked out, leaving the Communists stunned and goggle-eyed.

Apart from the name-calling, the talks had been virtually deadlocked anyway, over the Reds' insistence that Soviet Russia be permitted to sit at the conference table as a "neutral".

The United States was unalterably opposed to this. We could never, said Dean,

**SOME WELCOMED THE TRUCE.** Made by an enemy photographer in a Red P.O.W. camp, this picture shows how most prisoners reacted to word that soon they would be released

accept Soviet Russia as "a back-seat driver constantly telling everyone where to go, how to get there, what turn to take. . . . We can't have the Soviet Union there, like the proverbial mother-in-law, all gab and no responsibility."

At year's end, Dean had not returned to Panmunjom and the meetings were still recessed. It looked as if a political conference might never be called.

On the last Saturday of the year, President Eisenhower unexpectedly announced that two American divisions would be withdrawn from Korea and that American ground forces there would be "progressively reduced". He warned, however, that any renewal of Red aggression would be opposed "with even greater effort than heretofore".

In the quiet darkness of midnight, as the sands of turbulent 1953 ran out, one of the remaining reluctant twenty-two American G.I.'s approached a sleepy Indian guard.

"I've changed my mind," said Corporal Claude J. Batchelor. "I want to go home."

# Red China and Formosa

THE WAR IN KOREA HAD BEEN STALEMATED in the spring of 1952. Suddenly the headlines were big: IKE TAKES WRAPS OFF CHIANG! FORMOSA PREPARES INVASION OF MAINLAND.

"Now," said many Americans, "maybe we'll see some real action." They didn't.

As a campaign promise, Dwight D. Eisenhower had intimated that he would settle things in Korea one way or the other. Immediately after his election in November he flew there for a personal look-see. And six days after his inauguration, the new President told Congress he was rescinding ex-President Truman's order of June 27, 1950, which directed the U.S. Navy's Seventh Fleet to "neutralize" Formosa.

**ON MAY DAY** in Peiping, Chinese women (top) salute Red holiday, cheer Mao Tse-tung (right)

For two and a half years the Seventh Fleet had patrolled the 100-mile-wide Strait of Formosa. Its job was to restrain the Nationalists from attacking China's Communist mainland and to protect Formosa from the Reds. The new order freed the Nationalists to invade the mainland while our warships continued to protect Formosa.

Formosa is a sizeable (13,838 sq. mi.) tear-shaped island lying off the southeast coast of the mainland, with a population of over 7,000,000 who are racially Chinese. Ceded to Japan at the end of the Chinese-Japanese War of 1895, it was recovered by China at the end of World

**HUNGER** remains the rule in most of China despite the "new order". These poorly dressed peasants, mother and child, count themselves lucky to dine on bowls of rice-and-water gruel

**STUDENTS** "rate" in Red China. This group, on vacation, sun-bathes by a "people's swimming pool"

**VOTING,** however meaningless under one-party rule, still brings out 93-year-old painter (below)

**IN HONG KONG** a British sergeant supervises target practice of rookie Colony police

War II. On Dec. 9, 1949, when the Nationalists, headed by Generalissimo Chiang Kai-shek, were driven from the mainland by the Chinese Communists, they took refuge on Formosa. There they set up a regime-in-exile, which in 1953 was still recognized by the U.S. as the legitimate government of China.

Reputedly the Nationalists were eager to liberate the mainland from the Communists. But freedom of action and ability to follow through are two different things, and it was clear that unless the Nationalists received substantial U.S. naval and air support—not specifically contemplated in President Eisenhower's order—they could not possibly carry out a full-scale invasion of the mainland. Even if they established beachheads, their only hope for success would lie in an uprising of mainland Nationalists, which was unlikely.

To encourage the Generalissimo to launch an invasion without all-out mili-

Formosa. Further confounding the Reds, the administration speeded the tempo of military aid to Formosa during the year.

## Hong Kong

TO KEEP THE REDS GUESSING ABOUT WHAT we planned to do if they didn't quit stalling over the Korean cease fire, Secretary of State John Foster Dulles intimated in February that the administration was considering a naval blockade against the Chinese mainland. This threat to "enlarge the war" was attacked abroad.

The British were dead against it. In the first place, they said, it would be ineffective because of China's 2000-mile coast. Secondly, as an act of war it might bring Soviet Russia into action under its defense treaty with the Communists.

And the Reds would almost certainly retaliate by attacking the British Crown Colony of Hong Kong. An attack would kill Britain's valuable trade (in nonstrategic materials) with Red China, but would also mean losing to Communism another 2,000,000 free people.

At the least the blockade would mean the closing down of British business in Hong Kong. It might also mean starvation, for the rocky island depends almost entirely on surrounding Red-held areas for its meat, vegetables, and fruit.

Hong Kong, the New Orleans of China, is British territory, a seaport Crown Colony carved from the mainland by force of arms in 1842. It depends almost entirely on the commissions it makes as a transfer point for South China's foreign trade. Ample facilities are provided for loading and unloading cargoes which are transshipped inland in lighters, junks, and barges. It is also the terminus of a railway that runs up through China and Manchuria by way of Kwangchow (Canton), Hankow, Peiping, Mukden, and Manchouli, where

tary support from America would, as one Pentagon cynic said, be like "turning a Chihuahua loose in a den of lions".

At best, Eisenhower's new order injected new imponderables into the Korean conflict. Taking the wraps off Chiang's troops might puzzle the Communists about the administration's military intentions in the Far East. It might even worry the Reds enough to divert some of their military strength from Korea and the border of Indochina to man coastal defenses across the strait from

it connects with the Trans-Siberian Railway to Moscow.

Since 1951, exports to China have fallen by 70 percent. Even so, a lucrative trade with Red China still continues both by land and by sea from Hong Kong— and has continued all through the fighting in Korea, where British soldiers were members of the United Nations forces.

There was something ostrich-like in Britain's Far East policy. For, apart from Soviet Russia, Great Britain was the only other major power which had recognized the Red regime in China. The Reds, however, have never acknowledged the British move or, as the wags put it, have never "recognized Britain's recognition".

## Red China

RED CHINA'S MILITARY SHOWING IN KOREA had enormously increased her prestige throughout the Far East, but the effort had strained its underdeveloped economy. Weapons, of course, had been supplied by Soviet Russia, but not for free. The Chinese Reds paid for them with raw materials and foodstuffs badly needed for their own people.

Even so, by early 1953 there was increasing evidence that the Soviets had begun to reduce their material aid to Red China. Their probable reasons: increased preoccupation with their own defense to meet the growing strength of Western Europe; reluctance to throw more materiel into a stalemate in Korea; suspicion that not all Russian arms were going to Chinese troops in Korea, but instead were being diverted to build up Red China's over-all strength.

The last possibility was of particular concern to Moscow. No nation, not even the U.S.S.R., could feel secure with a re-awakened, ultra-nationalistic China of 500,000,000 people as a neighbor.

There was evidence, too, that non-military economic aid promised by Soviet Russia was not reaching China in sufficient quantities, or soon enough. This evidence was revealed by the Chinese when they admitted that their grandiose plans for large-scale industrialization were snarled. Confessed vice chairman Chia To-fu of the government's Economic and Financial Committee: "On the whole, our industrial foundations are very weak and our industrial technique backward." Industrialization goals for 1953 were scaled down drastically from those announced in 1952.

Chia To-fu disclosed that 60 percent of all Chinese industry was state-owned, but that the state was having trouble finding competent managers. Moreover, planning was sloppy, designing defective, and there was a serious shortage of skilled labor. It was clear that Red China was still a long way even from getting tooled up for industrialization.

The death of Stalin in March caused some soul-searching among Chinese Communist leaders. Outwardly there was no change in the close alliance of the two Communist nations or in their determination to drive "colonial exploiters" from Asia. But adulation of Malenkov was far less than that given Stalin.

The year 1953 marked the graduation from institutions of higher learning of 13,000 Communist-indoctrinated students, the first products of the nationwide Red reorganization of China's educational facilities. The shake-up had eliminated foreign missionary-run schools, removed all traces of American influence in colleges and universities, and brought teaching under the control of the central government.

The new graduates must accept whatever jobs the government assigns them, work hard, and show fanatical enthusiasm in the service of the Communist new order. These first graduates assumed their new posts in construction projects "consciously and joyfully"—according to the Peiping *Daily Worker*.

On Red China's farms, meanwhile, crop failures, in addition to inefficiency on enforced cooperatives, resulted in a spring famine which, according to a Peiping broadcast, threatened the nation's agricultural production as a whole and the grain harvest in particular. Tens of thousands of starving families had to "sell their land and unharvested crops to last out the famine, while others committed suicide or died from hunger."

Peasants streamed from famine-stricken farms to cities already burdened with unemployment, and with housing and food shortages. On April 17 Premier Chou En-lai ordered local authorities to dissuade the emigrants by "explaining to them that industrial construction in the cities is only at its start; the existing number of buildings for workers is insufficient and if they go to the cities freely they will be unable to find jobs, and will not only incur traveling expenses but will also hinder rural production".

The collection of an agricultural tax after the autumn harvest in southwest China, according to official "incompleted" statistics, resulted in sixty-nine deaths and 352 "casualties". Twenty-three deaths were suicides following official demands for "impossible amounts of grain". Forty-one deaths and 199 "other casualties" occurred among peasants "delivering rice over long distances to government granaries".

The government boasted about one "blessing" traceable to the West's "imperialist" invasion of Korea. America's alleged use of germ warfare had sparked a nationwide health campaign and an overdue cleanup of Chinese towns.

**DRIVEN OUT** of Chinese mainland, Chiang Kai-shek sits in his Formosa stronghold — and waits

**WEST EYES EAST:** This American sailor, on leave in Tokyo, seems to be a fan of Japanese movie actress Kaeko Awagi (who also has appeared in U.S. films)

# JAPAN

A SLIP OF THE TONGUE BY JAPAN'S COCKY, pro-American Premier Shigeru Yoshida threatened to sink the Japanese Ship of State. The incident indicated a dubious faith in the nation's new parliamentary government.

Serving continuously as Premier since October, 1948, scholarly, high-born Yoshida had held a delicately balanced government together by sheer strength of character. Then, on March 1, a member of the opposition needled him to outline Japan's foreign policy in his own words, "not those of Eisenhower or Churchill". The hot-tempered little Premier exploded.

"*Bakayaro!*" ("Stupid idiot!") he flung at his tormentor.

Though he apologized, the opposition pressed for a vote of censure. This action was followed by a vote of no confidence. Dissidents both within and without his Liberal party ganged up on Yoshida and forced him to dissolve the Diet and call for new elections. Although an indifferent public voted him back into office, the election turnout was small and Yoshida's political support in the Diet was slimmer than before.

The end of the Korean War created new and serious problems for the Yoshida regime. Tokyo's flashy neon lights, crowded night clubs, and streams of shiny new American cars jamming downtown streets were a dazzling deception.

The nation's economy had suffered grievously since the recovery of national independence in 1952. Floods and frost had cut the rice crop to the smallest in nineteen years. The heaviest rainfall in fifty years had all but wiped out thousands of small farmers. The population, meanwhile, had increased an additional million since 1952, and welfare officials noted an alarming increase in the sale of farm children to brokers for service as laborers, servants, or prostitutes. Even in normal years Japan has to import rice. Methods of making up for the disastrous drop in food production were of major concern to the government during 1953.

The Korean War had been a bonanza for Japan. "Special-procurement" buying, and heavy spending by the much-maligned American garrison and troops on leave, who converted about a million American dollars daily into Japanese yen, had provided a major prop for Japan's shaky postwar economy. The armistice, followed by a sharp drop in these war revenues, was a body blow.

From Washington came warnings that the U.S. would attach strings to further aid. There would be no more blank checks in exchange for pious avowals of democracy and loyalty to the anti-Communist West. Nonetheless, Washington recognized that unless sizeable subsidies were given to the Japanese, they would inevitably seek to reopen trade with

mainland China. They would have to, or starve.

On a visit in late November, Vice President Richard Nixon told the Japanese that the United States had "erred" in disarming them at the end of World War II. In Washington, Secretary of State Dulles agreed. "We assumed," he added, "that we were entering into an era of lasting peace, and that the Soviet Union would not be a threat."

Now the United States was encouraging Japan to rearm and to increase her American-sponsored embryo army, the National Safety Force, from 110,000 to 350,000 men. The Japanese were not enthusiastic; they scorned the National Safety Force as "American mercenaries".

At year's end the nation's military protection was provided almost entirely by American armed forces stationed there in accordance with the U.S. Security Treaty with Japan.

The year's end also brought a tragic toll when a crowd of 700,000, dressed in their holiday best, massed outside the Imperial Palace in the heart of Tokyo to sign the royal register and wish Emperor Hirohito a Happy New Year. As the gates of the palace began to close, protesting thousands pressed forward and swept away the police cordon. Men, women, and children were trampled underfoot. Sixteen persons were crushed to death, forty-three seriously injured.

An interesting development in Japan was the popular craze for *pachinko*, a kind of poor-man's pinball game.

The pachinko machine (cost, about $20) stands upright. A lever kicks a small steel ball around a board studded with nails. If the ball falls into one of the several nail-fenced cavities, the player wins ten, fifteen, or twenty steel balls. He may exchange these for cigarettes, candy, or other inexpensive prizes (the law forbids prizes worth more than 27¢).

More than a million pachinko machines already speckled Japan, with about 10,000 pachinko arcades in Tokyo alone. In less than a year the Japanese had spent 100 billion yen ($277 million),

or the equivalent of 11.7 percent of the national budget, on pachinko.

A day did not pass in 1953 that a tavern, candy store, restaurant, or shoeshop did not close, only to reopen again as a pachinko parlor. Special pachinko halls were reserved for school children.

The police frankly favored the craze. It kept people out of mischief.

Doctors reported cases of sprained thumbs resulting from overindulgence. A young wife was granted a divorce from her tailor husband, who spent all his time and lost all his money at pachinko. And a 72-year-old woman lost her temper at a noncooperative machine, smashed the glass, cut herself severely, and bled to death.

**PARACHUTE DROP** livens Indochina fighting as French troops raid remote Vietminh base, destroy stores brought from China

**VICE PRESIDENT NIXON,** back from global trip to 19 countries, discusses Southeast Asia

# Indochina and Malaya

IN 1953, AFTER MORE THAN SEVEN YEARS of conflict, the battle of Indochina was the world's oldest war.

When the Japanese surrendered in 1945, the French returned to Indochina to reclaim their colony, only to find that Moscow-trained Ho Chi Minh, the goat-eed leader of the Vietminh revolutionaries, had set up an independent native government.

By a series of political and military coups, the French regained control and Ho Chi Minh reluctantly agreed to head a provisional government until some form of self-rule within the French Union could be worked out for Indochina—the collective name for the French-dominated Associated States of Vietnam, Laos, and Cambodia.

The French, however, made no major

**ON LOOKOUT** for raiders and mined tracks, Vietnamese soldiers ride trains in attempt to maintain service through guerrilla-infested jungle

concessions, and on Dec. 19, 1946, Ho Chi Minh and his Vietminhese took the bit in their teeth. They attacked the French garrison in Hanoi (Indochina's northern capital), and in four days of vicious fighting massacred hundreds of French, both troops and civilians.

Even then it was not too late for the French to take a realistic attitude. The British had done so in India and Burma by granting full independence. But the French did nothing and, as a result, found themselves with an impossible war on their hands.

Even after dyed-in-the-wool native Communists moved in to hijack and mastermind Ho Chi Minh's rebellion, until then largely nationalistic, the people remained convinced that they could not achieve real independence until the French left the country. In consequence, millions remained sympathetic to the Vietminh.

In 1953, after seven years of fruitless warfare, the French grudgingly admitted that they had little hope of winning a decisive victory in Indochina. War-weary and fearful of a renascent Germany, France was anxious to liquidate her liability in Asia—if she could do so without loss of face.

Meanwhile, the drain in manpower and money was staggering. By 1953, some 40,000 French soldiers had been killed, another 120,000 wounded. Each year almost as many officers as graduate from St. Cyr (France's "West Point") were losing their lives in Indochina.

Six billion dollars had been poured into the struggle—twice as much as America's total Marshall Plan aid to France. And in 1953 the U.S. directly contributed $400 million—one half the annual cost—to help finance the Indochina war.

There were no clearly defined front lines in Indochina, nor were any sizeable blocks of territory exclusively controlled by either side. The French occupied most of the major cities and the Vietminh controlled much of the countryside, especially after dark when the French garrisons shut themselves up in their blockhouses. Much of Indochina was French by day and Vietminhese by night.

In this fluid, highly unorthodox war there had been no spectacular successes for either side. Outweaponed by the French, the Vietminh, with time as an ally, fought a guerrilla war. Their strategy and tactics resembled the hit-and-run resistance of the Chinese during the Japanese occupation of North China.

Early in 1953, for example, the Vietminh began digging tunnels under rice paddies for use as hiding places during the day. At night Vietminh regulars would come out and attack some nearby French post while their politicos held meetings in surrounding villages, collected food and taxes, and vanished like ghosts at cock's crow.

Once an exasperated French commander boiled out of his fortress in search of his tormentors. Leading a detachment of Legionnaires, he probed the darkness until he thought he had surrounded a company of about 120 Vietminhese in a flooded paddy field. When he closed in, however, the enemy had vanished. Later he learned the Reds had merely submerged themselves and breathed through hollow bamboo twigs.

Just before the spring rains began, while the Reds in Korea were talking peace, the Vietminh sent 40,000 crack troops driving into the Buddhist kingdom of Laos. At his capital of Luangprabang, gouty 68-year-old King Sisavang Vong sat stubbornly in his palace overlooking the palm-fringed Mekong River and refused to order his carefree, peace-loving subjects to mobilize. "This

is my country; this is my palace," he told the French. "I am too old to tremble before danger."

Laos is one of the most remote and backward areas in Asia—a rugged, mistily mountainous region about twice the size of Pennsylvania, with high plateaus and broad valleys and a population of 1,400,000, more than half of whom live on income from opium cultivation.

The invasion of Laos caught the French unprepared and revealed glaring French weaknesses—inadequate cross-country mobility and shocking apathy on the part of the native peoples. To meet the threat, they were obliged to withdraw badly needed troops from the vital rice bowl in the Red River delta, from Hanoi to the sea in the northeast, and airlift them to besieged outposts in the Laos mountains.

The high tide of the Laos invasion receded quickly, but not before the Viet-

minh had considerably enhanced their prestige and thrown a scare into the whole of southeast Asia, especially Thailand (Siam) and Burma, on the Indochinese border.

Summer rains brought a military respite for the harassed French, but on the political front new and more serious problems arose. On a trip around the world, Norodom Sihanouk, the plump 30-year-old bachelor King of Cambodia, who loves to play the saxophone, compose jazz, and act in plays, sounded off to New York reporters. Under the French colonial system, he said, his kingdom suffered many injustices which persisted even though Cambodia was supposed to be a full member of the French Union. Then he dropped a blockbuster.

"If we have an invasion of the sort that Laos suffered recently, I am not at all certain that I can call for a general mobilization. . . . If there is a menace, my

In a lightning thrust from coastal bases, two Vietminh divisions punched westward 100 miles across mountains and jungle to Thakhek on the Mekong River, cutting Indochina in two at its narrow waist. Hopelessly outnumbered, the French withdrew to the south.

The Red capture of Thakhek on the day after Christmas threw Thailand, just across the river, into a panic. A state of emergency was declared, and Thai troops rushed to the river border.

As French planes hammered at the Vietminh, the Communists appeared undecided whether to turn north or south from Thakhek. No one seriously expected them to cross the Mekong into Thailand. That would have constituted a clear case of aggression, with possible world-wide repercussions.

Did the Red offensive have political purposes? Was Ho Chi Minh reinforcing his military position so that he could bargain for peace from strength? In Communist Europe and in Asia speakers were already calling for a "just" peace in Indochina.

Ho's terms demanded that France give full recognition to his government, withdraw French troops from Indochina, and make the first official move for peace.

As the year ended, the French insisted Ho's price was too high. There was still no peace in Indochina.

## Malaya

ALTHOUGH THE WEST IN 1953 LOST GROUND in Indochina, it registered substantial gains in Malaya. Hostilities there continued, but vigorous efforts by the British brought the shooting phase of their anti-Communist campaign almost completely under control.

people will say that the French are encircled and their end has come."

In Paris the French purpled. But when tempers had cooled, they decided they could not afford to argue with Norodom, especially since he had threatened to take his case to the U.N. Hastily, they signed a new agreement with him, giving his government control of administration, justice, and other departments hitherto run by the French, in exchange for a Cambodian undertaking to help prosecute the war.

A similar agreement was signed with Laos and Vietnam, thus giving virtually complete sovereignty to all three Associated States within the French Union.

On Nov. 29 the Stockholm newspaper *Expressen* published a cable over the name of Ho Chi Minh, offering to discuss a possible armistice with the French. While Paris studied the proposal, Ho Chi Minh again sent his armies into action.

In five years the Communist-led rebellion in Malaya had taken a toll of 16,000 casualties—about 10,000 of them fatal. The cost had been more than $2 billion.

But time was running out for the Malayan Communists. Their only hope for ultimate success was the outbreak of a world war, or strong military and material aid from Red China. Nevertheless, waging a hit-and-run campaign from jungle hide-outs, they had forced the British to commit 250,000 heavily armed men, an air force of bombers, helicopters, and transports, and a squadron of naval units to patrol Malayan waters. In military terms, the Communists had been succeeding with one of the cheapest holding-down operations in the history of war.

Until 1953 the jungle-based Reds were able to obtain provisions by raiding or terrorizing squatter farmers living on isolated plots of land. Unable to protect these farmers on their own farms, the government uprooted half a million of them and moved them into barbed-wire-enclosed areas, where they were provided with new homes and parcels of government-owned land.

To check smuggling of food from the cities to the Reds, stringent measures were taken to control the sale, possession, and movement of all foodstuffs. Surplus rice stocks were bought up by the government, the weekly rice ration was reduced, and the sale of rice on the free market forbidden.

Only licensed dealers were permitted to purchase or possess more than specified amounts of sugar, cooking oil, dried fish, meat, and other provisions. Shopkeepers had to puncture every tin of canned food before handing it to a customer. In Malaya's tropical climate, an open tin of food spoils if not eaten at once.

**ANXIOUS KING** of Laos (a division of Indo China) faces possible attack by Vietminh army

**RARE PHOTO** of Ho Chi Minh, taken from a high-ranking Vietminh prisoner, shows the rebel leader reading by lamplight in one of his hideaways

Mere possession of unopened canned goods was enough to land a man in jail. Conviction of an offense under these regulations was punishable by a fine of up to $5000, or imprisonment for five years, or both. If a man was caught trying to smuggle food to the Communists, a death sentence might be imposed.

Harsh as these measures were, they paid off. In May, a captured Communist directive admitted that "shortage of food in various places has prevented us from concentrating large numbers of troops and launching large-scale operations". At all costs, it continued, priority must be given to the "critical" food question.

By June, more and more disillusioned and half-starved Reds were coming out of the jungle to surrender. One of these was Wong Kow, who staggered up to a police post mumbling, "I've been work-ing like a slave on a starvation diet." He was sent to a hospital.

Some days later, R.A.F. planes dropped leaflets with messages from Wong Kow to five Red comrades who had been working a tiny patch of jungle-cleared land with him. Four came out of the jungle clutching the leaflets in emaciated hands. The fifth man, they said, was too weak to travel. One of the Reds led a patrol in search of the missing man. They found him—dead of starvation.

## The Philippines

ON DEC. 30, 1953, RAMÓN MAGSAYSAY, A 46-year-old jungle fighter, took the oath of office as the third President of the Republic of the Philippines.

He was the "people's choice" in the

cleanest, calmest election in the nation's history, which he won by a 2-to-1 landslide. The world, and Asia especially, had watched this election with unusual interest, as the first real test of whether American-style democracy could work when a people had been prepared for it.

By Magsaysay's order, simplicity was the keynote at his inaugural. He ruled against formal Western garb. The rugged President-elect, who boasted he had swung a sledge hammer in his father's blacksmith shop at the age of six, broke precedent and prescribed the national dress: a translucent embroidered shirt, made of fine pineapple fiber, worn outside the trousers, which are either striped or plain gray. Women wore a colorful native gown with starched butterfly sleeves.

For the inauguration an estimated

quarter of a million Filipinos swarmed into Manila—on foot, by oxcart, in sailing junks from distant islands. Magsaysay, a symbol of nationalism to them all, had startled his opponents with a "whistle stop" campaign that took him to more than 1500 villages in every one of the archipelago's provinces. He seemed determined to leave no hand unshaken, no baby unkissed, no man's question unanswered. He was never too tired to make another speech or dance a "Magsaysay mambo" with the nearest girl.

"I love to shake hands—the dirty, muddy hands of the poor farmer," he said. "I love to shake the greasy hands of the mechanic rather than the hands of the Quirino [his opponent] politicians, who wash their hands ten times a day, perfumed hands washed with the best of soap."

From 1950 to February, 1953, Magsaysay, as Defense Secretary in outgoing President Quirino's Cabinet, had vigorously fought the armed Huks (Communist-led native revolutionaries). His personal courage, coupled with a lenient, understanding treatment of surrendered Reds, enabled him to reduce their numbers from some 25,000 to barely 3000, and their sympathizers from an estimated 2,500,000 to 40,000.

He disarmed many of the Huks simply by buying their rifles for cash and offering them land plus a carabao (water buffalo) and a house with electric light. "You say you are fighting for land?" he asked. "Well then, you can quit fighting, because I will give you land."

He gave one surrendered Huk commander $3000 to buy a car. In return, the Red gave him the names and addresses of the twenty-two members of the Communist Politburo in Manila. Moving

**IN A VILLAGE** loyal Vietnamese show scorn for Vietminh women sent in to try to win Red converts—a trick that augments propaganda with sex

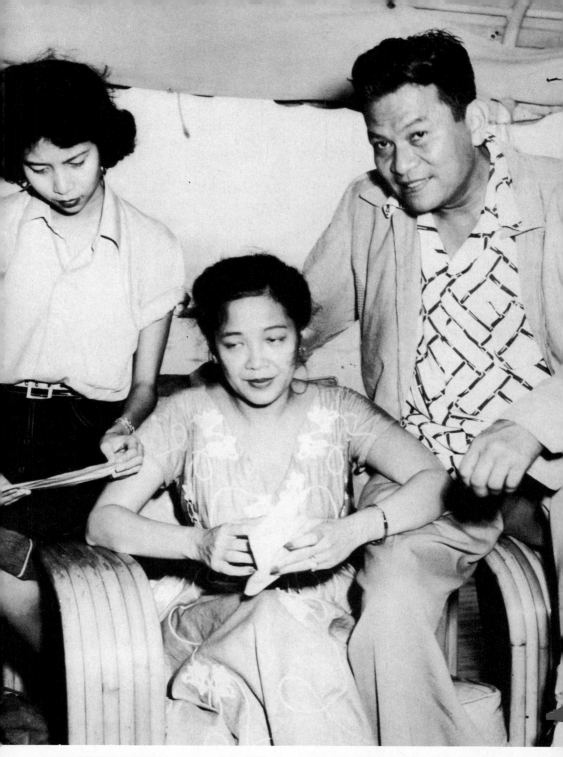

**NEW PRESIDENT** Magsaysay of the Philippines poses with wife (center) and daughter Teresita

swiftly, Magsaysay arrested the entire group except for one who was later killed in a gun battle.

He reorganized and revitalized a corruption-ridden army by meting out harsh punishment to offenders and rewarding honesty and devotion to duty. Three thousand cameras were passed out to key army units. Said Magsaysay, "When you claim five dead Huks, I want to see pictures of five dead Huks." Automatic promotion was assured to every soldier who killed ten Huks.

The task ahead for the new President was tough and challenging. Land reform had been his chief campaign platform. Poverty and oppression of the peasants had been the Huks' principal recruiting agents.

"Our people are restless and hungry," said Magsaysay. "We have millions of hectares of unworked government land that should be distributed. If that isn't enough, then we will break up big estates held by absentee landlords."

For all his honesty and energy, Magsaysay was relatively unskilled in politics and inexperienced in government administration. He couldn't do everything alone, and he had to find competent and trustworthy men for responsible posts. If he succeeded, the immediate future was indeed promising for the Philippines.

**OLD PRESIDENT** Quirino, out after four corruption-tainted years, wishes Magsaysay well

# BUSINESS

**TOUGHEST JOB** of 1953 was joint U.S.-Canadian laying of 711-mile, $94 million Trans Mountain pipeline (above) through Canadian Rockies to bring oil from new Alberta fields to Vancouver

# BUSINESS

EXPERTS SAID IT COULDN'T HAPPEN AGAIN—but it did. In 1953, as in 1952, farm prices slumped. Business failures mounted. Finance companies repossessed more goods bought on installment plans.

Despite these signs, through most of 1953 the boom zoomed along. Even though jobs weren't quite so plentiful at year's end, more people were at work than in 1952. The total of all incomes rose. Corporation earnings continued high. Gross national product, which is economists' lingo for the combined value of commodities produced and personal services rendered, shot above the 1952 figure. The American people spent more and saved more than they did the year before.

Over what would happen next, business and economic soothsayers disagreed.

Only a few predicted a major slump. Almost all expected a decline from the 1953 peak. The real disagreement was what to call the situation that developed toward the end of the year—a "mild recession", a "lull", or a "rolling readjustment". The rest of the year had to be called "prosperity".

To the usual reasons for continued good times, something new has been added: love and medicine. The last dozen years have seen the greatest baby boom ever. World War II sparked early marriages. High wages, steady employment, and greater leisure brought larger families. At the same time, development of "miracle drugs" and other advances in medical care lowered old folks' mortality rates and increased the span of life. And because of fewer filled graves and more

**YEAR'S WORST LABOR DISPUTE** saw rival unions trying to control New York waterfront workers. Here "old union" men hurl rocks at members of "new union" being escorted to work by police

filled cradles, the population grew twice as fast as expected.

Census calculators had figured that our 1950 population would be 140,000,-000, a gain of 8,000,000 over 1940. Instead, it was 151,700,000 and had leaped to more than 160,000,000 by 1953. At this rate, by 1960 there would be between 175,000,000 and 180,000,000 Americans.

Such population growth means more consumers, more production, and expanding markets for all sorts of consumer's goods. At the same time, the number of retired persons over 65 has increased, and their pensions and retirement funds already are creating new markets for small houses, travel, gardening, and other hobbies for older people.

Meanwhile, the postwar baby crop even now is influencing our economy.

Since 1940 the toy industry has grown from a midget $84 million a year to a giant $800 million. In 1940, some 270,-000,000 cans of baby food were sold; 1,500,000,000 cans were sold in 1953.

The banks of the country had an excellent year in 1953. The U.S. Treasury advanced interest rates on its new borrowings, private borrowings went up, and there were 500,000 more savings accounts, which meant more money to lend. The largest maker of depositors' passbooks enjoyed a 30 percent increase in business and was four months behind in filling orders.

The year's biggest innovation in banking was charge-it-to-the-bank systems. A bank first obtains cooperation of merchants. Next it signs up cardholders. When making a purchase, a customer shows his credit card and signs a sales slip. Daily, the merchant sends his sales slips to the bank, which credits his account with their total, minus a 3 to 5 percent discount. At the end of a month, the bank bills its cardholders for purchases made.

The scheme is a convenience for cardholders, who need make out only one check instead of several to pay a month's bills; and the bank's statement makes it easier to keep track of household expenses. The plan also helps merchants, who get their money immediately instead of waiting a month or longer for customers to pay. In particular, it helps small retailers, who cannot afford business machines and elaborate credit systems, to compete with larger stores.

The plan was inaugurated in the 1940's by Brooklyn's Flatbush National Bank, and by the beginning of 1953, six banks had taken it up. Before the end of the year the number was seventy-five.

Another 1953 innovation in banking was the doorbell-ringing technique of the Fuller Brush man. Fidelity-Philadelphia Trust Company, fourth-largest bank in the Quaker City, trained eight young women for door-to-door solicitation of new accounts from "the lady of the house". The result has been a large increase in depositors in the bank's branch offices.

More than half of the thousands of women interviewed also filled out applications for "personal credit accounts", the first step in establishing credit for personal loans.

## Law Business

BACK IN 1950, SEVENTEEN OF THE COUNtry's leading investment-banking houses went on trial on charges of conspiring to monopolize the securities business. Instead of one firm's submitting its own bid for a new issue of securities, a syndicate of firms would conduct negotiated bidding. The case was heard in a New York federal court by Judge Harold R. Medina, temporarily refreshed after a nine-month legal battle which ended in conviction of eleven Communist leaders.

Judge Medina sank his teeth into the new case for thirty-four long months. Court proceedings ran to 5,000,000 words, and, with briefs and exhibits, made a 108,646-page record. Only two witnesses for the government were heard. The rest of the time was devoted to the argument.

Aligned against the government's fifteen-member legal staff was a platoon of forty-seven defense lawyers. When the government rested its case, Judge Medina called a halt, said he found no evidence of collusive bidding, and dismissed the case "with prejudice", meaning that the government may appeal but cannot reopen. Estimated cost of this legal marathon was between $1.5 and $3 million for the government, and $4 to $7 million for the defendants.

During the trial, seventeen children and three grandchildren were born in the lawyers' families (all but three, future defense attorneys). Meanwhile, Judge Medina had been promoted to the United States Circuit Court of Appeals but had to continue as a district-court judge until the trial's end.

## Management

TWO THINGS WHICH TROUBLE AMERICAN business management became more apparent in 1953. First, there are not enough good top executives. Second, they are burning out and dying faster than other men of their age. Industry needs more leaders than it has been able to train.

By the end of 1953, nearly a score of colleges offered short courses in business administration for junior executives of large corporations.

Some big companies like General Motors and Esso Standard Oil grade their young executives for initiative, emotional stability, cooperation, and sense of responsibility. There is increasing belief in American industry that a man who is a good executive in one line can do equally well in another; that essentially the same qualities are needed for virtually all top jobs.

These fundamentals are: ability to make sound decisions with firmness and dispatch, to judge men accurately and pick the right subordinates, to work harmoniously with others, and to be readily adjustable to change.

Depressing figures came to light indicating that many in top management are literally working themselves to death. The American Fidelity and Casualty Company estimated that the average businessman has a life span six years shorter than other men of the same age in different occupations. Examining 25,000 executives who averaged 45.6 years, Life Extension Institute found only one out of five in normal health.

As a result, 1953 saw some 450 leading corporations with fairly comprehensive medical programs. Others send their officials for three days in bed at such diagnostic clinics as Boston's Lahey and Detroit's Henry Ford Hospital. Pleasantest of all such goings-over is at Greenbrier Hotel at White Sulphur Springs, W. Va. There, between medical tests, the temporary patients play golf or swim, and the company picks up the check—$100 for examination, plus hotel bill.

Last fall the federal government brought out a breakdown of incomes of top career people who receive more than $15,000 a year, not from investment but from their own efforts. Of the 452,000 in this category, only 25,000 are women.

Topflight women executives are neither "sweater girls" nor "old battle-axes". Nor, according to Assistant Secretary of the Treasury Catherine B. Cleary, are they "big-time operators".

Social Research, Inc., of Chicago, reported that "an abiding femininity is characteristic of the successful group" who get to the top not by imitating male aggressiveness, but by capitalizing on "their feminine skills of understanding, adapting to others, and comprehending emotional factors".

And what do women workers in business expect of a male executive? The New York chapter of the National Secretaries' Association named as "Boss of the Year" Mervin B. Cooksey, a district sales manager for a calendar and specialty firm. He led the field in these qualifications: regular hours for dictation, regular routine, and realization that a secretary has an outside life.

For every farmer in the U.S. there is one clerical worker. Before World War I there were four industrial workers for every paper shuffler; in 1953 the ratio was 2 to 1.

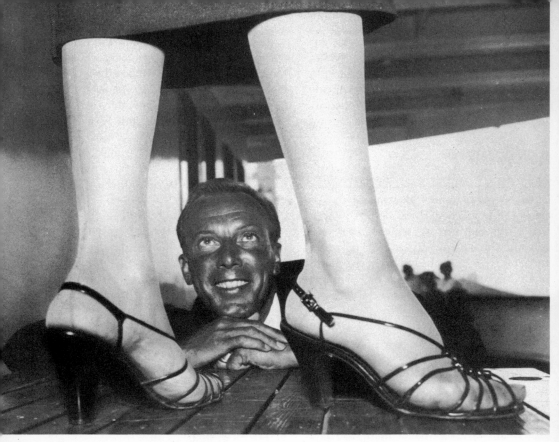

**FRENCH DESIGNER** Jacques Fath inspects the 15-inch hemline popularized in 1953 by his competitor Christian Dior. Fath himself favored slightly shorter skirts

In 1953, nearly 8,000,000 men and women wallowed in a slough of "Dear Sir" letters, invoices, payroll forms, tax returns, and so on. Emmet J. Leahy, head of the National Records Management Council, estimates that American business pays $35 billion a year for preparation of new records and preservation of old ones. He says the files of private business contain a trillion—that's 1000 billion —pieces of paper, 40 percent of which should be sold to the junkman.

Another Leahy finding: each new business paper costs 20¢ in stenography, materials, office handling, and equipment. Merely to keep that piece of paper in an office file costs 1¢ a year.

Federal government agencies have destroyed 2,500,000 cubic feet of records in the past year, thus reclaiming 135,000 files and transfer cases and about 36 square miles of floor space—equivalent to the area of a Midwest township.

Many big corporations are cutting down the number of their office forms. Mutual Life Insurance Company simplified its procedure and saved policyholders $80,000 a year on notary fees. It also translated into simple English the usual jabberwocky on insurance policies, and thereby figured an annual $25,000 saving in paper work.

Typical big-corporation stockholders' meetings used to be cut and dried. Many 1953 annual meetings pointed up a revo-

**ITALIAN MODEL** displays evidence of her country's growing importance in fashion design. She wears a creation entitled "Linen fantasy, in black and white"

lution in company-stockholder relations.

In a New York hotel ballroom, 400 stockholders of Sinclair Oil Company commented for an hour on their company's policies. American Airlines held its annual meeting in a hangar at La Guardia field, where all types of the company's equipment were on view before 1800 shareholders.

After its annual meeting in downtown New York, Tide Water Associated Oil Company herded 100 stockholders to the Whitehall Club atop a skyscraper for a sit-you-down of shrimp cocktail, creamed chicken, salad, dessert, and coffee. When cigars were passed, women shareholders, remembering menfolk at home, dipped into the box.

At Remington Rand's annual meeting, a former World War II corporal heckled the chairman of the board, General of the Army Douglas MacArthur. He was Lewis D. Gilbert, whose voice is upraised at many a stockholders' meeting, and he was "seriously concerned" because "the distinguished American who is president" owns no Remington Rand stock.

"Won't you sit down?" snapped the General. "I am an employee of the company and its servant, not one of its owners. Such money as I am able to invest, I have placed in defense bonds to help protect our beloved country. What I do with future funds is neither your business nor that of anyone else." The seventy stockholders applauded.

## Fads and Fashions

BY AND LARGE, THE AMERICAN PEOPLE have gone on a diet. More than a third of them are overweight by present-day standards, and a goodly proportion are trying, more or less seriously, to take off extra poundage.

The new "straight silhouette" in women's fashions demands greater slimness.

Among men, important diet factors are easier living, the performing of heavy manual labor by machines, and more sitting down at jobs—all things which necessitate fewer calories.

Chain restaurants famous for "gookie" desserts have added calorie specials to luncheon menus. Pennsylvania Railroad dining cars offer a 470-calorie "Streamliner". An executives' dining room at Westinghouse has a 350-calorie "Waistliner", and DuPont has developed special diets for its employees.

This new "battle of the bulge" scared the daylights out of bakers, brewers, and sugar and dairy people. There has been a slump in consumption of starchy foods. Before World War II the American people ate an average of two and a half pounds of potatoes apiece a week. Last year they ate two pounds. We are eating the equivalent of two slices less bread apiece a day; the flour involved in this difference adds up at the end of a year to nearly the entire wheat crop of Kansas.

In five years the country's flour consumption has dropped one quarter. Dozens of small mills have stopped grinding flour. Last year the world's biggest millers, General Mills, Inc., cut production 7 percent. On the other hand, Ralston Purina, makers of Ry-Krisp, an old dieting stand-by, reported its sales charts as "something beautiful to watch".

When Americans in great numbers began to take waistline warnings seriously, processors catering to diabetics with sugar-free, salt-free foods increased their output and added the magic word "non-fattening" to their labels. Their products ranged from soups to applesauce and peanut butter, and from canapés to puddings. They even reduced calorie quotients of canned beef stews and chicken dinners. By the end of 1953, eight out of ten supermarkets had low-calorie food displays.

Greatest boom of all was in low-calorie soft drinks. For the solace of diabetics, several thousand cases of unsweetened ginger ale and other bottled pops had been turned out each year. In 1952 the Brooklyn firm of Kirsh's Beverages placed on the market "No-Cal" ginger ale. Instead of an expected 100,000 cases, reducing dieters bought half a million. Last year No-Cal in five flavors sold more than 2,500,000 cases, sharing the 10,000,000-case no-sugar beverage market with fifty other firms.

Processors of foods of reputed high calorie content either fought back or joined the diet procession. Bakers added to their lines of protein breads, and their trade association launched a $1 million advertising campaign hailing bread as a reducing food. Breakfast-food and candy firms plugged their products as essential energy products. Domino Sugar bought advertising space to assert that "three teaspoons of sugar actually contain fewer calories than half a grapefruit". Brewers boasted of the low-sugar content of their beers, and a rum distributor screamed in thick, black type that "A Bacardi *Cuba Libre* has less calories than a lamb chop".

## Dior's "Old Look"

SOME WOMEN WANT TO LOOK DIFFERENT from others; other women want to look like the women who want to look different from them. And that's how fashions are born.

In 1953 the millinery trade was told by David Weisberg, one of its executives, that since the war "we have had nothing as radical as the Empress Eugénie silhouette, which made every existing fashion as dead as the dodo".

In women's fashions, however, Christian Dior obliged with a new silhouette again. Dior, who looks like a cross between Bing Crosby without toupee and

an embassy secretary, finds ideas for his creations in the bathtub. Every half year this 48-year-old bachelor goes off by himself to the French or Italian Riviera to daydream "in search of beauty". Then, some morning while he is lying in his tub, flash! comes an inspiration.

Pencil and drawing pad are on a stool beside the tub, in readiness for that electric moment, and sheet after sheet of paper is covered with sketches. Arising from his bath, M. Dior refines his scratch-pad work and is off to Paris with designs for a million dollars' worth of new Diors.

Son of a once-well-to-do family, Dior studied for the diplomatic service but launched out as an art dealer. Unsuccessful by the middle 1930's, he saw an artist friend's sketches for a dressmaking establishment. "Why," he exclaimed, "I can draw dresses too!" And he did—so well that by the time Hitler interrupted the business, Dior was working for leading fashion houses. In 1946, Marcel Boussac, a cotton manufacturer and one of France's richest men, staked him to his own establishment. A year later he took the lead in the fashion world with his "New Look".

Women who announced collectively that never, never would they be coerced into its acceptance then slipped into stores individually to buy it; but after six years, they were ready for a change. It was Old Look again in 1953.

M. Dior's 1953 models showed a raised hemline—not a revolutionary 6 inches and back to flapper-skirt days, but merely 1½ to 2 inches. His innovation reverberated around the world and provoked familiar reactions: women would not discard present wardrobes just because Paris said so; never, never would they be coerced into acceptance, and so on.

But Dior had started something. For the beginning of a new style era means hundreds of millions of dollars in new business, not only for women's-wear man-

**NONSTRIKING MEN** wait nervously on an Elizabeth, La. corner for their truck to be repaired. Hired during a work stoppage at local paper mill, they fear violence from strikers

ufacturers but for department stores and specialty shops. Also for textile weavers, yarn makers, dyers, fabric printers, and for the great chemical firms, which hopefully poured more than a half-billion dollars into development and manufacture of synthetic fabrics.

"How's business?" a New York garment-center man was asked.

"Fine! Fine!" replied the cloak-and-suiter. "Already we are 50 percent ahead of next year."

Biggest development in men's fashions during 1953 was also the raised hemline, only more so. There was a big run on "walking shorts", formerly known as "Bermuda shorts". For the first time, these bare-kneed garments, worn with long woollen stockings, seen in New York City offices and cocktail lounges. Before Father's Day was over, twice as many had been bought as in all of 1951 and '52.

Men's-furnishings dealers had the biggest-ever Father's Day sales. Gloomiest were necktie manufacturers. "Business," said one, "has gone completely to pot."

Women's fashions of 1953 continued to emphasize the bust, and the brassiere and foundation trade prospered. One successful firm is Peter Pan Foundations, a $13 million-a-year enterprise started a dozen years ago by Harry Plehn with $5000 of borrowed money.

Plehn, who looks like a movie actor, believes in promotion as well as in service. One of his smartest stunts was to sign up Joan Crawford as a consultant.

Much of his success with his "little numbers" came from choice of the right name. He struck it rich with his first creation, a built-in contour affair dubbed Hidden Treasure. Other Plehn offerings:

Inner Circle, Merry Go Round, Low 'N' Behold, Secret Scent-er.

Many brassieres change their shape after a few washings, and tend to follow the natural contour instead of uplifting it. Plehn claims that the Inner Circle can be washed again and again without

**STRIKING WOMAN** in Overland, Mo., keeps 14-month-old daughter with her on the picket line

collapsing, and there is a money-back guarantee if it fails to flatter after 100 washings. For those who don't fancy its rigid controls, Peter Pan brought out Merry Go Round, a softer bra. Secret Scent-er contained a perfumed pellet which gave off a pleasing aroma when warmed by the wearer's body. Women, however, disdained it, and Secret Scent-er was itself a bust.

So was Low 'N' Behold, a plunge-type affair. It came out just when necklines stopped going down and were on the way up. Plehn lost $250,000 on that venture.

Denim began as the sturdy pants cloth of cowpokes, hillbillies, and pick-and-shovelers. Later it became the uniform, with flapping shirttails, of the drugstore-soda-fountain set. Now it has gone high-hat. Production in 1953 was nearly three times that of prewar years, and was a shot in the arm for the swooning cotton-textile industry, moaning low from assaults by rayon, Dacron, and Orlon.

Repeated washing turns most dark-blue denim a soft, light blue, a color first favored by yachtsmen, and then by other members of the family. Whereupon denim makers turned out quantities of the light-colored stuff for men's slacks and women's playsuits. Next, stylists got busy with tailor-made dresses, men's suits, and all sorts of fancy pants for men and women.

For women factory workers there were slacks tapered at the ankles, in colors ranging from black to leopard skin. By the end of 1953, mills were turning out denim in nearly 100 different colors, stripes, and plaids. One stylist reached the pinnacle with a "limited collection" of denim creations trimmed with mink.

Mink madness continued to vex the $250 million fur industry. Insurance companies reported "very high" numbers of mink thefts. Mink accounted for two thirds of all 1953's retail fur dollar sales.

## Chemicals

UP WENT SYNTHETIC DETERGENTS; DOWN went chlorophyll. Out came polyethylene to compete with glass and cellophane; also new motor lubricants which double automobile mileage between overhauls. These were outstanding 1953 developments on America's greatest business frontier, the chemical industry.

For the first time, synthetic detergents outstripped fatty-oils soaps in manufacture and sales. During five previous years, soap production had dropped 40 percent, while detergent production and use increased nearly 400 percent.

Chlorophyll, the stuff which makes grass and other flora green, tumbled even faster than soap. Because of its touted, not wholly proven, powers of killing breath and body odors, its output, with an almost infinite variety of use, was going great guns in 1952. Everything from tooth paste, chewing gum, and dog food to baby diapers, men's shorts, toilet paper, and inner soles of shoes was doused with green chlorophyll and pushed out to market.

A pipe maker put on sale a chlorophyll-treated tobacco. For first aid to husbands and others in need of disguising alcoholic breaths, an Indiana distiller dashed chlorophyll into vodka and shipped "Vodka-fyll" to Los Angeles, vodka-consuming capital of the U.S.A.

Disillusionment came in 1953. Use of chlorophyll had been overdone, and firm after firm withdrew from the market. Manufacture fell to half capacity. Only chlorophyll-treated tooth paste, chewing gum, and dog food held their own or increased their sales.

Extravagant claims, freakish use, and customer dissatisfaction were main causes of the slump. The cautious American Medical Association, which had dismissed chlorophyll claims as "bunk", modified its attitude and announced that the internal-deodorizing value of the substance "has yet to be determined". Yet "so many observers have reported deodorizing effects that they cannot be dismissed lightly".

Uneven results came from tests of chlorophyll dog food. Quaker Oats Company found that large dogs, like Newfoundlands and bloodhounds, smell stronger than dachshunds and Chihuahuas. The company also warned that when excessive dosage of chlorophyll kills all canine odors, a dog's love life is thwarted. Company chemists hastened assurances that chlorophyll does not destroy romantic urge in people.

Both odors and deodorants are now sprayed in the air or on the person from squeezable plastic bottles. These are composed of polyethylene, lightest and one of the newest commercial plastics. In 1953 a few giants of the chemical industry laid out $100 million for new plants to increase polyethylene production and to enter new fields of competition.

First used in World War II as an insulating coating for electronic devices, polyethylene withstands extremes of heat and cold, and corrosion from most chemicals. It is already giving cellophane and other transparent wrappings stiff competition. Nurserymen wrap shrubs and plants in it before shipment because it is strong and holds moisture, and growers of garden truck find that it keeps vegetables fresh and marketable for nearly a fortnight.

Should increased production lower its price from 44¢ to 30¢ a pound, polyethylene might give glass manufacturers a run for their money. It is light and unbreakable, thereby lowering shipping costs and eliminating breakage losses. An even greater potential market is as a substitute for metal pipe in oil fields, public works, and household plumbing. A 100-foot, 2-inch poly pipe can be lifted with one hand, and two men can lay 1000 feet in the time eight men lay 200 feet of metal pipe.

Although bothered by price wars in 1953, big oil refiners intensified their search for new markets. Back in 1400 B.C., Egyptians had smeared beef or mutton tallow on their chariot axles—the beginning of lubricated motor parts. Last year, oil refiners souped up still further their heavy-duty lubricating motor oils in what rose to a $100 million business.

These special oils were developed when the Army sought an all-round lubricant suitable in all climates for all types of motor transport. Essentially, the lubricant is compounded like a druggist's prescription from such substances as turpentine, alcohol, barium, calcium, and inert sulphur, mixed with regular motor oil. These "additives" act in many ways to slow down engine wear. Tests indicate that cars lubricated by heavy-duty oils run nearly twice as far without motor overhauling, and with half the number of oil changes. Prices range from 4¢ to 50¢ more a quart than prices of untreated motor oils, but cars run longer between repairs.

## Transportation

CHANCES ARE THAT THE MIDNIGHT CHOO-choo which used to leave for Alabam' is no longer a chuffing steam locomotive but a diesel engine. Last year, three quarters of all passenger trains and two thirds of all freight hauled by American railroads were pulled by diesels.

The carriers had problems. Competition of airlines and buses for passengers, and motor trucks and trailers for freight, grew more serious. And the Post Office Department, hitherto a very dependable source of revenue, began experiments with hauling suburban mail by truck, and sending 3¢ first-class mail between big cities by air.

**THANKSGIVING PARADE** in New York, put on by Macy's department store, features gigantic balloons like 70-foot "Mighty Mouse"

Most Class I railroads—about 130 carriers doing an annual business of more than $1 million—figure on spending more money so as to lose less money. The $1 billion in new equipment acquired during the last few years helped to cut passenger traffic losses to $635 million last year, as compared with $680 million the year before.

According to Great Northern president John M. Budd, "passenger service should be excellent or given up". As fast as public-service commissions allow, the railroads are dropping thinly patronized runs and are sprucing up their other trains. Virtually every "name" train has been re-equipped since V-J Day, and the discarded equipment has been rebuilt for new "Chiefs" and "Zephyrs" on shorter routes.

There are more "penthouse" glass-domed observation cars, and some 600 living-room, bedroom Pullmans are on order. Train "butchers", peddling their wares, are being displaced by vending machines, and neat coupon booklets are now beginning to take the place of long tickets.

Airlines are not taking stepped-up railroad competition lying down. In 1953 they increased air-coach service to twice that of the year before, and it accounts for nearly one third of all passenger miles flown.

Some airline people predict that this type of travel, at 30 percent less than regular fares, will become the standard service of the future, while the present standard will become de luxe and extra fare. United Airlines already operates a super de luxe. It has inaugurated "The Executive", an after-business-hours flight between Chicago and New York for men only. Pipes and cigars permitted. The only women aboard are two stewardesses ready with market reports, business publications, steak dinners, and even slippers.

**MIDSUMMER STYLE** in men's wear prompts State Sec. Dulles to josh British Washington correspondent who came to press conference in shorts

Air-coach travel originated six years ago when Capital Airlines sought a paying use for equipment generally idle during night and early morning. It offered bargain rates to passengers willing to take off during normal lie-abed hours. At first, these cut-rate flights offered no frills such as free meals aloft. Now, meals and box lunches may be bought. Once air-coach travel was in old equipment, but in 1953 many an airline turned its newest, fastest planes into eighty-person air coaches, with as many daytime as night flights.

Overseas airlines adopted cut rates. El Al (Israel Airline) has nothing but. S.A.S. (Scandinavian Airlines System) has more than three times as many tourist flights as first-class ones. K.L.M. (Royal Dutch) has more tourist than first-class business. And B.O.A.C. (British Overseas Airlines) has 50-50 tourist and higher-fare traffic between the U.S. and London.

One big personnel airline problem continued in 1953—replacement of stewardesses. The turnover in 1953 was one third. Causes were paradoxical. Airlines have a rule against married stewardesses. At the same time, they seek intelligent, attractive young women for flight hostesses— the ones most likely to have first choice of husbands.

Most airline stewardess requirements are the same. Height: between 5 ft. 1 in. and 5 ft. 8 in. Weight: 135 pounds maximum. Age: between 21 and 28. Status: unmarried.

For reasons obvious to anyone within range of an air-hostess smile, good teeth are essential. Long hair and glasses generally are out. Some airlines prefer young women endowed with gifts which the sweater girl brought into prominence. Others, having uniforms with short jackets, are more interested in small hips.

These specifications explain why so many former beauty queens get airline-hostess jobs. Among the reported recruits of 1953 were Queen Yam, Toronto's Peanut Queen of 1950, Baylor Beauty, Miss Moose Jaw, and the Homecoming Queen of Slipping Rock State Teachers College.

All was not sweetness and light in the automobile industry. There were shutdowns and layoffs. Parts suppliers were vexed by unauthorized strikes. A $70 million fire in its Livonia plant halted General Motors' production of transmission units. Screams of anguish came from dealers, complaining that manufacturers were "forcing" more cars upon them than they could sell.

Dealers' stocks of unused cars at the end of 1953 were the highest ever. Prices on used, traded-in cars headed down-cellar; 1953 cars slipped from show windows to used-cars lots, at cut prices.

By midsummer, new passenger-car output was twice that of the year before. Noting that the federal government comes to the rescue of dairy farmers with purchase of surplus butter and cheese, tongue-in-cheek letter writers to *The Wall Street Journal* proposed similar relief to the overproductive automobile industry.

Admission and denial of overproduction came from the auto makers. "A normal historical competitive market," said one manufacturer. Paul Hoffman, Studebaker board chairman, pronounced the industry in an "unhealthy" state, with "chaos the order of the day".

As a whole, the 1954 models were not much different from the 1953's. The given reason was that fewer sales this year are expected, retooling is expensive, and buyers seemed satisfied with the models of 1953. Among the Big Three, General Motors' Cadillac, Buick, and Pontiac were restyled. Ford and Chrysler added more horsepower to their lines.

Organized motor-car users began talking back to the auto makers. At the fifty-first annual meeting of the American Automobile Association, comprising nearly 4,000,000 members in 700 clubs across the country, the delegates called upon the industry to "tone down the increasing emphasis on more and more horsepower and higher-speed potentials, and devote more thought and emphasis to ways and means of protecting the driver against his own mistakes".

## Merchandising

A WELL-TIMED NOTION ABOUT WHAT MAKES the American economy tick was put forward at year's end by Paul Mazur, Wall Street banker and chain-store consultant. The secret of our prosperity, he said, is not mass production, but mass consumption. Without it, mass-produced stuff piles up on store shelves and in warehouses, production declines, workers are laid off, and fewer people have money to buy things. This situation calls for stimulating all persuasive arts of attracting the consumer's dollars.

This was a highfalutin' way of saying that 1953 was the Year of the Huckster. The slogan was "Get out and Sell". There was greater demand for salesmen on commission, more replacement of salaried store clerks by supermarkets and vending machines, the biggest advertising outlay ($8 billion) in history, and a flood of new sales techniques.

The change-over from sellers' to buyers' markets caught many manufacturers flat-footed. A big Akron rubber concern was so short of trained salesmen that it sent laboratory chemists out on the road with samples and order books. Some employers reported no shortage of salesmen, but a lack of know-how. "We interview forty before we find one we think might make the grade," said one sales manager.

Though salesmen have earning possibilities higher than salaried technicians and junior executives, most young college graduates seek regular-paying, less competitive jobs. President R. E. Humphrey of United States Rubber Company gave two reasons. "First, folks think their children should get into something more secure than selling. Second, even our college professors have been known to preach that selling is an unnecessary evil."

But many manufacturers found ways to spur salesmen on. One is the travel-incentive campaign, which rewards top salesmen with all-expenses-paid vacation tours to Europe, the West Indies, and other foreign lands. The scheme mushroomed during 1953 to some 100,000 tourists a year.

The secret spark of these contests is that the winning salesmen's wives accompany them on the free tours. "If I hadn't won this contest, I would have been afraid to go home," one Chrysler dealer admitted. "My wife made up her mind we were going the first time she saw announcements about the trip. Then I had to get us on the boat to keep peace in the family."

For the 320 winners of the "Sell 'N' Sail" cruise of Chrysler dealers, factory officials, and wives to Bermuda and the Bahamas, the liner *Queen of Bermuda* was chartered, and everything from bar checks to porter tips was on the house.

At year's end, salesmen of Hallicrafter radio and TV sets were competing for three round-the-world flights, with four-day stopovers along the way. Trips like these give salesmen and their wives a taste of high living and the incentive to work twice as hard so as to afford another taste.

In 1953 the problem of retailers concerned dissatisfied salespeople. They don't like the hours, particularly Saturday and night work—one reason why more stores did not convert to evening hours during 1953.

High wages and the forty-hour week have remade American living and buying habits. Why, it is asked, should stores be open while most of their customers are at work? Why not 9 and 10 P.M. closings, and Saturday openings when customers have free time for shopping? But the retailer's dilemma is that his employees want to be off at the same times that other folks are.

By and large, retail sales more than held their own during 1953. Christmas buying was heavy. Retailers turned to new methods of store display and to at least one old method of stimulating sales: the 65-year-old trading stamp. By the end of 1953, at least 100,000 stores, supermarkets, and filling stations were offering stamps—usually one for every 10¢ purchase—as customer bait.

When a purchaser has accumulated a bookful of stamps, he turns it in for free merchandise—radios, household linens, desk sets, and the like. A book of 1200 stamps may be good for a bedspread, a four-piece saucepan set, or a set of highball glasses.

Oldest and largest trading-stamp system is that of Sperry & Hutchinson Company, whose familiar green stamps are doled out by 35,000 stores. S. & H. has 300 redemption stores, where customers exchange stamps for free merchandise. All in all, some 200 trading-stamp systems are in operation, of which twenty appeared during 1953.

One problem, however, is counterfeits. S. & H. found a flood of imitation stamps arriving for redemption. The spurious stuff was traced to a Pittsburgh barbershop, where operators were reselling the goods redeemed by their forged stamps. Now S. & H. green stamps are marked so that it is possible to determine where they are issued and almost the exact hour of sale.

**HAPPY WORD-MEN** who made Scrabble the parlor hit of 1953 — inventor Alfred Butts (left) and promoter James Brunot — play with outsize set

# Arts, Sciences, and Entertainment

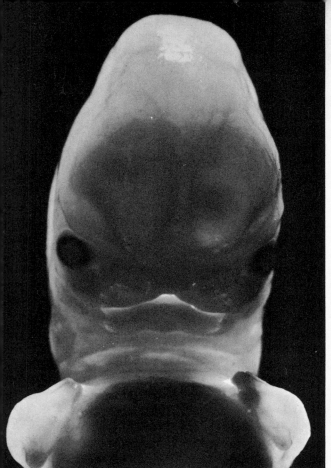

MAN remained science's No. 1 concern in 1953, a fact dramatized by these pictures of human embryo (left) and birth

# SCIENCE

In August of 1953 the average American awoke to the fact that he was living in the path of an impending avalanche. Soviet atomic scientists, just a year behind their American opposite numbers, had detonated a hydrogen bomb.

Premier Malenkov's triumphant announcement of the fact was confirmed three days later by the United States Atomic Energy Commission, whose scientists had analyzed samples of air wafted from the site of the explosion (probably in Siberia). In this air they found traces of uncommon isotopes, fragments of hydrogen fusion.

Scientists and civilian-defense officials

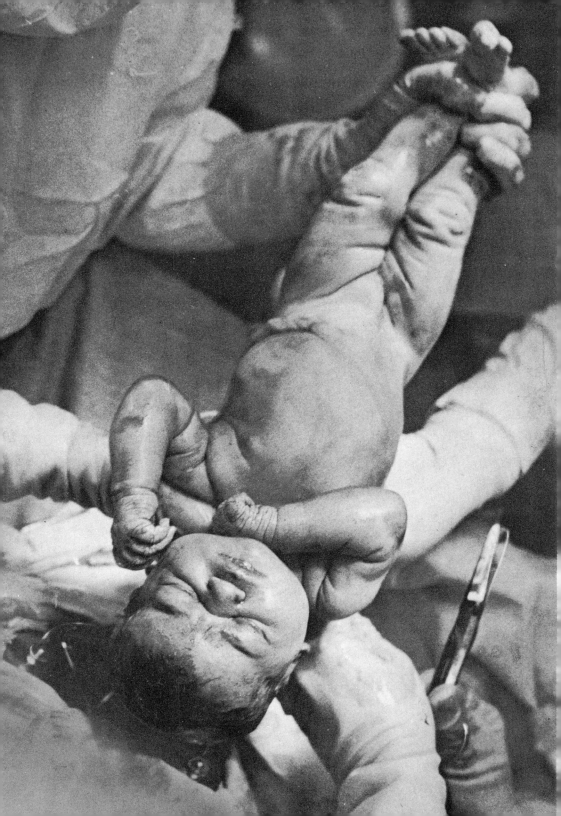

were virtually unanimous: The U.S. was in no way prepared to prevent or withstand an atomic onslaught.

Warned lean, graying Dr. J. Robert Oppenheimer, dean of U.S. atomic scientists: "The atomic clock ticks faster and faster."

Private industry was eying the atom with increasing concentration. University of Michigan food technologists had built a concrete cave in which they were sterilizing food with germ-killing rays from radioactive cobalt. The Monsanto and Dow Chemical companies were investigating the use of radioactivity to promote chemical reactions. And several power companies were studying atom-generated electricity. A consultant of the Detroit Edison Company estimated that within ten years industry could develop atomic power to compete with coal and oil.

At midyear the atom's economic prospects brightened overnight. The A.E.C. announced that its scientists at Arco, Idaho, had succeeding in "breeding" nuclear fuel. As ex-chairman Gordon Dean explained, in the breeder reactor each atom of uranium that fissions and yields its energy produces more than one atom of plutonium, another fissionable element. Thus, while such a reactor goes about its business of generating power, it simultaneously creates more fuel than it consumes. In any commercial venture, the breeder reactor could make all its own fuel, and the extra fissionable material could be sold to the government and written off against operating costs.

**Men of the Atom** Atomically speaking, the No. 1 human-interest story of 1953 concerned a stocky, smiling Greek named Nicholas Christofilos.

Back in 1950 he sent an application to the U.S. Patent Office from Athens, Greece. It outlined a scheme for vastly multiplying the power of atom smashers.

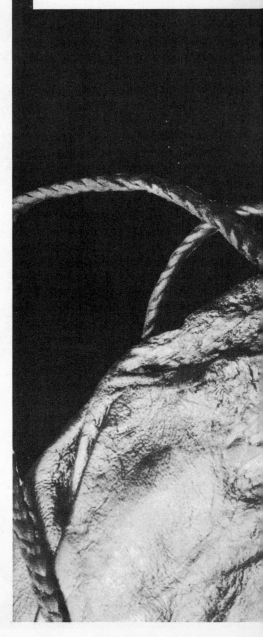

**2000 YEARS OLD,** this man became scientific "news" in 1953. Found in Tollund peat bog in Denmark, he apparently had been strangled as a religious sacrifice, then buried. Thereafter, bog preserved body almost intact

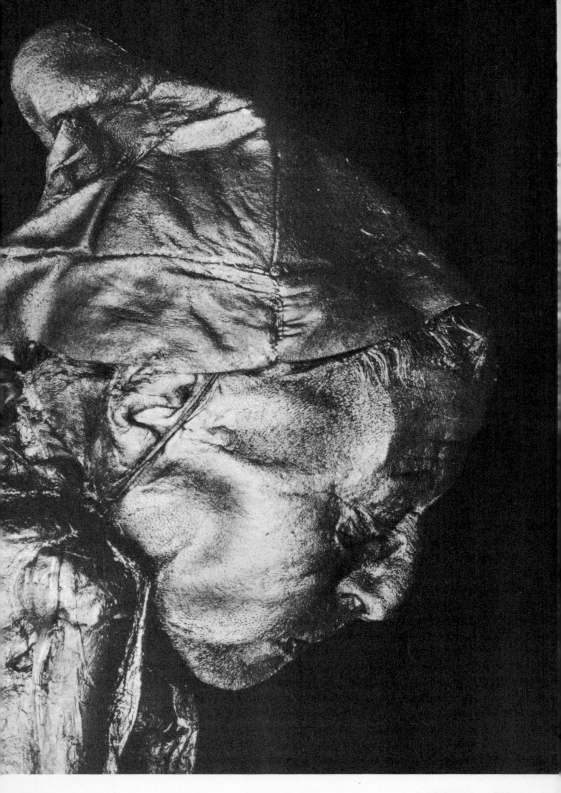

Ill-equipped to pass on the idea, the patent examiners forwarded it to the University of California Radiation Laboratory. Some of the world's most sophisticated scientists noted its original thinking but concluded that it was just the work of a well-meaning amateur. It ended up in a Patent Office pigeonhole.

Two years later, scientists at the Brookhaven National Laboratory developed a theoretical method for designing a 100,-000,000,000-volt atom smasher fifty times as powerful as Brookhaven's own fabulous cosmotron. When Christofilos read of their inspiration and recognized it as his own, he hurried to the United States. This, he told the A.E.C., was his idea. Oddly enough, he was right.

And who was Christofilos? Born in Boston, where his father ran a restaurant, he was taken to Greece at the age of seven. He studied electrical engineering, but when the Germans swarmed over Greece in World War II, he was ordered to become a truck mechanic.

Like most Greeks, Christofilos felt the full weight of the Nazi occupation. To take his mind off his troubles, he started reading books on physics, and, after Hiroshima, on atomics. It was heavy sledding, but he kept at it. When 1950 rolled around, this self-taught scientist proved he had learned his lessons well.

In 1953, with a shamefaced smile, the A.E.C. acknowledged Christofilos' abilities. When Brookhaven scientists admitted that he had, indeed, beaten them to their invention, the A.E.C. awarded him a bundle of cash for his patent rights —and a job at Brookhaven.

The post which dominates American atomic policies changed hands in 1953. After three years, Gordon E. Dean resigned as A.E.C. chairman and was succeeded by Rear Admiral Lewis L. Strauss. An investment banker and World War II Navy man, Strauss had been a member of the original Atomic Energy Commission appointed by President Truman in 1946. Clashing with fellow members, he had opposed sending radioactive materials to Norway and sharing atomic information with Britain. Some people felt his appointment as chairman indicated the U.S. was tending toward atomic isolation.

**Highbrow Science** Meanwhile, "pure" science had not been neglected. High above the level of most thought, scientific or otherwise, Dr. Albert Einstein was still groping for a super theory that would encompass all the forces of the universe. Perhaps he had found it in the universal-field equations which he published in 1950 and revised slightly in 1953.

The equations might be checked by physical experiments, but first would have to be simplified and interpreted. A few months after Einstein announced his revision, Dr. Vaclav Hlavaty, a Czech refugee teaching mathematics at Indiana University, tinkered with the enigmatic equations and came up with the conclusion that, if Einstein is right, everything is electromagnetism—that is to say, energy. Einstein has shown, in his theory of relativity, that matter is a form of energy, a fact dramatized by the atomic bomb. According to Hlavaty, gravitation is just part of the same package.

Again, at Stanford University a team of "pure science" physicists headed by Professor Robert Hofstadter began to scrutinize the atomic nucleus. Their tool was a sort of supermicroscope which fired a beam of electrons and focused the picture with a 2½-ton electromagnet. The scientists had expected that the heart of the atom would be uniformly solid, like a tiny marble. Instead, they found that the nucleus center is almost inconceivably heavy—130,000,000,000,000 (130 trillion) times as dense as water—whereas the surface thins down to a "cottony fluff".

**Gadgetry**  The world's fastest computing machine came into being in 1953. A $350,000 maze of wires, condensers, tubes, and other electronic bric-a-brac, it was named "Oracle" by its designers at the Argonne National Laboratory near Chicago. It started work at the Oak Ridge National Laboratory in Tennessee by multiplying 999,999,999,999 by 999,999,-999,999 in less than one twelve-hundredth of a second.

Of particular interest to tired motorists was a model automobile demonstrated by Dr. Vladimir K. Zworykin, the electronics wizard who developed the television tube for the Radio Corporation of America. In a low-ceilinged basement at the R.C.A. laboratories in Princeton, N.J., a little red car sped around an oval track of wires, swerving just in time to avoid a similar blue automobile parked in its path.

The trick was in the wires, which carried electronic impulses detectable by the car's steering mechanism. The signals guide the car and shunt it over another wire when the main track is blocked. Some day, Zworykin hopes, his experiment will serve as a model for superhighways on which a driver can read his morning newspaper, while wires buried in the concrete steer him more safely than he can steer himself.

**Above and Below**  Man keeps pushing upward into the air that envelops the earth, and downward into the seas that cover it. In 1953, records were set in both directions.

At Muroc Dry Lake, Calif., Lieutenant Colonel Marion E. Carl of the United States Air Force climbed to 83,235 feet—higher than anyone had ever flown before. His plane, a Douglas Skyrocket, was launched from a bomber at 33,500 feet, plummeted to 28,000 feet before its rockets caught fire, and then in three minutes zoomed to 75,000 feet. That flight ex-hausted his three tons of fuel. The final 8000 feet, Carl simply coasted.

In the Tyrrhenian Sea off southern Italy, Professor Auguste Piccard and his son Jacques dived more than 10,000 feet. It was quite a change for the aging (69) scientist, who, twenty-one years before, had established a balloon altitude record of 53,153 feet. This time his vehicle was a new "bathyscaphe", a steel sphere 8 feet in diameter with 3½-inch walls, suspended from a 60-foot-long cigar-shaped hull filled with gasoline.

Christened *Trieste,* the odd craft was started downward by flooding special compartments with sea water. Eventually it settled on the bottom "as if on a soft pad". The Piccards, peering out into darkness from a maze of instruments, took a few hundred feet of motion pictures and then jettisoned their iron ballast. Two hours and eighteen minutes after they had started, the *Trieste* bobbed to the surface. Whispered the elder Piccard: "It was very important, very lovely."

**A New Link**  For sheer patience, no fisherman ever rivaled ichthyologist James L. B. Smith of Rhodes University, South Africa. In 1938 a native caught a coelacanth (pronounced *see'-la-canth*), a hefty armored fish that supposedly became extinct 75,000,000 years ago. By the time Smith saw the "living fossil", it had rotted and only the thick scales and skeleton were left.

Excited by the thought that this fossil still swam the seas, Smith littered the southeast coast of Africa with pamphlets offering a reward of £100 for a fresh specimen. For fifteen years he had no luck. Then in January, 1953, the master of a small coastal ship cabled Smith that another coelacanth had been caught near Madagascar. Borrowing a plane from Prime Minister Malan, the ichthyologist rushed to the site of the catch.

There he found a bona fide coelacanth in fairly good shape. Native fishermen had damaged the brain in clubbing it to death, but the alert ship captain had preserved the rest with formaldehyde. The monster was five feet long, iridescent blue in color, with blue eyes and a clublike, triple-jointed tail. Its bulbous fins looked curiously like arms and legs.

Scientists agreed that Smith had filled an important gap in the evolutionary chain. The coelacanth is a direct descendant of the lobe-finned fishes, the first animals to leave the sea and try life on the land.

Out of gratitude, Smith named the species *Malania anjouanae* and presented Prime Minister Malan with a scale from his precious catch. Malan, a stanch orthodox minister of the Dutch Reformed Church, was dubious about the honor. His faith specifically denies the theory of evolution.

**Red Botanist Debunked** The greatest biologist in the Communist half of the world lost some of his luster. Trofim D. Lysenko, whose anti-Western genetics theories had become law for U.S.S.R. botanists, fell out of favor when Malenkov succeeded Stalin. Fellow Soviet scientists published articles that attacked Lysenko as a bigot and scientific monopolist. Then the Soviet Academy of Sciences charged that Lysenko had failed to make "contributions of practical value". This was a most serious accusation, since Lysenko had boasted that his brand of botany could breed oranges that would thrive in the Arctic, convert rye into wheat, and perform similar miracles.

Lysenko countered with perhaps the most unusual document of his strange career. He defended his research by claiming that Stalin himself had directed the experiments and interpreted the findings. Lysenko had proved again to Western scientists that Soviet biology is still strongly political.

On the lighter side, a California zoologist discovered in 1953 that desert rattlesnakes can't stand strong sunlight.

An Ohio bull got such a stubborn case of hiccups that despite care by Ohio State University veterinarians, it finally had to be slaughtered.

And a biologist at the University of California at Los Angeles reached the amazing conclusion that birds often sing simply because they are happy.

**Ancient Man Modern** An irreverent note was sounded at the staid old British Natural History Museum, where for forty years the skull of the so-called Piltdown man had been displayed as a unique anthropological trophy. Unearthed in a Sussex gravel pit, cranium fragments, teeth, and part of a jawbone had been painstakingly assembled by British specialists. Their owner was identified as some 500,000 years old, the earliest known true man.

Many scientists had reservations, however, about that jawbone. They felt it could not be so ancient, might indeed not even be human. Finally, Dr. Kenneth P. Oakley of the museum staff tried a new test on the skull, based on the fact that long-buried bones absorb fluorine from the soil: the more fluorine, the older the bone.

Last November, Dr. Oakley released his bombshell. The jawbone actually belongs to a modern ape, probably an orangutan, and looks old only because it had been expertly doctored with chemicals.

This discovery demoted Piltdown man —his cranium, at any rate—to a period perhaps 50,000 years ago. It did not explain who had faked the jawbone, nor why the hoax had been perpetrated. At year's end, red-faced museum officials still were looking for the answers.

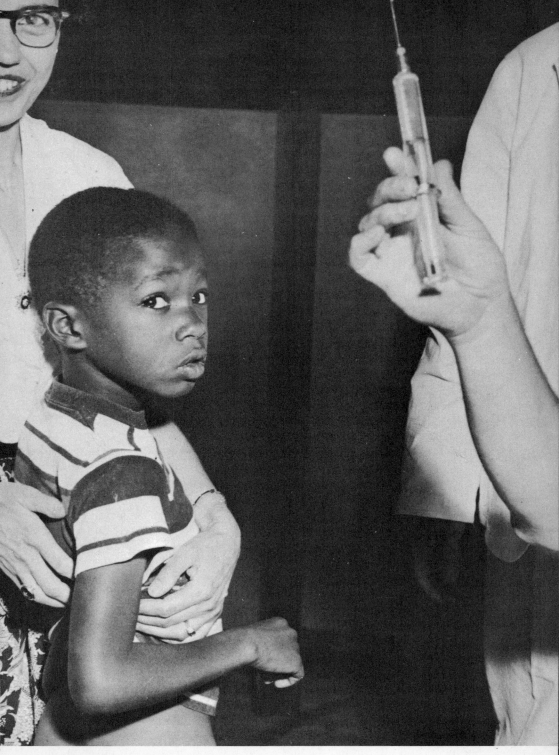

**IT WILL HURT** a little, but that big needle is basic to mass inoculation of children against polio

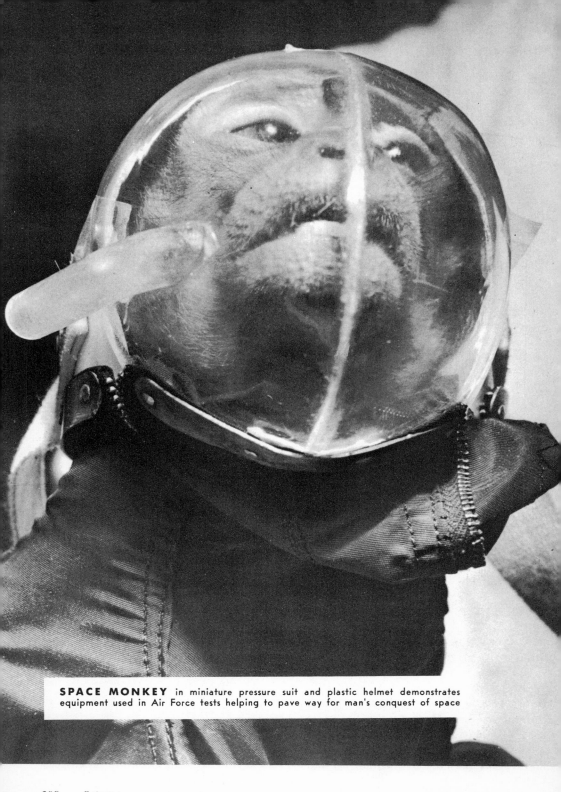

**SPACE MONKEY** in miniature pressure suit and plastic helmet demonstrates equipment used in Air Force tests helping to pave way for man's conquest of space

# Medicine

THE WOMAN WAS DRUNK, NO QUESTION
of that. She staggered as they brought
her in. Her lids kept drooping over her
bloodshot eyes, which she had trouble
focusing. Her slack lips loosed a string
of curses at the waiting doctor.

Then the hypodermic needle was
slipped in. It was as though a magic
wand had touched her. In three minutes
the woman was cold sober. Quietly she
apologized and walked out.

Such is the almost incredible effect of
vitamin B-6 pyridoxin, as reported last
year in the *British Medical Journal*. If not
1953's most important medical news, it
was perhaps the most dramatic. It did not
mean a cure for alcoholism, a disease
whose roots are as much psychological
as physiological. But it did offer a tool to
help halt the symptoms while the under-
lying condition is being treated.

Meanwhile, though it directly concerned far fewer people, research into
poliomyelitis attracted wider public notice. At last the dread crippler, object of
a fifteen-year, $18 million attack by the
National Foundation for Infantile Paralysis, seemed ready for the knockout blow.

Some progress had been made in 1952,
when mass tests of G.G. (gamma globu-
lin, a blood-plasma protein) seemed to
provide protection against polio for a five-
week period. In 1953, judicious use of
the scarce, expensive fluid undoubtedly
helped lower the total number of polio
cases. It also created a problem with
parents who wanted G.G. for their children.

Officially it was reserved for epidemic
areas or for individuals who had had direct contact with polio victims. But a
thriving G.G. black market sprang up on
the West Coast. Druggists charged as
much as $50 for one shot of an amber
fluid which in some cases was only tinted

**J. ROBERT OPPENHEIMER** headed World War II
Los Alamos project, helped create hydrogen bomb

gelatin. In New York City a score of embattled parents camped all night outside
the health commissioner's office, leaving
only when he robbed his slim stock of
enough G.G. for eighty children.

These developments pointed up the importance of the discovery, reported early
in the year, of the first really effective
antipolio vaccine. It was made by Dr.
Jonas E. Salk of the University of Pittsburgh, and came from live viruses, bred
in monkey kidneys. Salk inactivated the
viruses with formaldehyde to the point
where they no longer could cause disease
but still would inspire human blood to
generate polio-fighting antibodies.

His success with ninety patients cleared
the way for further experiment and, ultimately, mass production of his vaccine.
If further experiments proved equally
successful, man would then have the
weapon to lick polio—for keeps.

Cancer, on the other hand, was far from
licked. The causes and cures of most
forms remained mysteries. But in the
case of lung cancer, more and more doctors were pointing accusing fingers at

**CROSSED EYES** are uncrossed in this delicate operation on little Ana Martinez (left) of New York. Below: Muscle is cut for moving, resewing. Right: Surgery over, Ana's eyes begin to focus

the billion or more cigarettes Americans smoke each day. Some doctors thought it was no accident that as U.S. cigarette consumption rose (from 111,000,000,000 in 1933 to 433,000,000,000 in 1953), lung cancer, as a cause of death, was increasing faster than any other disease.

Then in November, 1953, came a resounding report which sent tobacco stocks tumbling and panicked both smokers and vendors. Dr. Evarts A. Graham of St. Louis said: "Dr. Ernest L. Wynder and I have reproduced cancer in mice by using merely the tars from tobacco smoke. This shows conclusively that there is something in cigarette smoke which can produce cancer. . . ."

Supporting evidence was contributed by Dr. Alton Ochsner, a New Orleans

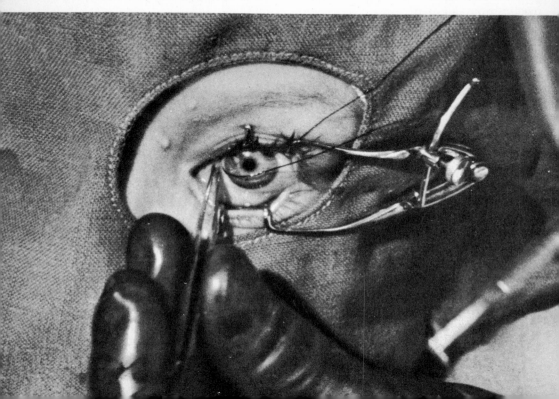

surgeon, most of whose patients had been men over forty who had been smoking heavily for years. Three National Cancer Institute researchers, reviewing 1990 cases of cancer of the mouth, throat, and lung, reported that regular cigarette smokers are four times as likely to get lung cancer as nonsmokers. In Britain, an elaborate study of lung cancer case histories had pointed to the same conclusion. And Danish physicians who had once judged cigarettes "not guilty" reversed their verdict.

The nonsmoking 47 percent of the adult population watched smugly as their smoking friends hung on fearfully to the one-to-three-packs-a-day habit of the average smoker. Even more fearful were the cigarette companies, whose advertisements had long made reassuring health claims.

The companies fought back, stepping up their campaigns to sell filter mouthpieces to a worried public. Puffs of cotton, wads of crepe paper, and chemical filters, advertisements stated, would screen impurities from the smoke. Finally, the companies, in full-page ads, announced that the cigarette industry would set up its own facilities for research into "tobacco use and health".

Meantime, there was a boom in the "how to stop smoking" business. Books and speakers on the subject, quick cures for the habit, and tobacco substitutes were in great demand.

Although Dr. Ochsner had gloomily predicted that "by 1970 one out of every ten or twelve men will have lung cancer", most veteran smokers kept on smoking. They remembered the hysteria in the '20's, when cigarettes were thought to cause tuberculosis, and their attitude about this latest tobacco scare was "wait and see".

**The Drug Parade** New drugs, and new uses for old ones, kept appearing in 1953.

One of the most exciting of the new ones was a chemical kin of a discarded poison. Called actinomycin, it was an early discovery of Dr. Selman A. Waksman of Rutgers University (who later won the Nobel Prize for his part in the discovery of streptomycin). On learning that one pinch of actinomycin would kill a man, Waksman destroyed all but a tiny sample and stuck that away in his desk.

Then a German biochemist, Professor Gerhard Domagk, began to re-tread Waksman's path. He probed through fungus cultures until he had isolated a new version of actinomycin, which he called actinomycin C. In 1953 he announced that his variation not only was nontoxic, but that it seemed to benefit patients who had cancer of the lymph glands.

Another unexpected dividend of research was the discovery by two California doctors that typhoid vaccine seems to be the best treatment for encephalitis, a brain infection. Just why remained to be seen. But it cured fifty patients who developed the infection after bouts with measles.

New drugs assaulted commoner ailments, too. Dr. William S. Hoffman of Chicago found that Probenecid eased the aching of gout. And Chlorpromazine, a drug that halts nausea and vomiting, was put on the market.

But for the commonest ailment of all, grandma's cold remedy still was best. At least that was the conclusion of Drs. Howard Traisman and Martin Hardy of Children's Memorial Hospital, Chicago. They rounded up 160 sniffling children. Some got a sulfa drug; others, antibiotics. But fifty-five were put to bed and given only aspirin. And that group recovered faster and with fewest complications.

**Fertility** In medical as well as journalistic circles sex was violently discussed in 1953 when Dr. Alfred C. Kinsey published his long-awaited study of the sex habits of the American female. The 850-page tome, at $8 per copy, quickly became a best seller.

The 5940 females who "told all" to Dr. Kinsey were from two to ninety years old, but critics said they were not representative of U.S. women. Three quarters of them had gone to college, most came from the Northeast, and the majority were Protestants. Some scientists ridiculed Kinsey's methods, but all that most people cared about were his more provocative findings. Some were as follows.

1) Almost half of the U.S. women have sexual intercourse before marriage, and one of every four wives has extramarital relations. The more educated the wife, the greater her infidelity (31 percent of college-goers, 24 percent of high-school graduates were unfaithful).

2) As a group, American women are not frigid. Their enjoyment of sex reaches a peak in their late 20's and is maintained for twenty or thirty years.

3) Almost every woman, before she reaches the age of eighteen, has some sort of sexual experience—necking, petting, or intercourse.

4) One fourth of the unmarried women have had homosexual relationships.

The search for an ideal birth-control method continued throughout the year and was illuminated by at least one gleam of success. Dr. Clarence Gamble of Milton, Mass., learned that common table salt effectively kills sperm cells. So he experimented with salt incorporated in a variety of jellies, and finally decided that the cheapest jelly could be made by boiling rice flour. Birth-control advocates in India and Japan, where both rice and babies abound, were immediately interested.

On the other hand, Dr. Raymond G. Cross of Dublin, Ireland, had some tips for men who want to raise families. Eating bananas, celery, garlic, honey, onions, and parsley will increase fertility, he advised. He also recommended discarding trousers and tight-fitting underwear, and switching to kilts.

**Dentistry** Tooth decay remained unconquered in 1953. Ammoniated dentifrices, once hailed as the solution to dental caries, were taken down another peg. Dr. B. G. Bibby of Rochester, N.Y., and Lieutenant R. R. Hawes, an Air Force dentist, completed a study of 400 children and concluded: "There is no satisfactory evidence, notwithstanding advertising claims, that a dentifrice with a high urea [ammonia] content reduces dental decay."

Late in the year another "miracle" dentifrice ingredient hit the market. Anti-enzyme was its name, and it was intended to neutralize the chemical action of bacteria on teeth. The American Dental Association was far from convinced. Its journal warned editorially: "Hope always prevails that someday, somehow, someone will discover a true preventive for dental caries. . . . Dentists, of course, will wisely withhold judgment of the product until scientific evidence proves its worth or worthlessness. It is hoped that the intelligent consumer will do likewise."

Meanwhile, a California orthodontist saw a new threat to dental health. He feared that children, lying on their stomachs and watching television with their chins propped on their cupped hands, would grow up with malformed jaws.

**Operations**  Everybody talks about his operation, and in 1953 there were several operations that everybody was talking about.

British Foreign Secretary Anthony Eden crossed the Atlantic to have a bile duct repaired by Dr. Richard Cattell of Lahey Clinic, Boston. During or after an earlier operation for the removal of gallstones, the outlet from the gall bladder had become blocked. As a result, bile was backing up into the blood stream and causing jaundice. Rebuilding the closed duct was a ticklish job in which Cattell specialized. So, though British papers protested the "insult" to British surgery, Eden flew to Boston for a wholly successful operation.

At Jefferson Hospital, Philadelphia, an 18-year-old college freshman, Cecelia Bavolek, made history. While her blood was detoured through a machine that served as both heart and lungs, Dr. John H. Gibbon Jr. performed a delicate operation to plug a leak in her heart. The machine, which was Dr. Gibbon's own invention, had never been used before on a human being, although he had tested it while operating on dogs.

Another historic operation also took place in Philadelphia. A 29-year-old waitress, blond Irma Miller, got a new set of thyroid and parathyroid glands after her own had been surgically removed.

Miss Miller's surgeon, Dr. Julian Sterling, knew that transplanted glands almost never take hold. But he reasoned that the operation would have a chance of success if only he could find a donor young enough. When a baby was born so misshapen that it could not hope to survive, its parents agreed that its glands should be given to Miss Miller. Four days later the infant died, and Sterling made the switch. The swift-growing, almost embryonic tissues took hold firmly.

The most astounding surgery of 1953 was performed by an amateur, a young Mississippi mechanic named Carl Cree. His automobile turned over, smashing his left arm and trapping it against the pavement. Afraid the car would catch fire, he pulled out a pocket knife and sawed off his own arm. Then he walked a mile to the nearest farmhouse and borrowed a towel for a tourniquet.

Yet in all 1953 perhaps no medical story topped the heart tug of the operation on Carolyn Anne and Catherine Ann Mouton of New Orleans. The two little girls, just two months old, had been born Siamese twins, joined awkwardly at the base of their spines. Medical history recorded no case in which twins so joined had been successfully cut apart. But surgeons at Ochsner Foundation Hospital decided to try.

For 135 minutes a team of eight doctors worked to sever the connection at the base of the spine and to reconstruct individual lower intestines for the girls. The operation succeeded. Then for the first time in their brief lives, Carolyn Anne and Catherine Anne slept in separate cribs.

# Music and The Dance

INTERNATIONALISM HAS ALL SORTS OF ASpects. In 1953 one of them was the music of that jiviest of jive men, Lionel Hampton. With his vibraharp, which he calls his "woodpile", and with his band, which he calls "my twenty-three boys", he set out from New York in early fall for a four-week tour of Europe.

The tour took fifteen weeks. Before he got home the Hamp had knocked them dead in such strange spots for bebop as Brussels, Zurich, Casablanca, Hamburg, and Oslo.

"Played one house in Copenhagen, held twelve thousand people, and we're sittin' and playin' and all of a sudden the spirit hits them and they're up and jumpin' and dancin', the whole twelve thou-

sand!" Hampton proclaimed. "They went gaga over us. They was all the time presentin' us with flowers."

Hamp and his bandsmen played eighty-seven concerts, and to judge from accounts in European newspapers, they could have played eighty-seven more, or ten times eighty-seven, before any European bopophile would cry out for mercy, or for quiet.

On the home front there were other noises. Toward the end of the year a slight and fair-haired child named Gayla Peevey, from Oklahoma City, turned up in New York with her mother and a song called "I Want a Hippopotamus for Christmas".

Mother stood by devotedly while Gayla, who is in her tenth year and her fifth grade, sang for her hippo for Columbia Records, Inc. The song sold about 400,-000 records, and Gayla pocketed close to 4¢ from each sale. For her, if not for those who prefer carols at that time of year, it was a merry and most profitable Christmas.

Ten months before Gayla's shining hour, a musical comedy called *Wonderful Town* opened on Broadway. It was a song-and-dance distillation of several works by Ruth McKenney, all of which had appeared under the title *My Sister Eileen*: short stories, book, play, and movie script.

**HUSH BEFORE SOUND** heightens the anticipation of his studio audience as conductor Dimitri Mitropoulos signals for the start of a rehearsal performance

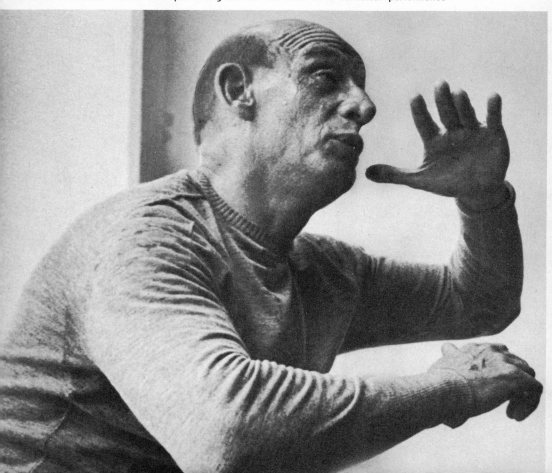

**ACTION WITHOUT WORDS** nears its dramatic peak as dancer John Franklin leaps high in the ballet "A Streetcar Named Desire"

**COMPOSER** Igor Stravinsky considers his opera, "The Rake's Progress", after premiere at Met

Versatile Leonard Bernstein wrote the music, Betty Comden and Adolph Green pieced the lyrics together, and Rosalind Russell, of Hollywood, supported by a cast without an incompetent in it, did the singing and dancing. New York critics told their readers that Broadway had a great big hit musical.

Some of the best music during 1953 was played at the Berkshire Festival at Lenox, Mass., where, in the summer months of July and August, the East Coast's music lovers—and tourists who want cultural trimmings with their travels—settle down to hear the Boston Symphony Orchestra at work.

There *Wonderful Town*'s Leonard Bernstein set about demonstrating that show tunes are among the least of his attainments. At the Berkshire Music Center, the educational adjunct of the festival, Bernstein taught orchestral conducting, and on a few nights during the summer he stood before the orchestra (which is in summer residence at the center) and proved he knows what he is teaching. In the summer of 1953 his best night's work came in early August when he conducted a memorial concert in memory of Serge Koussevitzky, the late, famed conductor of the Boston orchestra and the center's founder.

Bernstein is a young man, 36, with big talents and prodigious energy. After graduating from Harvard, where he studied music, he became a rehearsal pianist in New York and studied conducting on the side. His studies led to the job of assistant conductor of the New York Philharmonic Symphony Orchestra, and one afternoon when the regular conductor, Bruno Walter, was unable to work, Bernstein took over and did a magnificent job.

Between piano playing and conducting, he had worked at composing the score for a ballet called "Fancy Free", and songs for a musical comedy, *On the Town*. Both were hits. Bernstein could not make up his mind whether to give up podium and piano work or to become a composer.

He came to no decision. Since then he has written two symphonies, a few ballet scores, some song cycles, incidental theater music, and an opera called *Trouble in Tahiti*. He has also conducted just about every major symphony orchestra, not only in the United States but all over the world, and he has even conducted some of them while playing the piano concertos of Mozart, Beethoven, and Ravel.

His friends feel that he has spread himself too thin. Bernstein agrees. What he has done about it is to become a professor at Brandeis University in Boston, and producer-director of that institution's Festival of the Creative Arts.

The year 1953 will be remembered by many as the last year of life for brilliant young American pianist William Kapell, 31, and the towering Russian composer Sergei Prokofiev, 61. Critics the world over saw in Kapell, who was killed in the crash of an air liner, a masterful pianist who played crystalline Mozart, pure and precise Bach, and deeply lyric Brahms.

"He was winning, and would have gone on winning," Virgil Thomson of the *New York Herald-Tribune* wrote, "for he had a star."

Prokofiev had already won, especially the hearts of children. His "Peter and the Wolf", a musical tale of matchless charm,

**BELLY DANCER** Nedjla Ates (Turkish) shows form that led U.S. playboy Sheppard King 3d to seek divorce from belly dancer Samia Gamal (Egyptian)

has been an all-American favorite since shortly after it was introduced in Moscow in 1936. Seven symphonies and an array of operas, chamber works, cantatas, and movie scores were among his generous bequest to the world of music. A cerebral hemorrhage struck him down a few months after the American premiere of his Seventh symphony.

One of the most unstylized composing talents of the era is within Igor Stravinsky. In the spring of 1953 the Metropolitan Opera Company presented the American premiere of his opera *The Rake's Progress*. Critics did not turn from *The Rake*, but neither did they lavish praise on it.

Fritz Reiner, who later became permanent conductor of Chicago's symphony orchestra, was the conductor in the pit the afternoon *The Rake* opened, while Stravinsky drifted through the audience sampling the acoustics and public opinion.

But when it was time to put *The Rake* on records, it was not Reiner but Stravinsky who conducted. A reporter at the recording session asked the composer about the difficulties of reproducing the sound of the human voice on tape and records. "The human voice," Stravinsky told him after brooding for a while, "it is perfect on the telephone." His wasn't the last word. One of the singers in the opera's chorus had an opinion too. "Mr. Stravinsky's music," he volunteered after going through *The Rake* three times, "it is perfect for trombones."

## Top Pop Tunes

Money makes the music business go up, down, and around at the popular level, and a magazine with a spectacularly apt name—*The Cash Box*—each December publishes a list of the year's top pop music and musicians. The word "best", to *The Cash Box* and its adherents, means "probably made the most money" for jukebox owners.

The poll for 1953 revealed the following: the theme song from the movie *Moulin Rouge,* recorded by band leader Percy Faith, and "Till I Waltz Again with You", sung by Teresa Brewer, were the two best records.

Newcomer Joni James, ex-Pfc. Eddie Fisher, and ex-barber Perry Como were the three best vocalists. The best small instrumental group was Les Paul and Mary Ford, his wife, who contentedly sings and strums her guitar while he whacks his and superintends a battery of mikes and amplifiers. Their record titled "Vaya con Dios" was top seller during the year. When the sale topped 2,-000,000 disks, the recording company gave the couple a platinum recording of their work. In late December, song and sale were still going fairly strong.

But, according to *The Cash Box*, the most promising new female vocalist was the diminutive but earthy and beautiful Eartha Kitt. Eartha, a Negro from South Carolina, had spent most of her singing career in Europe, and much of her time declining offers of palaces from princes. She had gone there to dance with Katherine Dunham's troupe, but stayed on to sing in the Left Bank cabarets of Paris. Orson Welles worked her into his Paris production of *Faust.* Then Producer Leonard Sillman, a shrewd gambler with show talent, saw her onstage and induced her to come home for his revue *New Faces of 1952.*

The revue was good for more than a year, and in 1953 it advertised itself simply as *New Faces.* It still featured Miss Kitt's insinuating solo, "Monotonous", which, with monotonous regularity, drew an audience response that stopped the show until she had sung it again, and sometimes again.

In Los Angeles she sang two offbeat ditties—"Santa Baby" and "I Want to Be Evil"—for visiting King Paul and Queen Frederika of Greece. The mayor of Los Angeles deemed her songs not only offbeat but off-color, and said so. But the royal couple seemed to admire Eartha's earthiness. "We thought it was lovely," the Queen said.

Eartha couldn't understand the fuss. "I didn't think it was possible to shock politicians," she said. The mayor was not appeased. "The King and Queen," he said, "must wonder what kind of yo-yo heads we have in Los Angeles."

Meanwhile, other musical headliners were active in unexpected fields.

Frank Sinatra, who did not have a best-selling record all year, won acclaim for his acting in the movie *From Here to Eternity*. Rosemary Clooney, the Kentucky girl who, in semi-Armenian accents, entreated strangers to come on-a her house a year ago, dropped her dialects and concentrated on being a movie star, after marrying actor José Ferrer. Vaughn Monroe divested himself of his bandsmen and took to making radio shows and personal appearances in front of the Sauter Finegan band, an assortment of musicians who contrive sounds from a wide, wild, and un-dance-band-like assortment of instruments including recorders, violas, toy whistles, and tympani.

And there was Liberace, gentle-voiced and gentle-mannered, who, flanked by lighted candles, played a piano lavishly and winked into television cameras. When Liberace winked, impressionable ladies throughout the country presumably winked back.

Eye appeal has its place in music, as Liberace proved. Some years ago, the book-publishing business began snaring buyers by adorning jackets with a touch of voluptuousness, and editing titles to match. In 1953 this device spilled over into records. The ladies on the record jackets often wear little, and their relation to the music within is sometimes obscure. "Music for Dreaming", "Music for the Fireside", "Melodies for a Sentimental Mood", "Music by Starlight", and "Beautiful Music to Love By" were some of the titles thus merchandised. The albums, usually amorphous mélanges of "mood music", threatened to tap a whole new audience: one that buys its music by sight rather than sound.

Yet the "sight buyers" helped provide the profits that enabled record companies to offer distinguished performances of music's masterworks.

## Classical Recordings

Hundreds of excellent records were released in 1953. Among them were Ravel's "L'Heure Espagnole", sung by the Opera Comique of Paris under André Cluytens; the nine symphonies of Beethoven played by the N.B.C. Symphony Orchestra under Arturo Toscanini; and Verdi's *Otello* in a recorded transcription of a radio performance aired five years ago, with Ramon Vinay, Giuseppe Valdengo, and Herva Nelli in the vocal roles and with the N.B.C. Symphony Orchestra, again under Toscanini.

The Bach "Unaccompanied Sonatas and Partitas" were recorded by violinist Jascha Heifetz, who some months before was clubbed by an Israeli fanatic who objected to the violinist's performance of a Richard Strauss sonata in Jerusalem. Strauss was once president of the Nazi Kulturkammer (academy of arts), and in Israel that is not forgotten easily.

Bach's long, sublime *St. Matthew Passion* was made available in three recorded performances (by Westminster, Vox, Columbia). The Westminster set, made by the Vienna State Opera Orches-

**GERMAN PIANIST** Walter Gieseking looks up from keys during concert in Carnegie Hall

**GERMAN JITTERBUGS**
catch up with U.S. dance style.
Berliners call it "boogi-woogi"

tra and the Akademiechor and soloists conducted by Herman Scherchen, was generally considered superior to the other two.

Those were the year's musical heavyweights on records, but a set of wonderfully assorted songs sung on a television show by Mary Martin and Ethel Merman and transcribed to records may have outsold all of them. "I Get a Kick Out of You", "I Got Rhythm", "My Heart Belongs to Daddy", and "There's No Business Like Show Business" were among the medley of thirty poured out by the two fabled ladies of the musical-comedy stage.

Dancers flitted around and aloft in some new and many established attitudes during 1953. The New York City Ballet trekked about Europe after a transcontinental tour at home. In Milan, Italy, there was fighting in the streets for standing room to see the troupe, and the management at La Scala—where they danced—pressed them for an annual three-month engagement.

At their home base of operations, the cavernous City Center of Music and Drama in midtown Manhattan, the dancers and their artistic director, 50-year-old George Balanchine, are among the finer showpieces of the town's show business.

Ballet, as an art form, has been in transition in the United States for at least ten years. Only recently has it shown signs of settling down into a style of its own. The style is as lean and severe as the best of the dancers, and the staging of most of the ballets is as swift and adroit as a World Series double play.

Russian classical ballet, which dominated U.S. ballet fashions until Balanchine (born in Russia, but a renegade in dance styling) took over, has its fine moments of motion but it spreads them out, and the in-between is filled with static pageantry. Balanchine thinks pageantry has its place, but never lets it become static. He urges scenic designers to keep the stage clear of props because he feels that the customers have come to see flying bodies, not furniture.

Television began to do well with dancers during the year. Ray Bolger started a series in which he disported himself entertainingly in one way or another between dance routines. Maria Tallchief, the best serious dancer in the country and prima ballerina of the New York City Ballet, made a number of appearances. One of them, however, was remarkable in that it kept her dancing almost entirely out of camera range.

TV presents new problems to choreographers. When the camera is close to a single dancer, the viewer in his home can see as well as the ballet-goer in the theater's best seat. But when the camera widens out its focus to take in a line of whirling dancers, the scenery behind them, and possibly the soloists in front of them, the viewer in his home is peering at a blur of pygmies. Critics agreed that would not do, and TV's choreographers have been trying to do something about it.

Jeanmaire, the trim French dancer, pranced through an authentic cancan on Ed Sullivan's "Toast of the Town". A few weeks later, that same unsmiling master of ceremonies introduced to the country a pair of Moscow-trained Hungarians named Nora Kavach and Istavan Rabovsky. The two seemed to have a dispensation from the laws of gravity. They would leap into the air and not descend until long after they were expected to.

Fred Astaire, in the old movie *Top Hat,* danced with Ginger Rogers—which was as it should be. On a different lot, a girl named Jane Russell danced in a movie called *Gentlemen Prefer Blondes.* There was another girl with her, some girl called Marilyn Monroe. Some girl.

**ON HOLLYWOOD SET** petite dancer Leslie Caron shows lithe grace during rehearsal routine

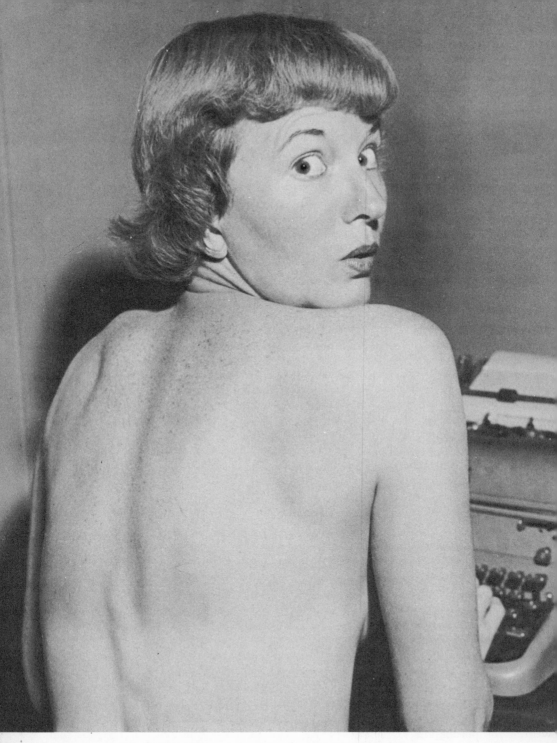

**DEVOTED TO DUTY,** U.P. correspondent Aline Mosby, following local rules, uncovers herself to cover California convention of the American Sunbathing Association

# PRESS

THE THREE-LETTER WORD "SEX" PROVIDED the hottest news story of 1953. Editors knew that the report on female sex behavior on which Dr. Alfred C. Kinsey of Indiana University had been working since 1947 would be sure-fire reading fare. In their eagerness to get at it, they began running "previews" (guesses) as early as 1950.

By the time 1953 rolled around, Kinsey was wary. Some 160 "newsmen" had written for permission to see proofs of the study ahead of public release. In his air-conditioned basement office on the Indiana campus, Kinsey and his colleagues limited this group to representatives of forty-seven publications and wire services. Each writer would come for a thorough briefing. Then, bound to secrecy by a three-page contract, he was permitted to read and take notes on the galley proofs.

When the K-bomb exploded on Aug. 20, the U.S. press ran amuck. Though the same day brought the news that Soviet Russia had exploded an H-bomb, that dread event was blown right off most top page 1 spots by the Kinsey report. "Big-

**LIFE AND DEATH:** in notable examples of 1953 press photography, a New York patrolman saves a would-be suicide (left), and another New Yorker, apparently deranged, falls from fifth-floor roof where he ran after killing his wife

**KEEPING COOLER** than he might like, this San Franciscan wrestles with trousers—and amuses news readers—after a fire broke out in his hotel

gest news prominence ever to greet a new book," said the Associated Press.

From front-page banner headlines, the story bounced along to back-page follow-ups in which scurrying reporters got the comments of every available savant or citizen.

Many took exception to the report on scientific or moral grounds, but that did not stop the editors: the public was eating it up.

Some papers, however, believing the report might offend readers, played it down. Said the *Fort Wayne News-Senti-*

*nel:* "If interested, buy the book. . . . About sex, this newspaper has two convictions: God designed it, and it is here to stay."

Sex also brought front pages to lurid life in February, when playboy Mickey Jelke went on trial in New York on prostitution charges. The young oleo heir (who was given a three-to-six-year sentence), the glossy young ladies, and the prominent male names in the case added up to a newspaper "natural", even to the Communist *Daily Worker*. CAPITALIST MORALITY IS DEFENDANT AT THE JELKE PROSTITUTION TRIAL, its headline pontificated.

Just as the press was winding up for all-out coverage, however, the presiding judge shut the courtroom doors. His thought was that children should be spared the sordid details. Newspaper and wire services howled, but the ruling stood.

The reporters did not. They ran. Each day, as testimony ended, they stampeded through the courthouse corridors seeking anyone—lawyers, courtroom attachés, witnesses—who might have heard the day's proceedings. Women reporters even trapped female witnesses in the washrooms. The result was a fairly complete account of the trial—second hand.

More journalistic razzle-dazzle came in September, on an international scale, when headline writers played with the hottest rumor of the year. Lavrenti Beria, deposed head of the dreaded Soviet secret police, was "reported" to have "possibly", "maybe", "conceivably" escaped from the Soviet Union and to be seeking political asylum in the U.S.

On Saturday, Sept. 19, an A.P. reporter, nosing around for week-end news in Washington, picked up word that officialdom was agog over Beria's reported escape. The reporter wrote a cautious story, stressing the hearsay nature of his news.

Three thousand miles away, the A.P. wire caused a sensation. For several weeks the *San Diego Union* had been tracking down the same story. Reporter Gene Fuson had picked up a Beria lead while investigating Communism in Latin America. A man who said he represented Beria had come to Fuson. The idea, apparently, was to work out a deal guaranteeing Beria safety in America. Fuson turned it over to government intelligence officers.

When the A.P. broke its tip, the *Union* opened up. In a copyrighted story, it took credit for the major role in the Beria case.

New York's mammoth tabloid, the *Daily News,* got into the act. Editor R. W. Clarke had heard a Beria rumor and had passed it on to columnist Ed Sullivan, who printed it on July 30. Now Clarke sent one of his best Washington reporters,

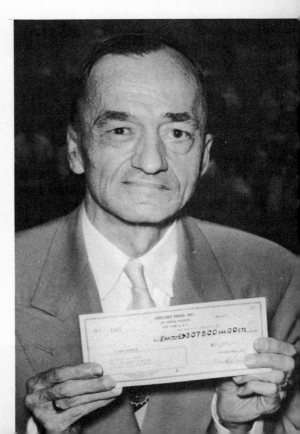

**BIGGEST PAYOFF** in any puzzle contest, $307,500 awarded by Unicorn Press, is displayed by winner, Chicago civil engineer Herbert J. Idle

**LUCKY SURVIVORS** of an Army plane crash appear in this amateur-made news photo. Scene: Louisville, Ky., where a chartered C-46 carrying 38 G.I.'s fell from 200 feet up, killing 24

For a while, similar lack of corroborative detail bid fair to kill off an even bigger story. That was in March, when, at 12:15 E.S.T. on a Wednesday morning, Radio Moscow crackled with electrifying news: Joseph Stalin was ill and near death.

Radio monitors in London got the first word. Within minutes, American wire services had it. Soon their London offices were bombarding the handful of American correspondents in Moscow. But censorship was rapidly in force. All the newsmen could do was to repeat the meager news that Radio Moscow had issued.

Editors sweated to keep the story alive. The *New York Journal-American,* for example, made it STALIN'S CONDITION INCREASINGLY GRAVE, and then, a few hours later, STALIN'S CONDITION STEADILY GETS WORSE.

A flood of articles sought to forecast the immediate future. On page 7 of one edition of the *New York World-Telegram and Sun* appeared a heading: "Heir to Stalin May Need War to Hold Power." On page 8, another story was headed: "Kremlin's New Rulers Need Peace to Solve Problems."

Then, Thursday night, technicians monitoring Radio Moscow for the Agence France Presse in Paris heard a startling sound: the tolling of bells in the Kremlin. Immediately the French wire service flashed the word to a waiting world. Stalin was dead.

A daily paper in Mexico City heralded the news with the shortest headline possible: YA (finally).

Meanwhile the press of the free world was concerned over William Oatis, ex-chief of the A.P. bureau in Prague,

Jerry Greene, to check with Senator McCarthy's investigating committee (where the leak apparently had originated).

Getting nothing there, Greene went to a free-lance specialist in Iron Curtain intelligence work, an ex-O.S.S. colonel named Amoss, who vowed that a man who *might* be Beria *was* in hiding and dickering for asylum. Top-level consideration was being given the deal, Amoss indicated, and Greene printed that in the *News.*

Then, as reporters hammered at the doors of government offices, the facts began to trickle out. Sure enough, there had been reports of persons purporting to represent Beria. Most officials, however, were skeptical. Thereafter the big rumor of 1953 died of malnutrition. A few months later, it was buried when Moscow officially announced that Beria had been executed for treason.

Czechoslovakia. The shy young reporter had got into serious trouble because of his habit of keeping notes on stories. He went about his job in Prague as though he were still back home in Indiana. When he was curious about military plans or maneuvers, he asked questions. For his pains he was arrested and charged with espionage. After a mock trial, at which the brain-washed Oatis numbly echoed the charges made against him, he was sentenced to ten years in prison.

For two years the Western press fought in Bill Oatis' behalf, but his captors would not soften the sentence. Finally, on May 16, 1953, a short item in *Pravda*, official Communist party newspaper in Moscow, reported that Oatis had been pardoned.

The reason was said to be a moving letter Mrs. Oatis had written asking for her husband's freedom. Most observers, however, felt that the release was an attempt to relieve American trade restrictions imposed against the Czechs because of Oatis' imprisonment.

As soon as Oatis was escorted across the German border, newsmen rushed to interview him. Strangely, he had little to say. He did not protest against his trial or imprisonment. The Czechs, he said, had not mistreated him. There was even "justification" for his sentence. "In that country," he said, "certain standards of journalism could amount to espionage."

His version of the case had to wait while he spent months poring over records of his trial, and recovering the health that an attack of tuberculosis had sapped from him in prison. Finally, in September, the A.P. released his story. Quietly, Oatis told of his trials and tribulations. The Czechs, he said, had led him to believe

**AMATEUR SHOT** that won $500 prize in New York newspaper contest depicts a "gag" situation: a modern William Tell, an arrow badly aimed, an apple still unhit

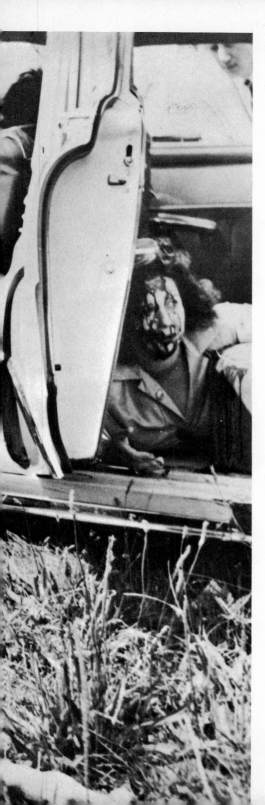

that his reporting had involved slight technical violations of security laws. Probably a legal slap on the wrist would follow.

By the time he realized that he had been misled, it was too late. Automatically, often after sleepless nights of questioning, he had signed a drawerful of confessions. He didn't even know the gist of some.

At the end of his story, he set down chilling words: "Living in [the Red prison] is like being buried alive. The inmate there is like a man in Purgatory. . . . He is waiting, and his problem is to get through time."

Other newsmen, too, left a sort of Red confinement when Russian officials finally agreed to let two American correspondents in Moscow return to America, accompanied by their Russian wives. Until then, if the husbands had left, the wives would have been held. The West concluded that both the Prague and Moscow releases were part of a Soviet peace offensive. Only the Red Chinese kept aloof from such gestures, still holding captive two American reporters picked up as they sailed a boat from Tokyo to Hong Kong.

During 1953, Communist newspapers had trouble holding readers. In Paris, *Ce Soir*—once France's largest daily, with a circulation of 620,000—ceased publication after its readership dropped to 80,000. In East Berlin, three more Communist papers suspended. A Communist Bulgarian journal ran a cartoon showing a railway station piled high with undelivered Red publications.

To U.S. newspapers, the year's No. 1 headache was the relationship between President Eisenhower and the press.

**THE CAMERA LIES** in this striking news photo of New Jersey crackup. The whole scene—wrecked car, bloody bodies, child sobbing for his family—spells fatality. Yet no one was killed

When President Truman had begun to spat with reporters, the presidential press conferences had changed from a simple source of information to a testing ground where newsmen struggled to learn more than they were told.

President Eisenhower had assured reporters that he would stick to his predecessor's once-a-week schedule of news conferences. Instead, his average was one a month. And he walked into a squabble with the press such as Harry Truman used to have.

The fight blazed up in October when newsmen tried to learn who would fill the vacancy left by the death of Chief Justice Vinson.

Attorney General Herbert Brownell told regular reporters he knew nothing. Then, quietly, he called in top representatives of five papers which had been most influential in their support of Eisenhower for President, and told them Earl Warren would get the job. They printed it without revealing the source.

Next day, when Eisenhower confirmed the leak at a regular press conference, reporters were angry. Would the President, they irately demanded, continue to favor certain friendly papers over the rest of the American press? Just as irately, Eisenhower said that if his trusted subordinates wanted to do just that, they had his blessing.

Next to Eisenhower, the hottest figure in Washington, journalistically, was the junior Senator from Wisconsin, Joseph R. McCarthy. Particularly memorable was his joust with editor James A. Wechsler of the *New York Post*. Out of the blue, while investigating Communist-line books in U.S. propaganda libraries overseas, McCarthy called Wechsler, one of his outspoken critics, to appear for questioning.

McCarthy said he simply wanted to ask Wechsler about things the editor had written during a brief, collegiate membership in the Young Communist League. Wechsler's version was that he was being harassed in retaliation for his paper's constant criticism of the Senator. He asked the American Society of Newspaper Editors (A.S.N.E.) to investigate the investigator.

The A.S.N.E. appointed a committee of editors to look into Wechsler's charges, but its conclusions were inconclusive. Had freedom of the press been endangered by the McCarthy action? A minority said "yes". The majority, expressing varying degrees of criticism of McCarthy himself, said they felt that it was a personal fight.

The year's top personnel shift came in Washington, at the bureau of the *New York Times*. The widely respected senior pundit of the Washington press corps, Arthur Krock, resigned as the bureau's chief. James ("Scotty") Reston, a *Times* correspondent already rivaling Krock in stature, took his place.

The former President, Harry Truman, signed up for the year's top writing assignment. For upwards of half a million dollars, he agreed to write his memoirs for *Life* magazine.

Cowles Magazines (*Look*) folded up their pocket-size newsweekly, *Quick*, after four years. Despite a circulation of 1,300,000, *Quick* never attracted enough advertising revenue. Its title was sold to another company, to be used on a biweekly "feature" magazine, and most of the former *Quick* staff became stockholders in a modest new firm publishing *Tempo*—a pocket newsweekly much like the original *Quick*.

The Crowell-Collier Company (*Woman's Home Companion, The American Magazine*) finally faced up to the fact that its weekly, *Collier's*, had fallen on evil days. Its drastic solution was to leave the "general" weekly field to *Life* and

**LOOKING DOWN** 20 stories to street, a Chicago news photographer got this exceptional shot of a woman being led from a suicidal ledge by a fire marshal (not shown)

*The Saturday Evening Post* and convert *Collier's* to a biweekly (like *Look*). Within a few months, *Collier's* claimed a circulation jump of 500,000-plus per issue.

A new magazine, *The Democratic Digest,* official organ of the Democratic National Committee, appeared. Unlike most party organs, which are given away or sent to subscribers, it went right on the newsstands and, loaded with material reflecting the party's viewpoint, became a big seller.

# THEATER

*The theater is dying,*
*The theater is dying,*
*The theater is practically dead. . .*

SO SANG A MOCK CHORUS IN A RICHARD Rodgers and Oscar Hammerstein musical about backstage love, *Me and Juliet*, which hit Broadway in 1953.

Living refutation to this lament was the most successful team in show business—composer Rodgers and lyricist Hammerstein themselves. No other creative team in history has made such enormous fortunes from the theater. During 1953 their musicals *Oklahoma!, South Pacific, The King and I,* and *Me and Juliet* all were running simultaneously on Broadway. Of the $30 million grossed by the eighty-odd Broadway productions during the year, by far the largest single slice went to Rodgers and Hammerstein.

At the year's end, *The King and I* and *Me and Juliet* were still playing to standees in New York. Both *Oklahoma!* and *South Pacific* were earning $30,000 a week touring the nation. *Oklahoma!,* which had enjoyed a nostalgic return visit to New York in 1953, was entertaining audiences for the eleventh year with its lilting melodies and homely poetry.

*South Pacific* brightly illustrated the Rodgers-Hammerstein saga. This tune-

**HIGH-KICKING** chorus girls tread the measures of a "Can-Can" number. Cole Porter wrote show's music

ful tale, which departed from Broadway at the end of 1953 after nearly five years, was still invading the forty-eight states, and enjoying long runs in England and Australia. During its long tenure on Broadway, it had grossed $10 million. In its first year, *South Pacific* had set a new box-office record ($2,635,000), topping Florenz Ziegfeld's *Show Boat*.

Who were these two magic-makers of the theater? They were sharply dissimilar. Richard Rodgers was small (5 ft. 7 in.), urbane, impeccably dressed. Oscar Hammerstein 2d was bulky (6 ft. 2 in. and 200 lbs.), homey, carelessly garbed in rumpled suits and shirts.

Rodgers relaxed in his handsome fifteen-room Park Avenue duplex; Hammerstein preferred his Bucks County, Pa., farm, where he raised prize cattle. Rodgers enjoyed cocktail parties; Hammerstein liked sarsaparilla and ice cream more than Martinis, and never smoked. Rodgers' father was a prosperous doctor, and the theater was not in the family tradition. Hammerstein was the third generation of one of the most formidable theater dynasties.

His uncle, Oscar Hammerstein, was a large-scale impresario, once owned and managed the Manhattan Opera House (forerunner of the Metropolitan) and the Philadelphia Opera House. His father, William, was a well-known theatrical agent. Uncle Arthur was a producer.

But in addition to talent and wealth, Rodgers and Hammerstein had much in common. Both were native New Yorkers, and both attended Columbia University, where—separately—they wrote college plays. Both had had their quota of Broadway successes and failures before they teamed up, in 1943, to create *Oklahoma!* That initial joint effort enjoyed Broadway's fourth-longest run, topped only by *Life with Father*, *Tobacco Road*, and *Abie's Irish Rose*, in that order.

**ONE-MAN SHOW:** During nationwide tour and Broadway run, Victor Borge's "Comedy in Music" rolled packed houses in the aisles

Queried about their riches and their $2 million annual payroll, Rodgers smilingly commented: "I'd be a fool to say it wasn't wonderful, but it is frightening to have so many dependents."

Of their methods of work, Hammerstein said: "We are not temperamental at all. If one of us were, he'd get the big horse laugh from the other. I do insist on one eccentricity, though. I like to write standing, leaning on my desk. My lyrics and plots come easier that way."

Rodgers answered the perennial question: which comes first, the words or the music? "In our case, we never know. . . . Whoever gets the Muse's message first."

While Rodgers and Hammerstein were mopping up with musicals, two top movie actresses invaded the theater—one the queen of four-handkerchief films, Bette Davis, and the other the eternal Tailored Woman, Rosalind Russell. Miss Davis flopped in the musical *Two's Company* (a $32,000 loss), while Miss Russell scored in *Wonderful Town*.

Since breaking into pictures in 1931 as the harassed heroine of *The Man Who Played God*, Miss Davis had portrayed seventy-three overwrought ladies, to the delight of millions. Back on the Broadway stage after twenty-one years, the 45-year-old actress from Lowell, Mass., sang, joked, performed modified bumps and a shimmy.

In New York with her fourth husband, film actor Gary Merrill, and her three adopted children, Miss Davis explained her return: "You've got to take chances to get anywhere today. This income-tax bite . . . is putting us all back to work."

It soon became obvious that the actress was ill, and *Two's Company* closed after a brief, unhappy engagement.

Miss Russell's return to Broadway, after an eighteen-year absence, was quite another story. Her gravelly voice ("I don't sing; I gargle"), her uninhibited

**UNRELATED KERRS,** England's Deborah and America's John, star in drama "Tea and Sympathy"

conga, and her warm, shining personality made her Manhattan's darling.

Born forty-five years ago in Waterbury, Conn., the daughter of a prosperous lawyer, Miss Russell was graduated in 1929 from New York's American Academy of Dramatic Arts. After a couple of stage flops, she toured a cut-rate theatrical circuit at $45 a week, augmented her income by beating the producer at pinochle.

In Hollywood she was type-cast as the career woman. "The plot was always the same, and I used to get the same desk in each picture," she recalls. Married to Danish-born theatrical agent Frederick Brisson (son of night-club baritone Carl Brisson), she won respect by her earnest efforts for various charities. More than any other entertainer, she popularized the work of the late Sister Kenny in infantile paralysis therapy. She practically browbeat Hollywood into making a film biography about the Australian nurse.

Here is how she explains the difference between film and theater work: "The stage demands that you use forty-two new muscles. And you must relearn how to work with other actors and get a laugh. You have to build it from the snickers to the belly to the boff."

## Death of Eugene O'Neill

Saddest theater news in 1953 was the death at 65 of playwright Eugene O'Neill, of bronchial pneumonia. Three-time Pulitzer Prize winner and Nobel Prize ($40,000) recipient, O'Neill had made more than a million from his stark, elemental tragedies.

No modern playwright, with the possible exception of George Bernard Shaw, has been more widely produced. His *Hairy Ape*, for example, was a hit in Russia and Japan and was performed by Zulu actors in South Africa. His plays of life in the raw—*Emperor Jones, Desire Under the Elms, The Iceman Cometh*—were preoccupied with human destruction. In his tragedies there were eight suicides, one attempted suicide, twelve murders, twenty-three deaths, and seven instances of mental derangement.

He was born at New York's Broadway and Forty-third Street in a seedy theatrical rooming house, and was the son of famed and alcohol-tortured actor James O'Neill, who made a fortune playing Edmond Dantès 6000 times in *The Count of Monte Cristo*.

Young O'Neill, who displayed his father's temperament, was once suspended from Princeton University for throwing a beer bottle through a window. He never completed his college courses, instead roamed the world on tramp steamers and cattle boats. A patient at a sanatorium for tuberculars, O'Neill read Shakespeare and Ibsen and decided to become a playwright. He first shook up the genteel world with violently emotional plays at the Provincetown Playhouse, a converted stable in New York's Greenwich Village.

O'Neill's own life was filled with tragedy. As he aged, he suffered from Parkinson's disease, a form of palsy which made writing extremely difficult. Married three times, he was survived by a daughter, Oona, wife of the controversial funnyman Charles Chaplin. In his will he left his daughter nothing. A son, Eugene Jr., had committed suicide in 1950.

During an interview a few years ago, the embittered playwright declared: "If the whole human race were to go down the drain like drowning insects, it might be a good thing."

One of his plays, *Long Day's Journey into Night*, reportedly dealt with his own tragic family life. He decreed that it was not to be produced until twenty-five years after his death.

A happy event in 1953 was the rise of a new star over the gaudy, paper-moon world of Broadway—Geraldine Page, 28, leading lady of a trifle entitled *Midsummer*. Not within recent memory had any other performer making a debut been garlanded with such spectacular notices.

Tall, pale, with a wistful face, fluttery hands, and odd, faltering speech, she modestly described herself as "an ordinary dishwater blonde". At her one-room Greenwich Village apartment, the Kirksville, Mo., girl, who had struggled for eleven years in small stock companies, seemed bewildered by her sudden fame: "What has happened to me is not at all rational, and I'm not sure it is the best way. Is stardom overnight good for an actor?"

Miss Page, who had acted in groups at Lake Zurich (35 miles outside Chicago), at Woodstock, Ill., and in off-Broadway companies in New York, offered this advice to novitiates: "I don't go for the phony *theatah* nonsense. The best way to become an actress is to act. If there is no acting group in your neighborhood, create one. I never got anywhere by visiting producers' offices, showing off glossy glamour photographs. . . . And take another job so you can eat. I was a hat-check girl, a theater usher, a negligee model, a book clerk."

All that was over. She was soon to be seen in films, for she signed a seven-year contract with independent producer Charles Feldman.

"Thank God," she said, "I don't have to save cigarette butts any more."

Broadway discovered the intense young star when she was playing leads in a converted Greenwich Village night club renamed Circle-in-the-Square. Her discovery pointed up a new trend in the New York theater.

Irritated by high prices for Broadway tickets and often mediocre fare, theater-goers were taxi-ing to unlikely places all over the city, and were sitting on hard benches in converted churches and defunct saloons to view solid and inexpensive drama. Twenty companies were competing for attention off Broadway.

## The Phoenix Theater

At year's end, the most successful was the Phoenix Theater, located in a former movie palace on the teeming East Side, once the city's worst slum. There the noted husband-wife acting team, Hume Cronyn and Jessica Tandy, scored in a comedy by the late Sidney Howard, *Madam, Will You Walk*. Incredulous East-Siders stared at the procession of limousines and taxis in front of the new theater. Top salary for the performers, including the stars, was $100 a week. Maximum ticket price: $3. Phoenix backers included such luminaries as Rodgers and Hammerstein, director Elia Kazan, actress Peggy Wood.

T. Edward Hambleton, wealthy cofounder of the Phoenix, explained his reasons for investing in the new showcase: "On Broadway, a play is a flop unless it is a sure-fire colossal hit. There is no in-between. Many good, important plays cannot get a hearing because they do not fit into the commercial hit pattern. To insure that such plays are seen, the Phoenix was born. And, happily, it's amazing how many actors will work for peanuts for something they can believe in wholeheartedly." He was right about actors. At the end of 1953, Hollywood's Robert Ryan announced he would star in a Phoenix production, Shakespeare's *Coriolanus*—at $100 a week.

Broadway sentimentalists had a field day on the evening of May 24, 1953. That date marked the closing of the Empire Theater, New York's most beloved and oldest operating playhouse. At its open-

**"ROZ FOR PRESIDENT"** raved "N. Y. Times" critic in review of musical comedy "Wonderful Town". Movie star Rosalind Russell sings, dances, grinds, charms in first Broadway appearance

ing in 1893, the elegant carriage parade had been led by society arbiter Mrs. Cornelius Vanderbilt. Sleeping-car magnate Pullman had been the first to present his ducats to the ticket taker. Opening bill was Edna Wallace (Hopper) in David Belasco's *The Girl I Left Behind Me*. Since that time, every important name in the American theater had played the Empire.

On that nostalgic evening in 1953, Cornelia Otis Skinner, as mistress of ceremonies, introduced Edna Wallace Hopper to the audience. The old lady skipped out—gingham dress, sunbonnet, and all—and performed a scene from the

ancient Belasco play. There was not a dry eye in the marble-and-gilt Empire.

Shortly afterward the wreckers began dismantling the landmark. It would be replaced by a spanking-new office skyscraper.

Most important new producer in 1953 was handsome, 31-year-old Paul Gregory.

He had introduced a new and successful formula on Broadway: productions with small casts and no scenery, most of them readings from great literature.

In 1952 he had made a name—and a fortune—with his bare-staged production of Shaw's *Don Juan in Hell*, read by Charles Laughton, Agnes Moorehead, Charles Boyer, and Sir Cedric Hardwicke. In 1953 he scored a second time with Stephen Vincent Benét's compassionate Civil War ode, *John Brown's Body*, recited by Judith Anderson, Tyrone Power (Hollywood's perennial pretty boy emerged as an actor of stature), and Raymond Massey.

At year's end, Gregory's production of *The Caine Mutiny Court Martial*, which Herman Wouk had dramatized from his own best-selling novel, was touring the nation preparing for a Broadway opening. It starred Henry Fonda, Lloyd Nolan, and John Hodiak, had an advance sale in New York of $500,000, and probably would become a smash hit.

Producer Gregory started his theater career early. At 13 he organized the Iowa Young Artists League and presented a concert in Des Moines. He was a failure as an actor in Hollywood—to pay for lunches, he once collected pop bottles on the beach for 2¢ apiece. An idea dawned when he happened to hear Charles Laughton read selections from Shakespeare and the Bible to hospitalized vets —why not present Laughton in these readings on the stage? That idea made him rich. Laughton, incidentally, has directed all of the plays produced by Mr. Gregory, including *The Caine Mutiny Court Martial*.

Gregory believed he had proved an important point: "All my productions have toured the nation before coming to Broadway. I think I have made it clear that hits don't need to originate in New York."

The biggest theater news of 1953 was the passing of Lee Shubert, who died Dec. 25, at 78. He was the undisputed ruler of the American theater. At one time his theater empire was valued at $400 million.

For half a century Mr. Lee (as the theater-wise referred to him) looked upon Broadway's lucre-laden acres as a feudal lord might survey his fiefdom. Sitting in his turret-shaped office overlooking Shubert Alley (in the heart of the theater district), he could leaf through the deeds to most of Broadway's and the nation's legitimate theaters. As both landlord and producer, he had hired practically every important entertainer in America at one time or another.

The famed Shubert brothers, Sam, Jacob (always called J. J.), and Lee, were sons of a Syracuse, N.Y., peddler. Although stage-struck while still in their teens, they did not become actors. Instead they bought a small upstate chain of theaters in Syracuse, Utica, and Rochester. They soon began acquiring other theaters all over the East.

In 1906 Sam was killed in a train wreck (his gold-framed photograph hangs in Shubert lobbies all over the nation). The two other brothers waged a bitter war with the ruthless "Syndicate" (Klaw and Erlanger), which had controlled most of the nation's theaters up to that time.

The Syndicate operated on an economy of shortage: the fewer theaters, the more crowded those few would be. The Shuberts, borrowing Wall Street money in enormous quantities, operated otherwise. Mr. Lee, who seldom talked to the press, once described his method in a moment of frankness: "Because I own a number of theaters, the profit I earn in one theater goes to pay the losses in another. That way, I can keep them all open."

Several times in those early years, it looked as if the Shubert brothers would be broken by the Syndicate. "But we always pulled through," declared Mr. Lee. "Sarah Bernhardt once made an American tour under our management, and the Syndicate denied her bookings in any of their theaters. But we played her any place we could hire—town halls, school auditoriums, even tents."

When the battle with the Syndicate was won in the '20's, Lee Shubert showed no mercy. "I never sought or gave it," he once declared. He was contemptuous of rival tycoons who whined when defeated.

Tense, small, melancholy, almost Oriental in appearance, Mr. Lee was always darkly tanned from a sun lamp in his office. He liked to work after midnight, parked his foreign cars in his famed Shubert Alley. He was secretive, uncommunicative to all but family friends. Nobody knew what he thought of the plays he produced.

At year's end, his published will read like a timetable of feuds with his brother J. J., with whom he had had some harsh, secret battle years before. The canny and embittered old man had even made provisions in his will for veteran subordinates who had once been fired by his brother.

He favored his nephew Milton to take his place in the Shubert dynasty, but it was anybody's guess how the struggle within the great theater empire would turn out.

Ironically, five days after his death, an antitrust suit brought against the Shuberts by the U.S. government was dismissed. The emperor had not lived to see that triumph.

**BOX-OFFICE MAGIC** gladdens film comic Danny Kaye (right), whose one-man show at Palace Theater in New York grossed $743,000 in 14 weeks

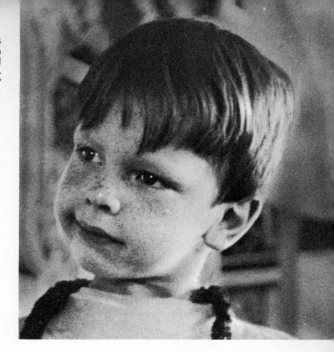

# MOVIES

NINETEEN FIFTY-THREE WAS THE YEAR OF the Long Wail, in which Hollywood complained that business was awful and movies were done for. Actually it proved to be Hollywood's best year since 1947. Most companies paid dividends, worldwide sales mounted, "big" pictures rolled up record-breaking box-office grosses, and lesser ones didn't do badly.

It was a year of awakening, of challenge and decision. Hollywood tightened its belt, cut expenses, and decided that since it couldn't beat television, it might as well use TV to its own advantage. Thus it permitted its biggest stars to appear on TV screens. It used video for free publicity and for paid picture plugs. It even made several movies showing families sitting around home TV sets.

But in the economic confusion, producers cut stories, production, and payrolls, as well as their lists of stars and contract players. Some cut their actor lists from 1000 to 300.

The result was not all hardship. Many actors sought other fields. Some made movies abroad. Some chose to adventure in vaudeville and night clubs. Some returned to their old love, the Broadway stage. And almost every actor who had the opportunity appeared on radio or TV, preferably in a regular program.

Their names read like a Hollywood *Who's Who:* Clark Gable, Ava Gardner,

**TYPICAL SCENE** in year's best Western, "Shane", finds hero Alan Ladd battling villains

Gregory Peck, Danny Kaye, Charles Boyer, Ray Milland, Ann Sothern, and Douglas Fairbanks Jr., to name only a few.

Youth found it harder to get into movies in 1953 than in previous years. There were fewer grade-B films, traditional tryout areas for new talent. "Big" pictures, requiring big investments, needed big names for box-office insurance. Hollywood therefore relied on veterans who through the years had proved they could entice the public to the box-office wickets.

This situation made 1953 a big year for oldsters: Gary Cooper, 52; Humphrey Bogart, 54; Charles Boyer, 54; Cary Grant, 49; James Cagney, 49; Bing Crosby, 49; Fred Astaire, 54. Not to mention actors in their mid-40's: James Stewart, Robert Taylor, Errol Flynn, John Wayne, and many more.

However, some among a younger Hollywood group did get a chance. Elaine Stewart, a 23-year-old brunette from Montclair, N.J., created a flurry in a brief role in *The Bad and the Beautiful,* and then whipped up a veritable storm as an army camp follower in *Take the High Ground.* At year's end, M.G.M. was touting Miss Stewart as their answer to Twentieth Century-Fox's blond bombshell, Marilyn Monroe.

Other youngsters who were discovered or rediscovered included Robert Wagner, Debbie Reynolds, Rock Hudson, Tony Curtis, and Audrey Hepburn—although Miss Hepburn had already established herself on Broadway.

Meanwhile, screens in American movie theaters were having growing pains. In New York, Cinerama had begun the transition in September, 1952. Its curved, three-sectional screen stretched to nearly

**NEW FACE:** Audrey Hepburn bowled cities over in "Roman Holiday", year's No. I romantic comedy

three times normal length. As one wit remarked at the time: "Some of the scenes are so big it takes two customers to look at them."

By the end of 1953, Cinerama had been exhibited in five cities, taken in over $6 million, and started a flood of movie innovations, among them scores of three-dimensional films, accompanied by stunts, gadgets, and half a dozen ever expanding screen styles.

Three-dimensional movies were hailed with loud hoopla. Moviegoers were promised "a lion in your lap and a lady in your arms". Movie critics blasted the poor quality and the nuisance of 3-D Polaroid eyeglasses for the audience, but the public, excited by the producers' sensational advertising and the novelty of three dimensions, refused to listen.

The theater weekly *Variety* commented on this with a characteristic *Variety*-style-English headline: CRIX CACKLE AT 3-D PIX TRIX; PUBLIC DOESN'T GIVE 1-D HOOT! By the end of the summer, however, the 3-Ds began to run out of box-office steam.

Even as 3-D interest ran down, Big Screen interest began to gather momentum. "Giant" screens were tried—much higher and wider than normal—but all they showed was an enlarged image sometimes disastrously chopped off at top or bottom.

Then Twentieth Century-Fox brought out CinemaScope.

The net result was an enormous picture. With "stereophonic sound" coming at the audience from all parts of the screen, the total sight-and-sound effect was overwhelming. Hollywood producers, as well as hundreds of theater owners, jumped on Twentieth Century-Fox's big-screen band wagon.

The first CinemaScope picture was *The Robe,* derived from Lloyd C. Douglas' novel about a Roman centurion who, according to legend, gambled for and won Christ's robe at the foot of the Cross. It opened in September before a gala audience in New York's 6000-seat Roxy Theater. In one month it earned $1 million. By the year's end it had earned well over $12 million all around the country—and was still going strong.

Soon other U.S. theaters joined the big-screen parade, and the race was on. In New York, Radio City Music Hall ordered a new screen 70 feet long and 28 feet high —biggest in the world. Amid all the excitement, one fact stood out: the public would be the ultimate gainer. For as time went by, not only would movie techniques improve but so would the movies. For the first time since the 1930's, the moviegoer was in the bargaining seat: Hollywood was trying desperately to please him.

In movieland the years that followed World War II brought in their train a raft of films with a religious or Biblical background.

In 1949 there was *Samson and Delilah,* followed in 1951 by *David and Bathsheba* and *Quo Vadis.* In 1953 *The Robe* was not the only reminder that religion was still big box office. In *Salome,* Rita Hayworth danced the torrid Dance of the Seven Veils—and lost six of them. In a more restrained but controversial vein was *Martin Luther,* a dramatic and historically detailed biography of a leader of the Reformation.

Even the Italians got into the act with a tremendous spectacle, *Queen of Sheba,* based vaguely on the Bible's brief account of her visit to King Solomon. U.S. filmgoers didn't like it much.

By the end of 1953 a score of Biblical

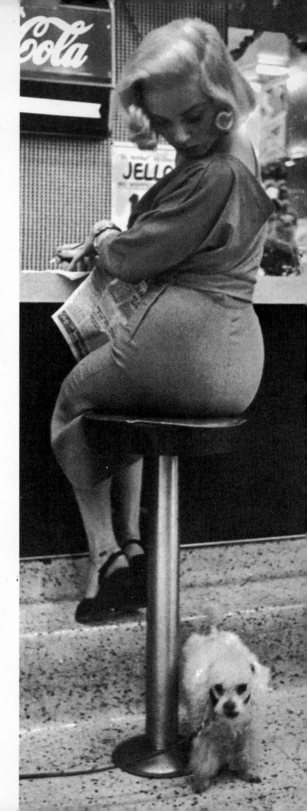

**NEW "BODY":** Mamie Van Doren was groomed as potential rival for eye-catcher Marilyn Monroe

dramas were being prepared. Among them: a gigantic Cecil B. DeMille remake of his 1923 *The Ten Commandments* (to be filmed "on location" in Egypt and Israel); *The Story of Mary Magdalene* (with Rita Hayworth); *Pilate's Wife; Joseph and His Brethren;* and at least three more examinations of the royal idolatress, Queen Jezebel.

## Movies in the News

Elsewhere around the world, movie events continued to make news.

In Berlin a strange coincidence developed when a Russian Army deserter, fleeing into the U.S. Zone, ran smack into a crew of Hollywood movie makers shooting a picture called *No Way Back*. The story is about a Russian in the East Berlin zone who escapes into the American sector. The dramatic real-life scene in which this racing soldier sought sanctuary—photographed just as it happened—was incorporated into the finished film.

In Ireland the powerful, patriotic, and very sensitive Gaelic League tried to ban newsreels of Queen Elizabeth II's coronation—"to prevent popular riots". The picture was shown. There were no riots.

In Hollywood, twenty-six persons who had testified before the House Un-American Activities Committee filed suit against the committee (and certain producers), alleging that "individually and collectively" they had been "maliciously, oppressively, wilfully, fraudulently, and wantonly" black-listed. They estimated their hurt feelings at $51,750,000.

In Ohio, drive-in theaters were castigated by the local clergy, who referred to them as "passion pits". The ministers complained that on Saturday nights their parishioners (especially the younger ones) stayed up so late they couldn't attend Sunday school next morning.

In Texas, drive-ins showed five feature pictures on a single program, stayed open all night, and served free breakfast at dawn. Ministers demanded that the police take action. "Nobody," they claimed, "stays up all night just to look at movies."

Movie people, as well as events, helped to make news, too. Tenor Mario Lanza, the roly-poly bad boy of the studios, who had begun and abandoned *The Student Prince* at M.G.M., sued his manager for "appropriations" of his money. Golden-throated Mario claimed that in a year when he earned $1 million, he received only $70 a week to live on. (In 1953 he bought himself a specially designed, custom-built, oversized white automobile, with a carful of fancy gadgets, including a gold-plated dashboard.)

Lovely June Haver, Twentieth Century-Fox's musical-comedy star, went directly from her "last" picture, *The Girl Next Door,* into the Kansas City convent of the Sisters of Charity, as a novice. Six months later she came out and went back to Hollywood. "It wasn't for me," she said.

Danny Kaye came to New York, played a one-man vaudeville show at the famous Palace Theater on Broadway, and broke all box-office records. In fourteen weeks the theater raked in $744,000 in admissions.

Marilyn Monroe, who created quite a stir in 1952, increased her box-office draw in 1953. She stirred comment all over the world—even behind the Iron Curtain. The Russians pictured popular response to Miss Monroe's charms as "typical American imperialist, sex-ridden, moral decadence". A Paris movie magazine sounded a patriotic clarion call for a "French answer to la Marilyn", and Italian producers boasted of Italian-born stars who out-Monroe Monroe in several obvious ways.

The Monroe legends that came out of Hollywood were carefully planted and nourished, and grew up like beanstalks overnight. A reporter, meeting Miss Monroe for the first time, stared at her fluttery blue eyes and asked, "Are those really your own eyelashes?" Marilyn replied softly, "Everything I have is my own."

An alleged rivalry between Miss Monroe and Jane Russell led to challenges from both camps. A famed Hollywood photographer summed it up: "Marilyn looks best walking away, while Jane takes first place in passing."

Perhaps the most interesting remark made by a movie star in 1953 was Marlon Brando's: "Acting is popular with a certain type of person because it offers the only legal expression of schizophrenia accepted in polite society. . . . The stage is a wonderful refuge for neurotics, and the theater's full of them. . . . But of course you understand that for every actor this always means the other fellow. . . ."

Censorship, always a thorn in the side of the movies, made headlines in 1953.

A commission of U.S. admirals banned *From Here to Eternity* from all Navy and Marine installations. The gold-braided brass felt that the picture was "derogatory to a sister service". The sister service, the Army, was surprised by the Navy's deli-

**DEARLY BELOVED:** Rita Hayworth and Dick Haymes say "I do." Among witnesses were her daughters Yasmin (left) and Rebecca, whose dads are Aly Khan and Orson Welles

cate courtesy, since the Army itself had not banned the picture, but on the contrary had O.K.'d it for showing at army posts all over the world.

But the Army had its own share of bluenoses. They banned *The Moon Is Blue,* a romantic comedy in which a boy chases a girl and vice versa, and in which the players say such naughty words as "pregnant", "seduce", and "professional virgins".

The usual bags of letters were also received in Hollywood from lawyers protesting against stereotypes of lawyer-villains in the movies, from bankers protesting against banker-villains, and in similar vein from Mexicans, Indians, and other minorities. Manufacturers, retailers, laborers, and professional people who fancied their special groups had been insulted, slurred, or in some way injured were also heard from. Those protests recalled producer Samuel Goldwyn's classic remark: "I'd like to make a movie of *Beverly of Graustark,* but I'm afraid some mythical kingdom might complain!"

As 1953 rolled to a close the nation's movie exhibitors prepared their list of box-office winners. The new technological gadgets—3-D, big screen, CinemaScope, and the rest—didn't seem to make any difference. As reported by the *Motion Picture Herald,* the line-up of the Top Ten ran in the order of their box-office appeal and earnings: Gary Cooper, Martin and Lewis, John Wayne, Alan Ladd, Bing Crosby, Marilyn Monroe, James Stewart, Bob Hope, Susan Hayward, and Randolph Scott.

Many distinguished motion pictures crossed the screens in 1953. Best to many minds was Columbia's film version of James Jones' novel, *From Here to Eter-*

*nity,* a powerful story of peacetime soldiers.

The picture, with Montgomery Clift and Burt Lancaster heading the cast, was also notable for another performance. Crooner Frank Sinatra, never before celebrated as a dramatic actor, showed in his handling of the role of the ill-fated Maggio that he had sensitivity and skill and could act with the best of them.

Best-liked musical of the year was M.G.M.'s *Kiss Me Kate,* based on the Broadway musical hit. Characteristically, in view of the technique confusion that hampered the movie industry this year, *Kate* was made and offered to theaters in four versions: 3-D regular screen, 3-D large screen, normal (2-D) regular size, and big screen. M.G.M. was taking no chances.

In contrast to previous years, there were very few "controversial" films, and these were of minor interest. Hollywood emphasized "entertainment", and that meant action dramas, adventure, Westerns, comedy, musicals, romance, fantasy, and science-fiction films. In the last group, *War of the Worlds* horrified audiences with a foretaste of what might happen if invaders from outer space (in this case Mars) attacked the earth.

The "outer-space" aspects reminded some of the rich lady who, when asked what she was going to do about her vacation, replied: "Well, last year we took a trip around the world. This year, I think we'll go somewhere else."

Hollywood was in somewhat the same position. In 1953 it tried everything: Cinerama, CinemaScope, 3-D, and a dozen other camera, film, and screen processes designed to lure the "lost audience" back again into the movie theaters.

Having tried nearly everything else, Hollywood indicated it was going back to first principles: good stories. If so, that might be the big movie news for 1954.

**TOP FILM** of 1953, "From Here to Eternity", had many dramatic moments. Among them: surf-washed love scene between Burt Lancaster and Deborah Kerr

# RADIO-TV

MUCH MADNESS AND A LITTLE BLISS HIGH-lighted radio and television in 1953.

Most headlined TV event was the firing of 23-year-old singer Julius La Rosa by Arthur Godfrey. At the end of his show one morning, just after La Rosa had completed a number, Godfrey suddenly said: "That was Julie's swan song with us." It must have been the first time anyone ever got fired in the sight of millions.

"Julius lost his humility," Godfrey explained later. He had changed from a "shy, bashful, scared-to-death kid" into an "obstreperous" one. Worse, he had hired his own agent. "One thing I will not have is interference by outside agents," said Godfrey.

La Rosa declined to do battle with his former boss. But he hardly needed to. For him, the publicity attending his discharge proved a godsend. Godfrey had

paid him about $900 a week. A few days after the firing, he was on the Ed Sullivan show getting $3000 for one performance. He also started his own radio program. All told, he would make at least $100,000 in the next year.

Godfrey swung the ax again only an hour or so after firing La Rosa. His second target: 44-year-old Archie Bleyer, his long-time orchestra leader. Bleyer's crime had been to make a phonograph recording with Don McNeill, a radio personality whom Godfrey considers a rival.

"It's like being married to a woman for twenty years," said Godfrey, "and then coming home and finding a cigar butt in the ash tray."

The whole episode was disconcerting to many people, who saw an unfamiliar side of Godfrey, once called the Huck Finn of the air. They had forgotten that Godfrey heads and personally directs a

**HOSPITALIZED** for hip surgery, TV star Arthur Godfrey grips overhead pulleys to adjust his position in bed—unconsciously aping another TV star, J. Fred Muggs (opposite)

multimillion-dollar empire and that in big business the gentle touch is a rare thing.

Television's next most publicized 1953 event was the coronation of Queen Elizabeth II. The two major networks, C.B.S. and N.B.C., each reportedly spent $250,-000 trying to be first with coronation films in this country. Neither won.

They had planned the stunt for a year. They sent camera crews to London to record the coronation, hired transatlantic planes to speed the films westward, set up transmitting equipment at the Boston airport so that the films could go on the air the moment they arrived.

On the morning of the coronation, the first films—including some made by the

**TV BABY OF 1953** was Desiderio Alberto Arnaz IV. Preparations for his arrival were written into parents' program "I Love Lucy". Here he is seen with mother Lucille Ball and sister Lucie Désirée

**MARTHA RAYE:** Expert delivery and shapely figure made this comedienne a top 1953 TV star

British Broadcasting Corporation—left London aboard a Royal Air Force bomber. At Goose Bay, Labrador, the C.B.S. films were transferred to a P-51 Mustang piloted by Joe De Bona, winner of the 1949 Bendix Trophy race. The N.B.C. films were placed in another Mustang flown by Stanley Reaver, who had finished second in the same race. The B.B.C. films were relayed by a Canadian jet to Montreal.

De Bona and Reaver raced to Boston; De Bona (and the C.B.S. films) won by twenty-four minutes. But his arrival was an anticlimax. U.S. viewers had been

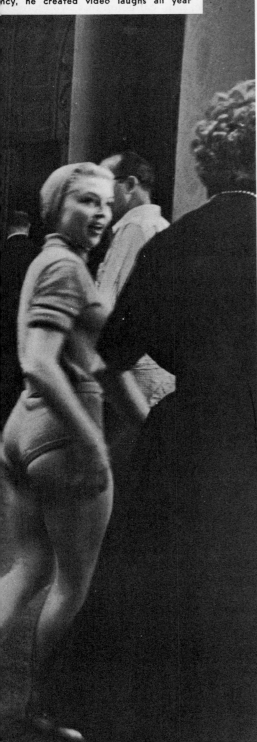

**CKIE GLEASON:** Big, brash, and ncy, he created video laughs all year

watching the B.B.C. films of the coronation for about ten minutes on telecasts relayed from Canada.

Meanwhile, the American Broadcasting Company also had arranged to telecast the Canadian relay of the B.B.C. film. When N.B.C. learned this, it asked to share the relay. The next morning, in full-page newspaper ads, N.B.C. exclaimed: "N.B.C.'s Coronation Coverage Topped All Networks". A shocked A.B.C. spokesman replied: "They should have spelled it 'tapped'."

Some Englishmen fumed at what they considered excessive advertising inserted into the American coronation programs. And they didn't like the fact that J. Fred Muggs, a chimpanzee featured on Dave Garroway's "Today" show (N.B.C.) was on the same program with their Queen.

No one was made unhappy, however, by another big TV story of 1953. This one involved Lucille Ball and her husband, Desi Arnaz, who became the parents of the year's most publicized baby. For

**FAYE EMERSON:** No longer relying on low-cut gowns, she did well as panel-show moderator

weeks the script of their television show, "I Love Lucy", had called for the couple to have a baby. What heightened the interest was that in private life they were also scheduled to have a baby (their second).

Jess Oppenheimer, producer of the show, decided to have the television script parallel Miss Ball's expected motherhood. Since "I Love Lucy" is filmed long before it goes on the air, the script writers guessed that Miss Ball would have a boy, and wrote the Jan. 19 show accordingly (the baby was to be delivered by Caesarean section).

Naturally, the television public waited eagerly to see whether Miss Ball would abide by her script. Sure enough, on Jan. 19 she had a boy. He weighed 8½ pounds and was given a name almost as heavy: Desiderio Alberto Arnaz IV.

The next month Philip Morris & Company, sponsors of "I Love Lucy", showed how much they loved Lucille. They signed an $8 million contract, guaranteeing the show's run for another two and a half years.

On Jan. 20, 1953, by means of TV, about half of the U.S. population "attended" the inauguration of Dwight D. Eisenhower as President. Some state legislatures recessed to watch, school children were dismissed, and trading on the New York Stock Exchange slackened.

In June the President starred in another TV production: a seemingly informal chat with some of his Cabinet members. Actually, the whole thing was carefully planned by a big New York City advertising agency (Batten, Barton, Durstine & Osborn, Inc.). Eisenhower himself showed up for an hour's rehearsal the day before. Cue cards were placed around the room to guide the Cabinet heads in their remarks.

On the air the President took a homey approach to the government's complex problems, but seemed ill at ease. The show itself drew mixed reactions. David Lawrence, political columnist, wondered "whether the American people like to see their President acting as a sort of master of ceremonies in a piece of obviously rehearsed showmanship". Bernard C. Duffy, president of the advertising agency, called it the best program his firm had ever handled.

## Color Television

The year's big TV story, technically, was color. After a decade of confusion and controversy, the industry finally came up with a "compatible" system that would not outmode the 25,000,000 black-and-white receivers already in use. This meant that an existing set could receive a color broadcast in black and white without any adjustment.

The Federal Communications Commission promised to approve the new system, which had been proposed by the industry-wide National Television System Committee and the Radio Corporation of America. Thereupon C.B.S. decided to shelve its "incompatible" system, previously the only one approved by the F.C.C. In so doing it jettisoned a "technical monopoly" which theoretically was worth millions of dollars.

Toward year's end C.B.S. put on a weekly color program and N.B.C. tried out all its major programs in color. But it appeared that color sets in quantity would not be marketed for several years.

The first coast-to-coast color telecast took place in 1953. In Burbank, Calif., an invited audience of 900 (including a number of movie executives) watched a musical program given in a New York theater, followed by some color films. The viewers broke into frequent applause.

Contributing to the development of

color processes was a redhead with blue-green eyes, 27-year-old Marie McNamara. For two and a half years she had been a live "test pattern" for R.C.A. engineers. She would sit for hours smiling into a camera while they adjusted their color controls to reproduce exactly her natural complexion. To relieve the monotony of staring endlessly into the camera, Marie made small talk with the engineers and stagehands. Occasionally someone came up with a risqué story.

"And that's bad," said Marie, "because I always blush and it louses up the engineers."

Other personalities made the air hum in 1953. Ageless Alben W. Barkley became a television commentator on N.B.C. less than two weeks after he stepped down as Vice President. Said Mr. Barkley: "I try to give constructive comments on current problems, drawing on my forty years in public life. I also work in a little humor to keep the audience from going to sleep."

Barkley's former boss, Harry S. Truman, was offered $10,000 to play the piano for Arthur Murray's television show. He declined, but later did appear on a children's program with an inspirational talk to youth. His reported fee: $8000.

Fred Allen, who calls television "a triumph of equipment over people", had another go at the medium after a two-year layoff. His new N.B.C. show, "Judge for Yourself", had elements of various quiz, audience-participation, and give-away programs.

Many critics panned it. They said Allen had made a mistake in getting mixed up with a lowly quiz program. Fred answered: "If criticism ever hurt anybody, the skunk would be extinct. I don't care if the critics pan the show as long as they don't pan the sponsor."

Nor was Allen worried about building a steady audience for his new show. He remarked: "In radio I always said that if you blow your nose long enough you'll get an audience. Television is the same."

The highest-paid TV performers for a single appearance were not actors but boxers: Rocky Marciano and Jersey Joe Walcott. Their Chicago championship bout was sponsored on radio and TV by the Gillette Safety Razor Company to the tune of $300,000. The bout did not go one round. Winner Marciano got $166,038 from radio and TV. Loser Walcott got $250,000, most of which came from broadcasting rights.

Football coach Frank Leahy used television to coach his Notre Dame team from a hospital bed when he was taken sick. So that Leahy could watch squad practice, a station in South Bend, Ind., sent a truck-mounted television camera up and down the sidelines. The picture was beamed to a microwave station atop Leahy's hospital, and then fed by wire to his bedside receiver.

This arrangement showed Leahy defects in his team he had never noticed before. He cited an example.

"For weeks I'd been watching Johnny Lattner punt, wondering why he wasn't getting much distance to his kicks this year. But on television I spotted his flaw instantly. He wasn't following through."

### The "Teleflush" Index

In 1953, television, which has been accused of many things, was blamed for something new. People in charge of waterworks in various cities had been mystified at the sudden rises and falls in amounts of water used from seven to eleven o'clock in the evening. On the hour and half-hour the water demand would shoot up—sometimes as much as 30 percent during a five-minute period. George J. Van Dorp, water commis-

**UNEASY WEDDING** of TV and movies brought first televising of "Oscar" awards. Program even had TV-within-TV. Here Ronald Colman and Bob Hope watch Shirley Booth, on big video screen, accept acting prize 3000 miles away

sioner of Toledo, Ohio, supplied the answer. The fluctuations, said Van Dorp, were caused by televiewers who, "having their interest held by the program on the air, were, at the end of the program or during the commercial, suddenly released. They then became engaged in many activities which were water consuming."

Van Dorp thought that if video producers came around every night and read his water meter they could get a quick rating on the popularity of their programs. One wag suggested the rating system could be called Teleflush. In Toledo, Teleflush showed that "I Love Lucy" was in top place.

What was probably the biggest business transaction in broadcasting history occurred in February, when the American Broadcasting Company merged with United Paramount Theaters, Inc., operator of 644 movie houses. The deal involved a $25 million exchange of stock. The new company was called American Broadcasting-Paramount Theaters, Inc.

The merger was an economic lifesaver for A.B.C., which had fallen behind N.B.C. and C.B.S. in the race for audiences and sponsors. Now it signed up television talent right and left: George Jessel, Ray Bolger, Danny Thomas, Paul Hartman, and others. And when the fall season began, A.B.C. rang up $20 million worth of new radio and TV business—all from new sponsors.

In 1953 the makers of Admiral receivers found that there were more television sets than bathtubs in Chicago, Los Angeles, Philadelphia, Cleveland, St. Louis, Washington, and Columbus. Even Boston had 730,000 sets but only 719,056 bathtubs.

Pay-as-you-see television was ballyhooed during the year by three different companies. Each had its own way of "scrambling" the incoming signal and arranging for the home viewer to pay to have it "unscrambled".

Subscriber-Vision, which uses a decoding card to unscramble the picture, was given a public demonstration in New York City by its developer, the Skiatron Electronics and Television Corporation. Arthur Levey, president, said that 93.6 percent of the people who saw it said they were willing to pay a "nominal fee for outstanding programs not now otherwise available".

In Palm Springs, Calif., the International Telemeter Corporation allowed the public to test its coin-in-the-slot gadget. The set owner drops his "admission fee" into an electronic coin box attached to his set and is allowed to see the picture free of blur. The test in Palm Springs featured the premiere of a Ginger Rogers movie entitled *Forever Female.*

The Zenith Radio Corporation, which owns Phonovision, announced that its system could be adapted for any means of decoding a picture and collecting money from the set owner. Originally, Phonovision was to operate through telephone companies only.

However received, what did televiewers see in 1953? Among other things they saw the following.

Actor Maurice Evans had his television christening in a two-hour N.B.C. production of *Hamlet.* Staging the play cost $180,000, required eighty tons of scenery, five cameras, three weeks of rehearsal (more than three times as much as most drama programs), and a cast of twenty-eight.

## Hamlet on TV

Evans wondered how a mass TV audience would take to Shakespeare, but decided that "*Hamlet* may fit into television's formula of violence. It rivals the goriest of whodunits in its blood-letting."

He had played Hamlet 777 times on the stage, but for video he had to unlearn many things about stagecraft. "In television, it's all cheek to cheek," he noted. "You can't stand away from another actor and project, as you do on the stage."

Still, most critics liked his TV *Hamlet*. Encouraged, he decided to have another go at Shakespeare with *Richard II*.

A New York City advertising agency licked the problem of how to demonstrate a girdle on a live model without offending televiewers. The model was sheathed in black tights. Over the tights she wore a girdle coated with phosphorescent paint. Then she was photographed under black light. When the film was televised, the audience saw only a girdle walking and twirling—no girl. The agency called it a "union of modesty and merchandising".

The year's biggest, and in many ways best, single TV show was an extravaganza entitled "The American Road". In observance of its fiftieth anniversary, the Ford Motor Company spent the record total of $500,000 to sponsor a breath-taking and nostalgic review of the last half century. The two-hour show was presented over the C.B.S. and N.B.C. networks simultaneously.

From the opening scene of an excerpt from the play *Life with Father* to Marian Anderson's closing rendition of "Battle Hymn of the Republic", the review never lacked imagination or showmanship. It had color, flavor, zest. Ethel Merman and Mary Martin sang their hearts out, and the dancers in Jerome Robbins' ballets worked themselves into a frenzy of brilliant movement. Other stars included Bing Crosby, Rudy Vallee, Eddie Fisher, Howard Lindsay, Dorothy Stickney, Frank Sinatra, Wally Cox, and the puppets Kukla and Ollie.

The show was produced by Broadway impresario Leland Hayward (*South Pacific, Mister Roberts*). N.B.C. later put him under contract as a television producer and production consultant.

For its half million, Ford settled for a single, almost unrecognizable, commercial. This was an hilarious scene of Kukla and Ollie driving through the streets in the days of the old Model T.

In its first venture into television, the Metropolitan Opera did a tailored (sixty-two mins.) version of *Die Fledermaus* (in English) for C.B.S.'s "Omnibus" program. Opera had been televised before from the stage of the Met, but this was the first time the company had performed in a television studio solely for home viewers. What emerged was generally agreeable, often gay.

## Montana in Philadelphia

Western movies are standard fare on television, but C.B.S. hit a new note (an old one in Hollywood) by building an outdoor set on the back lot of its affiliated station W.C.A.U.-TV in Philadelphia. It christened the result "Huberle, Montana".

Huberle's block-long street had a bank, blacksmith shop, newspaper office, general store, jail, saloon, and other structures—all with false fronts, just as in the movies. There were many cowboys—some good men and a lot of bad men. From Huberle a show called "Action in the Afternoon" went on five days a week, rain or shine.

The presentation of Hollywood's annual Academy Awards was televised for the first time. R.C.A., which paid $250,000 for the privilege, may have done itself a disservice in one way: a regular TV fan who saw the Oscars handed out might suddenly realize he had been missing a lot of good movies by staying home to watch TV.

R.C.A., however, also had an an-

nouncement that impressed everyone: Hollywood, the radio-TV industry, and the public. This was the development of magnetic tape for recording both color and black-and-white television pictures. Instead of being recorded on film, a show could be recorded on a roll of tape half an inch wide.

"It does away with all chemical processing," said Brigadier General David Sarnoff, chairman of R.C.A. "The pictures can be viewed the instant they are taken, which adds new flexibility in the making of motion pictures."

With Bing Crosby Enterprises also experimenting with magnetic tape recording, it looked as though home picture recorders might some day be as familiar as home sound recorders.

Meanwhile, according to the show-business weekly *Variety*, TV itself had become the "greatest free show on earth". *Variety* pointed out that video entertainment budgets hit the stratosphere in the 1953-54 season.

There were no figures to show TV's total costs, but five programs were spending a total of $300,000 a week for talent and production expenses. They were "Colgate Comedy Hour", the "Jackie Gleason Show", the "Milton Berle Show", "Toast of the Town", and "Your Show of Shows". It would take a Broadway musical two years to get back what the "Big Five" were spending in one week, *Variety* said.

While it was free entertainment for the public, sponsors were footing record-breaking bills. The total costs—including air time—of the Big Five for a full season came to $24 million. It seemed to prove that television is here to stay—if sponsors don't run out of money.

**NATIONAL POPULARITY** of TV crime show, "Dragnet", led to numerous TV burlesques—including this ballet grouping of net, corpse, gunman

**HUMAN FLY,** 10,000 feet up; Alpine climber Gaston Rebuffat traverses underside of rock overhang by driving nails into seam to hold nylon line, which supports him as he drives more nails

ATOP 10,227-foot pinnacle in French Alps, veteran mountaineer Rebuffat waves his hat in triumph

# SPORTS

SPORTS IN 1953, WITH WELCOMING COM-
mittees, scrolls of honor, and confetti-
spattered motorcades, was a throwback
to the Golden Age of the '20's. It was not
the general level of performance, which
was high, that caught the public's fancy,
but the performance of a few individuals.
As in the days of Dempsey, Grange, and
Tilden, the crowd went wild over sports
heroes, and particularly over golfer Ben
Hogan.

Early in the summer, Hogan, a tight-
lipped, grim little Texan with thick arms
and heavy shoulders, looked out across
a rolling meadow to the undulating,
treacherously fast green marking the
eighteenth hole of the Oakmont (Pa.)
Country Club.

Smoothly "The Mechanical Man" lifted
his second shot to within eight feet of
the pin, and then, with a feathery touch,
putted out for a birdie 3 and a course
record of 283, to win his fourth United
States Open.

**GAME BUT GROGGY** after pounding from champ Rocky Marciano (note follow-through), Roland LaStarza is counted out in 11th round of battle for heavyweight crown

**BASEBALL BALLET:** In fourth game of 1953 World Series, Billy Martin of Yankees is third out as Dodgers' Roy Campanella cuts him off at plate

At 40, Ben Hogan, small by athletic standards (5 ft. 8½ ins., 156 lbs.), had won every major professional tournament in America.

He was born William Ben Hogan. His father, a blacksmith in Dublin, Tex., died when Ben was eight. Mrs. Hogan moved her three youngsters to Fort Worth, where Ben caddied at the country club for 65¢ a round.

Golf intrigued the boy, but he was a leftie, and pick-me-up left-handed golf clubs were rare. Ben learned to play right-handed and though not a natural athlete, practiced with fierce fanaticism.

In 1932 he hit the winter circuit with a band of professionals traveling from one country-club tournament to another. Only half a dozen of the players met expenses; twice Ben had to sell his car to eat. Back to Fort Worth he went, and for four years slaved to perfect his game.

Those years paid off. By 1942 he had been golfdom's top money winner three times, and in 1948, for the first time, he won the big title, the U.S. Open.

Then tragedy struck. On a highway outside El Paso, his car collided with a forty-passenger bus, severely injuring him, and friends feared he would never play golf again. Hogan beat the odds. Not fully recovered, he entered the 1950 U.S. Open and won.

Even off the course, Hogan's manner was grim. One time he won a tournament and was handed a check and a shiny silver cup. His acceptance speech: "Thanks for the check."

Yet most Americans rooted for Ben Hogan in June, 1953, when, preparing to face a tricky course and the world's best players, he set out for Carnoustie, Scotland, and the British Open championship. No Yankee had ever won it on his first try.

Ben did. First he criticized Carnoustie's rock-hard fairways, pitted sand traps, and unkempt greens. Then, leaving a trail of cigarette butts behind him, he went out and played as if the course were perfect. Starting slowly but increasing the pressure relentlessly, he wound up with a scorching 68 on the last eighteen holes, to break Carnoustie's competitive record. His winning score of 282 shattered a mark that had stood since 1937.

When Hogan got back to New York he was paraded up Broadway in a blizzard of ticker tape. In front of City Hall a crowd cheered him. Even Ben Hogan could not resist such a tribute.

"I have a tough skin but a soft heart," he told the crowd, "and right now I feel like crying. . . . God bless you all."

New York's reception for Hogan lasted one day. In Milwaukee, a reception rolled throughout the summer for a doughty band of athletes who, the year before, had been known as the Boston Braves.

When owner Lou Perini moved his money-losing ball club to Milwaukee—first such major-league shift in fifty years—many considered the Wisconsin brewing capital (pop. 600,000) too small to support major-league baseball. Milwaukee soon showed them they were wrong.

From the first pitch on opening day, the Braves were treated like demigods. Merchants deluged them with everything from groceries to automobiles. Cab drivers, bellhops, and barbers refused their tips. Newspapers front-paged their slightest actions.

Fans from all over the State helped jam the new County Stadium, cheering ordinary plays and saluting brilliant ones with bells and sirens. During baseball broadcasts, crime decreased. After road trips, the team was met by parades and brass bands.

"I know sophisticated people will wonder why we have a celebration every time the team comes home," said Mayor Frank Zeidler. "To tell the truth, we never had so much fun in our lives."

The Braves responded nobly. Though they had finished a dreary seventh in Boston the year before, this time—with practically the same personnel—they led the National League for months and finished a respectable second. Their 21-year-old slugger, Ed Mathews, hit forty-seven home runs. And, with a ball park seating only 35,000, they set a new National League attendance record of 1,-826,397, topping the world's champion New York Yankees by more than a quarter million.

All this helped persuade the American League to grant permission for a similar franchise move. It converted the long-ailing St. Louis Browns into the Baltimore Orioles, reviving a once-famous major-league name.

For the Yanks, 1953 brought an all-

**DEFYING CENTRIFUGAL FORCE** on sharp curve, motor-cyclists keep all three wheels down during Grand Prix races in France

time record: the fifth World Series victory in a row. Much of the credit went to manager Casey Stengel, who, at 63, was the game's reigning wizard. In 1953 Stengel juggled lineups, switched pitchers, shifted batting orders until the opposition was ready to scream. But he got results.

Brooklyn began the Series with five regulars batting over .300, and outfielder Carl Furillo (.344) leading the league. The Dodgers had power, pitching, and an A-1 manager. The Yankees had only two regulars batting over .300.

Yet New York won, four games to two. The key player was tough, cocky Yankee Billy Martin, a spindly-legged kid from California whose season batting mark was .257. In the series he hit .500 and carried on a one-man guerrilla war against the Dodgers.

There were other Series stars, of course. Dodger pitcher Carl Erskine, knocked out in the first inning of the first game, came back in the third game to pace a Brooklyn victory with fourteen strike-outs, a Series record. Yankee outfielder Mickey Mantle hit a grand-slam homer to help win the fifth game. In the ninth inning of the sixth game, the Dodgers' Furillo, playing with a bandaged hand, walloped a two-run homer that evened the score and skyrocketed Brooklyn hopes for a showdown seventh game the next day.

But in that same inning the Yankees got a runner on second base. Billy Martin singled him home to victory—one that meant $8280 (a new record) to every New York player.

After that when Chuck Dressen, the able but talkative manager who had led the Dodgers to two successive National League pennants, asked for a new two-year contract, the management refused to go above one year. So Dressen quit, later signed on with Oakland, Calif. His successor was Walter (Smokey) Alston, 42, who for four years had run Montreal, the top Dodger farm team, with marked success.

In August the Red Sox welcomed back their great yet curiously unpopular slugger, lanky Ted Williams. Released at the age of 35 from the Marines after thirty-eight combat flying missions in Korea, Williams in the next six weeks batted ninety-one times and made thirty-seven hits (including thirteen homers) for a phenomenal .407 average.

## Sport or Business?

The year's last big baseball story took place in the U.S. Supreme Court, which had been asked to settle the long-standing question: is baseball a sport or a business?

The bone of contention was the so-called "reserve clause", which in effect gives club owners complete control over the careers of players. Back in 1922, Associate Justice Oliver Wendell Holmes had decided that baseball is not engaged in interstate commerce, and hence is not covered by federal antitrust laws. In 1953 the court confirmed Holmes' ruling, 7 to 2, and left any further action up to Congress.

Boxing also had its problems. Early in the year a big TV audience was horrified when, in a fight broadcast from Boston, lightweight champion Jimmy Carter made mincemeat of a frail, overmatched featherweight named Tommy Collins, who had once been temporarily blinded in a preliminary bout. The bewildered Collins was knocked down ten times (seven in the fourth round) before the slaughter was stopped. Said George Barton, chairman of the National Boxing Association: "If Collins had been crippled, it might have sounded the death knell of professional boxing."

Yet just one month later the fans were howling, for a diametrically opposed reason. Defending his title in a return bout with Jersey Joe Walcott, heavyweight champion Rocky Marciano dumped his aging opponent with a short uppercut. It was only the first round, but Walcott sat on the ring floor seemingly lost in thought until counted out; then he got up to a barrage of boos. Tommy Collins had been beaten too much; Jersey Joe not enough.

In 1953, Marciano established himself as a deserving champion. After he had knocked out Roland LaStarza for his forty-fifth straight professional victory (and a purse of $187,000), it looked as though the 29-year-old from Brockton, Mass., would rule the roost indefinitely.

More immediately exciting to millions was the hope of a meeting between two race horses, Native Dancer and Tom Fool.

The Dancer, a 3-year-old gray owned by Alfred G. Vanderbilt, had "color". Powerful, graceful, with a driving finish and a 29-foot stride at top speed, he made people push and shove to get near him, touch him, snap his picture. As one onlooker observed, "That's the way they act when the President goes by."

When Native Dancer was entered in the 1953 Kentucky Derby, he became a prohibitive favorite. One young man took his mother's life savings and bet them on the horse. "I figured it was a sure thing," he said later. Unfortunately, of the nineteen races the Dancer entered, the Derby was the only one he didn't win.

Eric Guerin, the Dancer's regular jockey, was given a ten-day suspension just prior to the $112,600 American Derby at Chicago's Washington Park, and Eddie Arcaro was hired to ride the gray. After his first workout, Arcaro stood in front of the big horse and peered up at his face.

"You know," he said, "this is the first time I've ever seen the Dancer from in front. I've seen plenty of him from behind."

Tom Fool, a 4-year-old bay, had an even better record than Native Dancer in 1953: ten straight wins. His specialty was carrying a heavy handicap. In one race he carried 136 lbs.—26 to 31 lbs. more than any other mount entered—and still romped in ahead. When he was named to meet Native Dancer in the Sysonby Stakes, an early-fall feature at New York's Belmont Park, $2 bettors picked the Dancer, but much of the wise money backed the Fool.

Then, in quick succession, Native Dancer hurt his foot and was withdrawn from competition; Tom Fool, after winning the Sysonby unchallenged, was retired to stud; and the public reluctantly accepted the fact that the "race of the century" would never be run.

## Earl Sande Returns

Fans still had a racing figure to cheer, however: no one less than Earl Sande, a true Golden Age personality who had won more than $3 million as a jockey, but later got rid of it as only jockeys can. In the fall of 1953, Sande, now 54 but still wiry and wily, returned to the tracks and proved he still knew how to boot those winners in—as writer Damon Runyon put it.

Track owners also had cause for joy. In 1953, for the first time, more than $2 billion was handed in at the betting windows.

In the water, a unique record was set by Florence Chadwick, a 33-year-old ex-stenographer of San Diego, Calif. She swam four world-famous channels—English, Gibraltar, Borporus, Dardanelles—within five weeks. In the English Channel she not only completed the west-to-

**UPSIDE DOWN,** this expert skier is executing a back flip high in the Blue Mountains of Oregon

east crossing in record time (14 hrs. 42 min.) but was 2½ miles out on the return trip when a school of stinging jellyfish forced her to stop.

Another San Diego girl also had gone about as far as she could go. She was Maureen Connolly, 18, who in 1953 made a clean sweep of the "big four" women's tennis championships: Australian, French, English, and American. "Little Mo" had begun to play tennis at eight, entered tournaments at ten, and competed at Forest Hills, tennis capital of the East, when she was fourteen. The world's top woman player nonetheless told a sportswriter that in tennis a good man could beat a good woman every time.

"He would simply annihilate her," she said. "I know. I was annihilated myself the other day by a pro no one ever heard of."

Meanwhile men's tennis was dominated by the continuing rivalry between Australia (pop. 7,000,000) and the U.S. (pop. 160,000,000). Despite its numerical advantage, the U.S. had seen the Aussies win both the American title and the Davis Cup in 1952. A year later, pleased galleryites at Forest Hills watched an unexpected all-American final in the national singles, with Cincinnati's Tony Trabert overpowering Philadelphia's Vic Seixas.

Still another heartwarming victory was chalked up by a 17-year-old Boston girl, Tenley Albright. Partially paralyzed by polio at eleven, Tenley had concentrated on skating to rebuild her strength. Her big moment came in the spring of 1953. At mile-high Davos, Switzerland, against the toughest possible competition, she became the first American ever to win the women's world figure-skating crown.

In football, after several years of the "two-platoon" game, the rule permitting unlimited substitutions was abolished. No longer could whole offensive and defensive teams be shuttled in and out as needed—not to mention single players who had been used only to run back punts, say, or kick extra points.

Instead, the game returned to fundamentals. Some teams, short on personnel, produced "sixty-minute men", as in days of yore. Others spent most of the season waiting for former defensive backs to learn how to run, pass, or block.

In basketball there was great interest in a sallow, stoop-shouldered, ham-handed youngster who had brought national headlines to tiny Rio Grande (Ohio) College.

His name was Clarence Francis. His father, a miner, had been nicknamed "Bevo", after a prohibition soft drink, and the son was called "Little Bevo". While still in high school, Bevo had received offers from sixty-three colleges and one professional team. He chose to follow his high-school coach to Rio Grande (*rye-o grand*). In a student body of ninety-two, including forty girls, 6 ft. 8 in. Bevo was bound to stand out.

In his freshman season, Bevo Francis scored 1954 points, a new record for any college. In one game he racked up an amazing 116, a larger total than is usually scored by an entire team.

Such were the outstanding sports events and personalities of 1953. It remained only for the almost legendary Leroy (Satchel) Paige—who at something close to fifty still was pitching major-league baseball—to offer the year's outstanding piece of advice: a distillation of his own painfully acquired experience for players, fans, or anyone else.

"If your stomach disputes you, lie down and pacify it with cool thoughts.

"Go very light on the vices, such as carrying on in society. The social ramble ain't restful.

"Don't look back. Something may be gaining on you."

**ICE QUEEN** Barbara Scott, now a pro, works out. In 1953, U.S. girl, Tenley Albright, 17, won world's figure-skating crown

**OLDSTERS** made big art news in 1953. At 84, architect Frank Lloyd Wright (above) captured New York with show tracing development of his pioneering designs

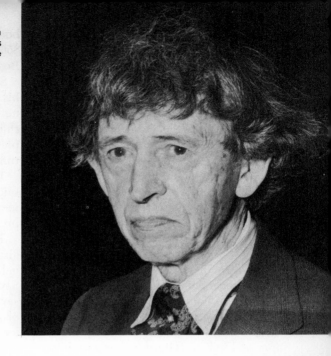

# Art and Architecture

ACROSS THE HUDSON RIVER FROM NEW YORK City, at Cliffside Park, N. J., a thin, alert man, with a face wrinkled like a winter apple and wispy hair combed in a pageboy bob, painted some of the finest canvases any American has produced.

He was John Marin, who died Oct. 1, at 83. His passing was the year's greatest art loss. Marin oils, water colors, etchings, or drawings are in almost every important collection of modern art and in more than fifty American museums. Reproductions of his Manhattan skylines are becoming as numerous on apartment walls as Van Gogh's "Sunflowers" or Degas' ballet girls.

America did not always honor him. His first work, exhibited in 1909 by *avant-garde* photographer Alfred Stieglitz, was jeered by public and critics alike. But Marin resolutely stuck to his highly original style, a kind of artistic shorthand whose delicate line suggested, rather than literally depicted, his subject matter.

He was fascinated by New York's skyline. To Americans accustomed to canvases of classic nymphs and sentimental landscapes, his poetic, semiabstract views of skyscrapers were startling. Gradually they won acceptance.

His early "Woolworth Building" and "Lower Manhattan from the River" are prized today. By the '40's he had become America's Old Master of the moderns.

In 1943 he was elected to life membership in the American Academy of Arts and Letters. Membership is limited to fifty persons whom that august body considers most likely to achieve a permanent place in American culture. (John Marin's Academy chair, No. 22, will now be filled by another John, novelist-reporter John Hersey.)

The next most important art event in 1953 concerned not a painter but a shrewd, brilliant art dealer, 72-year-old Paul Rosenberg. Long a giant in the fabulous field of buying and selling art, he opened his first gallery in Paris in 1897. Even after he came to New York in 1941, he still did not exhibit his private stock. But he did in 1953, and his collection was reported to be worth nearly $2 million dollars.

His New York show, impressively entitled "The First and Only Exhibition of Mr. and Mrs. Paul Rosenberg's 'Private Collection of Paintings", revealed a spate of splendid early Picassos, Braques, and Matisses. The venerable art dealer had helped make this triumvirate famous during the preceding half century, and in return they made him rich. Mr. Rosenberg, who sold modern masterpieces to the world's top museums, kept some of the finest canvases for himself.

Rosenberg's career started when, at eighteen, he journeyed from Paris to London to buy art for his father, also a dealer. Among his first wise investments were two Van Gogh drawings, bought for $20 apiece, and Edouard Manet's "Portrait of Victorine Meurend", bought for $200. He soon sold the Manet painting for more than triple that amount. In 1928 he re-

bought it for $40,000, sold it again for $56,000. "Victorine" now hangs in the Boston Museum of Fine Arts.

Septuagenarian Rosenberg, reviewing his colorful career, stated that he had never tried to sell anything. "Salesmanship is useless," he commented. "Great pictures sell themselves. I don't sell anything I wouldn't like to keep myself."

The paintings he kept for himself, he said, could not be bought for all the money in the world. "They are the expression of my life."

The unveiling of his private collection also celebrated the opening of his new gallery in New York's fashionable East Seventies. His exodus from famed Fifty-seventh Street to the former town house of collector Maud Dale signaled a new location for American art. The nation's art capital, for decades Fifty-seventh Street, will probably settle itself farther uptown in Manhattan, for where Rosenberg leads, other galleries dutifully follow.

Another New York art showcase, the Solomon R. Guggenheim Museum, changed its stripes in 1953. Under the forbidding subtitle of Museum of Non-Objective Art, it had previously been operated by Baroness Hilla Rebay von Ehrenwiesen. A protégée of millionaire art patron Solomon Guggenheim, and an artist herself, the imperious baroness favored nonobjective art (paintings with no recognizable subject matter) and showed a large number of her own works in the gallery rooms. The public called the paintings wallpaper designs, and stayed away in droves.

In 1953 the harassed museum changed its name and came under the directorship of enterprising, Brooklyn-born James Johnson Sweeney, formerly director of the Museum of Modern Art. He at once dropped the emphasis on nonobjective paintings and opened the building to

**EYE-FOOLER:** Up-to-the-minute kitchen of Frank Lloyd Wright house, seen in his New York show, actually was created back in 1900

**HIDDEN POWER:** Auctioneer exhibits controversial semi-nude portraits of actor Tyrone Power and wife Linda Christian. Works went on sale in New York

modern art of all types—an indication that his former employer, long the leading temple of the "latest word", might soon have a serious rival.

At year's end the new policy was paying off. As a tribute to 84-year-old Frank Lloyd Wright, the new Guggenheim Museum put on view 800 drawings, plans, photomurals, and scale models which

traced the lifework of the most influential architect of the twentieth century. A completely furnished two-bedroom house adjoined the main exhibition building. The house, as modern as today, had been created by Wright in 1900.

The show made New York Wright-conscious. Overflow crowds queued up at the museum. The architect was inter-

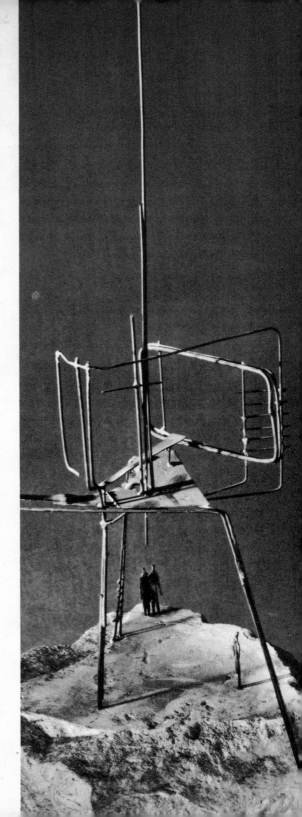

viewed in print and on the air. Similar reactions were expected at the show's next stops: Tokyo, Manila, and New Delhi.

Wright himself, a lifelong iconoclast, added to the fun with a pamphlet blasting the "international style" in architecture. He called it "nothing but the old architecture of the box, with its face lifted", and named the Museum of Modern Art in New York as its U.S. agent. Architects were still battling over that declaration as 1953 closed.

A unique painter, one who pleases both moderns and conservatives, was tapped in 1953 for a full-length retrospective show at New York's Knoedler Galleries. He was Andrew Wyeth of Chadd's Ford, Pa., a 36-year-old realist who paints farm life and outdoor scenes.

Mr. Wyeth is fast becoming a national best seller. Every canvas he paints is avidly purchased. Executed in meticulous detail, his work exhibits an elusive moodiness. Son of famed children's book illustrator N. C. Wyeth (whose illustrations for *Treasure Island* are classics), the painter had been a sickly child and had spent months in lonely isolation.

In 1953, living with his wife and two children in a white-stone converted schoolhouse of the 1820's, he was happiest when painting his haunting studies of loneliness. "Painting is living to me," he said. "If I had to stop painting, I'd just as soon die."

Meanwhile, all the embattled factions of contemporary art hailed him as one of their own. The realists praised him as a rallying point against the all-powerful nonobjective artists. The experimentalists replied that his paintings have surrealist, dream-world overtones. Either

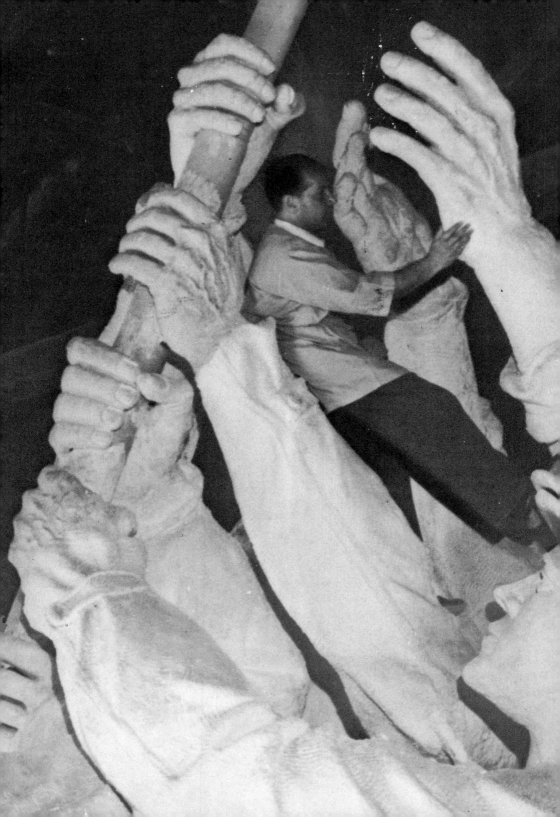

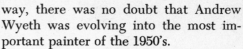

way, there was no doubt that Andrew Wyeth was evolving into the most important painter of the 1950's.

Internationally speaking, perhaps the event of the year was the mammoth display at the São Paulo Museum of Modern Art in Brazil. Marking the city's 400th birthday, the show added to São Paulo's repute as a South American art center. Works from thirty-nine countries competed for $54,175 in prizes, with rooms of honor reserved for France's Pablo Picasso and the U.S.'s Alexander Calder, inventor of "mobiles".

Alexander ("Sandy") Calder has long been grouped with Picasso as a pioneer of modern art. Europeans consider him America's greatest living artist. In the U.S. his mobiles, or imitations of them, have become a decorating fad and adorn countless numbers of apartments and homes.

They are constructed from bits of metal, wood, and wire in a balanced system of weights and counterweights, teetering, swaying, and bobbing in the breeze. Calder often incorporates taillights, bedsprings, even parts of toilets in his creations. He executes about forty a year, sells most of them for prices ranging from $200 to $3000 apiece.

Calder descends from a famed family of artists. His father, A. Stirling Calder, sculpted the conventional statue of George Washington on New York's Washington Arch; his grandfather created the statue of William Penn atop Philadelphia's City Hall.

Queried about the importance of his world-famed mobiles, Calder, who looks like a beardless Santa Claus, commented: "All I know is that they give pleasure to me; I like to play with them."

London was the scene of one of 1953's biggest art controversies. Its Institute of Contemporary Art sponsored the biggest sculpture contest ever held: an inter-

national competition for a proposed monument to "The Unknown Political Prisoner". Artists from fifty-seven countries entered works, mostly abstractions, and first prize ($12,500) went to England's Reg Butler for a prisonerless wire cage.

A young Hungarian, Laslo Szilvassy, whose parents had been killed by the Nazis and who had become stateless after the Communist victory in his native land, visited the exhibition and was so incensed by what he saw that he smashed Butler's prize-winning opus. London—and world—opinion was sharply divided over his action. The London courts made no comments on the value of modern art. They did describe the 28-year-old refugee's act as "wicked, malicious, and calculated hooliganism". He pleaded guilty and was placed on a year's probation.

Publishers in the United States were amazed when one of the best sellers of 1953 proved to be a 661-page art book retailing for $25. *Voices of Silence* was written by André Malraux, onetime archaeologist in the Far East, former Communist sympathizer, novelist, and currently adviser to Rightist French General de Gaulle. A magnificent prose poem in praise of art, the book made the important point that, with today's creative photography, no one need be ignorant of the art of one's country, or even of the world. Photography had created a "museum without walls".

The publishing industry was also rubbing its eyes at the enormous success of the Skira and Abrams art books. Albert Skira, a slender, sandy-haired Swiss who once taught dancing, had successfully operated his art-publishing business in

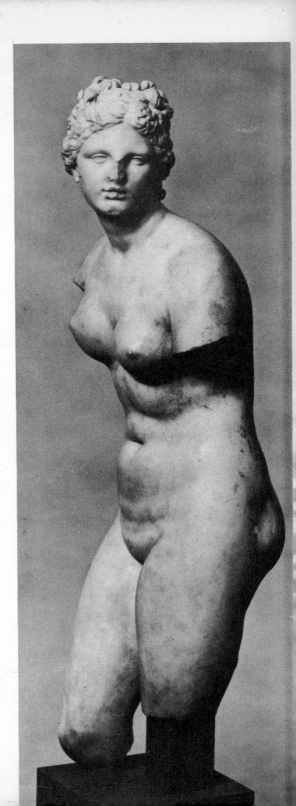

**GODDESS OF LOVE:** In 1953 New York's Metropolitan Museum bought this Aphrodite, by an unknown Greek sculptor (100 B.C.). It is a copy of a copy of a lost work by the celebrated Praxiteles

Europe for twenty-five years before opening a New York office. His art reproductions were better than those Americans were accustomed to seeing. Harry N. Abrams, formerly a part owner of the Book-of-the-Month Club, and still a member of its board of directors, countered with his own series of magnificent art books, starting in 1952 with studies of Van Gogh, Renoir, El Greco, at $10 apiece. By the end of 1953 it was a draw as to which publisher was issuing the better color reproductions. Meanwhile, America was being treated to the best art prints it had ever known.

## Le Corbusier's "Green City"

Unquestionably, the new city arising on the hot, dusty plains of northwest India was the architectural event of 1953. There, famed French architect Le Corbusier (real name: Charles-Edouard Jeanneret-Gris) had designed a modern capital for the state of Punjab.

Named "Chandigarh" for the Goddess of Power, it will be completed in 1956 at a cost of more than $35 million. French, American, and British consultants are working with Le Corbusier, who in 1953 released some photographs and drawings of the new city, then almost half completed.

Le Corbusier, whom architects the world over call simply "Corbu", spoke of the new capital as "the green city". Of its 14 square miles, he commented: "It is a new conception, a city of sky, space, and trees."

A series of contiguous open green spaces will run the length of the capital toward its backdrop, the Himalayas. All its 150,000 residents will live within a few minutes of trees and grass. The city will be planned on the grid pattern, each residential section (a half mile wide, three quarters of a mile long) containing its own schools, shops, playgrounds, and theaters. To combat the fierce Indian sun, Le Corbusier has devised deep concrete slabs, which jut outwards from the buildings, allowing air to circulate under them. But France's architectural genius has not ignored Indian traditions. He has employed the colorful and decorative brick studs from old Indian architecture in many of his modern structures.

In the center of the new city, a giant sculpture, an open hand 60 feet tall, will symbolize give-and-take. It will be a symbol not only for India but, its builders hope, for the world as well.

At year's end the U.S. could look to another kind of Indian—from Oklahoma. His name was Thomas Gilcrease, and he was part Creek.

In 1906, oil was found on his land, part of the acreage distributed among the Indians in Oklahoma by the federal government soon after the turn of the century. Eventually it flowed in such profusion that Gilcrease, proud of his blended heritage, was able to gather a unique collection: paintings of the Old West, pre-Columbian relics, items relating to the American Indian, and 70,000 rare books and manuscripts. Total value: between $4 and $8 million.

But Gilcrease found oil a mixed blessing. In recent years, thanks to government production curbs, his royalties had fallen behind his collecting urge. By 1953 he was $2.2 million in debt.

In December, 1953, he finally found the answer. At one swoop he turned over his treasure-trove to a nonprofit group formed by citizens of Claremore, Okla. (birthplace of another noted part Indian, Will Rogers). The group floated a bond issue to retire Gilcrease's debts and to start a new museum for his collection. Fittingly, it planned to name the museum after Gilcrease and make him its director.

# RELIGION

CHURCH AND STATE CONTINUED TO WRESTLE for men's souls in 1953. In Communism, Christianity faced its most relentless adversary since the days of the Roman Empire.

If the story of Hungarian refugees who escaped to the United States were true, the atheistic Reds would go to any extreme to wipe out belief in the Divine. The following Christless Christmas story, they said, was now being taught to Hungary's school children.

"There was once a poor married couple who had nothing to eat or wear. They asked the rich people for help, but the rich people sent them away. Their baby was born in a stable and covered with rags in a manger.

"The day after the baby was born, some shepherds who had come from Russia brought the baby some gifts. 'We come from a country where poverty and misery are unknown,' said the shepherds. 'In Russia the babies grow in liberty because there is no unemployment or suffering.' Joseph, the unemployed worker, asked the shepherds how they had found the house. The shepherds replied that a red star had guided them.

"Then the poor family took to the road. The shepherds covered the little baby with furs, and they all set out for the Soviet paradise."

## Godless Dictionary

The rulers of the Soviet paradise weren't missing any tricks. For example, the newest edition of the *Dictionary of the Russian Language* came up with some startling definitions. The expression "for God's sake", as a request, was termed obsolete. "Glory be to God"—which was translated as "fine, excellent"—became a "colloquialism". The "Second Coming" was defined as "an event which will never take place".

From the Red Zone of Germany came word that Martin Luther was not the "real leader" of the Protestant Reformation. The "real" one was an Anabaptist named Thomas Münzer—born in 1489 and executed in 1525—who advocated "Communist theocracy".

The battle was not only for the minds and souls of the young. Persecution and death for adult advocates of religion were also parts of the Soviet plan. Throughout the U.S.S.R., as well as in Hungary, Romania, Bulgaria, and Albania, clergymen of all faiths disappeared or were shot. Red China managed to eject or murder most of the foreign missionaries there, and in Communist Yugoslavia, Aloysius Cardinal Stepinac —although out of prison—was not free to carry on his archiepiscopal duties. At the year's beginning, only in Poland did the Red schedule seem to be delayed. The crackdown there came in September.

Then the Warsaw radio announced that the Polish government had deposed Stefan Cardinal Wyszinski of Gniezno and Warsaw. The 52-year-old-prelate— who had been raised to the cardinalate only months before—had been "allowed to retire to a monastery", said the Red radio. The semiofficial Vatican newspaper *l'Osservatore Romano,* on the other hand, stated flatly that he had been arrested. He disappeared, leaving ringing in his people's ears a prophetic statement made before his arrest: "Today one speaks of criminals, but history tomorrow may speak of saints."

Religious controversy—between faiths and between people—took many forms in 1953. In Colombia, Protestant missionaries documented dozens of cases of attacks on churches by Roman Catholics, and disruption of services by mobs led by Catholic priests. The South American country's Catholic authorities publicly deplored these incidents, but even a new, liberal Colombian government did little to halt them.

## The Finaly Case

A world-wide controversy was stirred up by two Austrian Jewish war orphans, Robert and Gerald Finaly. The two boys, aged ten and eleven, whose parents were murdered in Nazi gas chambers, had been in a Roman Catholic orphanage in France since 1944. Their aunt in Israel, Mrs. Hedwig Rosner, sought to bring them there.

Suddenly the boys disappeared. For five months they were shunted from one convent to another in France and Spain. Because the boys had been baptized in

**MELODRAMA** touched these brothers, the war-orphaned Finaly boys. Born Jews, they were raised as Catholics — but now are with aunt in Israel

**POLYGAMOUS CULTISTS** rounded up by police in isolated Short Creek, Ariz.; included men alleged to have as many as five wives. Here, bearded "elder" caught in raid is comforted by nephew

1948, Catholics did not want to give them up, fearing that in Israel they would lose the Christian faith. Both rabbis and Catholic prelates appealed for return of the boys. Finally, in June, they were turned over to their aunt in Paris, to which she had flown from Tel Aviv.

Mrs. Rosner declined to press charges against the fifteen priests and nuns who had spirited the boys away. She agreed that the children should choose their own faith when they came of age. Then Mrs.

Rosner and the boys flew back to live in Israel.

In Roman Catholic circles, the year's most troublesome figure was Father Leonard Feeney, a Jesuit of Boston, who had set up St. Benedict's Center there to strengthen the faith, especially that of Harvard students. In 1949 he had been suspended from his priestly functions for declaring that there is no salvation outside the Catholic Church. Later he refused a summons to Rome to explain his position. In March he was publicly excommunicated.

Undaunted, Feeney continued his teachings. A group of his followers, known as the Slaves of the Immaculate Heart of Mary, carried his word to the campus of Catholic Notre Dame University in Indiana. Before they were forcibly ejected from the campus, one of the group predicted: "The first sign of your approaching damnation is that Notre Dame has Protestants on its football team."

Father Feeney was only one of the colorful religious personalities to catch the public eye. Back for a good share of publicity was Negro Father Divine (born George Baker about 1880), who claims 20,000,000 followers throughout the world. His life story was told by a white non-Divinite, Mrs. Sara Harris (assisted by Harriet Crittenden) in the book *Father Divine: Holy Husband*.

Typical of the affection Father's followers bear him and show at religious services, said the authors, was "a trembling woman in a skin-tight black satin dress [who] keeps whispering: 'I love you, Father, I love you, my sweetheart, I love you. I love you. . . .' Her body

**DETROIT EVANGELIST** Prophet Jones wears followers' gifts as he prays. Among them: $17,000 diamond bracelet, $693 wrist-watch, 51-carat topaz ring, topaz earring

jerks in spasms. A middle-aged woman in a red coat starts to snake her way up and down the aisle of standees. She is half dancing, half stumbling. She cries: 'God, God, God!' . . . Nobody pays any particular attention."

The book also reported that Divine's real-estate holdings in New York, Newark, and Philadelphia (where he lives) are worth more than $6 million—although Father has never paid any income tax. He claims he personally owns not a cent,

six secretaries record his every word. Negro and white followers alike believe that he will never die.

After the book's publication, Father Divine issued a "divine prophecy, prediction, declaration, and ultimatum!"

"I curse all who believe or read its lies," he thundered. In his all-embracing malediction, Father was specific: "[Many] will be obliged to go in sorrow, misery, disappointment, and failure! Many of them will have accidents and be broken up! Many of them are cursed with infantile paralysis! I am cursing them now! Many are cursed with paralytic strokes. . . . And I will not consume them off of the face of the earth immediately—a good many of them. I will let them see me in my glory in this body!"

During the year, Father Divine found time for a courtly meeting with another Negro divinity, the Prophet Jones, Dominion Ruler of the Church of the Universal Triumph in Detroit. The tall and handsome Detroit leader journeyed to Philadelphia with countless suitcases and followers. Wearing the $12,900 white mink coat recently given him by a grateful believer, he towered over the short, plump Father Divine. Father's greeting: "Your Holiness . . ." The Prophet's reply: "Your Godliness . . ."

The biggest scandal ever in the Swedish State Lutheran Church came into the spotlight at year's end. Bishop Dick Helander, 57, of the diocese of Strangnas, was convicted of slander. His crime: writing anonymous poison-pen letters against other candidates for his office.

Pope Pius XII, 77, set a landmark in August, when his representatives and those of Spain's Generalissimo Francisco Franco concluded a concordat (a church-state agreement dealing with religious

and the Bureau of Internal Revenue has never proved otherwise. Angels flock to fill his heavens—angels with names like Miss Smile All the While, Mr. Universal Cheerfulness, Miss Buncha Love, and Miss Rapid Integration—and his twenty-

matters) after twenty-two years.

Spain's 20,000 Protestants had been eagerly watching the two-year negotiations, for, as a minority group, they felt they had few rights in that Catholic country. They could not seek converts or publicly advertise their services, and some of their meetings had been broken up by angry mobs. To their relief, they got some protection in the new concordat.

It ratified Article 6 of the Spanish constitution, which states that "no one will be molested on account of his religious creed or the private practice of his cult". Franco retained the right to appoint all Spanish archbishops and bishops, provided the Pope approved his choice.

During the year, Pope Pius also made public his views on psychoanalysis and its methods. Catholic theologians had been split on the subject. Although some had deemed it a mortal sin to make use of the science, the Pope formally approved psychoanalysis as a healing device. But he emphatically warned against abuse of it by both psychiatrists and patients. Psychiatrists, he said, should not try to usurp priestly functions, and patients should not reveal secrets which they frequently have "no right whatever" to give away. Where there is a sense of guilt, Pope Pius said, "the means of eliminating the fault, as every Christian knows, consist in contrition and sacramental absolution by a priest".

Pope Pius liberalized the rules of fasting in January, 1953, allowing water to be taken by everyone before the reception of communion, and other liquid nourishment by those who must work hard or are too ill to fast. Out of consideration for the working classes, he also ruled that Mass may be celebrated in the afternoon for those who find it difficult or impossible to attend in the morning.

In 1953, Dwight D. Eisenhower joined the National Presbyterian Church in Washington, thus becoming the fifth President to embrace a formal faith while in office.

American church membership rose to a new high—more than 92,000,000 members, a gain of more than 4 percent over the previous year. The Roman Catholics led the list, with more than 30,000,000 members, while the Methodist Church was the largest Protestant body, with 9,000,000-odd. The Southern Baptist Convention—fastest-growing Protestant denomination—was next, with some 7,600,-000 adherents. Jewish congregations could count about 5,000,000.

Increased American interest in religion became evident in other ways. At the top of the nonfiction best-seller list for most of the year was a religious book, Dr. Norman Vincent Peale's *The Power of Positive Thinking*. The Revised Standard Version Bible, published in 1952, had sold more than 2,500,000 copies by the end of its second year—enough to fill a bookshelf sixty miles long.

Even the old, half-forgotten custom of grace before meals was undergoing a revival. The American Legion and the nondenominational Laymen's National Committee conducted intensive campaigns to get Americans to say grace. They sent prayer cards with three graces (Protestant, Catholic, and Jewish) to thousands of restaurants and eating places, where they were displayed on menus or tables. And in Los Angeles a printer named Owen B. Shoemaker ran off some old-fashioned prayers on paper napkins—for parents whose children ask them to say grace but who cannot remember the words.

**HOLY WEEK IN SPAIN :** Hooded Brothers, a 16th-century religious order, parades in Seville. The Cowl originated as protective device during service in medieval plague epidemics.

# BOOKS

HOW MUCH OF A WOMAN'S BREAST MAY be shown on a book jacket? Is the story of Robin Hood Communist propaganda in disguise? Dare we let the Germans read about the exploits of Sam Spade, Dashiell Hammett's famous detective? Do books become dangerous when bound in paper covers?

These questions, and others like them, shook the book world in 1953. They were not asked in jest; instead, they gave rise to serious controversy. They were symp-toms of a growing trend in the United States toward censorship of books.

In Detroit, for example, police brought pressure on news dealers to restrain them from selling paper-back editions of some of Ernest Hemingway's books. Hard-cover editions were O.K. Apparently the man with a quarter to spend on a book was susceptible to corruption; the man with $3 was not.

In Youngstown, Ohio, the chief of police furnished the local distributor of

reprints with a list of titles which could not be sold (although many of the same books could be borrowed from the public library). When the distributor balked, he was arrested. And the State librarian of Illinois, acting upon the complaint of an obscure county sheriff, ordered all books of an "obscene, salacious, and vulgar" nature rooted out of the State library units.

When bewildered but obedient librarians got through complying, some 8000 books, representing 500 to 600 titles, were no longer available to borrowers. Mounting criticism resulted in a reversal of the order, however, and most of the books went back on the shelves.

**RECORDING** their work for a $100 L P album, noted authors run a gamut of expressions. Left and right: England's poetess Edith Sitwell, novelist Somerset Maugham. Below: American novelists Truman Capote, John Steinbeck, Edna Ferber

"Book burning"—the phrase was President Eisenhower's—became a burning issue. In point of fact, the number of books burned—figuratively or otherwise —was small. But as a rallying cry the phrase was effective. All over the country, it put librarians, bookdealers, teachers, and public officials on guard.

The American Library Association drafted a "Freedom to Read" statement justifying the inclusion of politically un—popular books in public libraries.

Said the conservative American Bar Association's Special Committee on Individual Rights: "Any fear that our people have become so softheaded that they must now be protected against an opportunity to examine the books of authors whose personal views or conduct are obnoxious is unfounded."

Still, the movement spread. The issue was broadened to include not only what books Americans might read, but those

which foreigners might be permitted to read about America. Senator Joseph McCarthy's investigators, poking into the State Department's overseas libraries, discovered many books written by U.S. "left-wing" and—a few—Communist authors. Should the taxpayer's money be used to stock books written by men and women who were undermining America's security? the Senator asked.

Many people thought not. The State Department itself, to forestall further criticism, issued a directive instructing its librarians overseas to remove books by questionable or "controversial" authors. The discretion permitted was wide. In many cases the baby was thrown out with the bath water.

So libraries were stripped of books by authors whose loyalty was unquestioned, but who disagreed with certain aspects of American policy abroad. Eleven books in the department's Berlin library were actually burned. But when the *New York Times* revealed that many volumes under attack were by such unquestionably loyal Americans as Vera Micheles Dean, editor of the Foreign Policy Association, and Walter Duranty, former *Times* correspondent in Moscow, the Secretary of State canceled the directive.

President Eisenhower himself got into the scrap. He said he had some mystery novels by Dashiell Hammett, one of the banned authors, around the White House, and didn't think the Germans would turn Communist from reading them.

Self-appointed local censors were not so easy to influence as overseas libraries. In not a few cases, police chiefs could cite elastic city ordinances against the sale of "obscene" reading matter. Booksellers resorted to the courts.

In the Youngstown case, for example, a news distributor sued for a restraining order to prevent the police chief from enforcing the ban, and won his case in federal court. Declared Federal District Judge Charles McNamee: "Freedom of the press is not limited to freedom to publish, but includes the liberty to circulate publications. . . . Censorship in any form is an assault upon freedom of the press. A censorship that suppresses books in circulation is an infringement of that freedom."

A stranger in the United States, pondering our controversy over books, might conclude that the country reads only the works of its most "unpopular" authors. Actually, the 9724 new titles published in 1953 included only a sprinkling of "controversial" products. U.S. readers continued to favor the mixture-as-before: fiction, with a dash of sex; and sex, with a dash of fiction.

In this latter category was Dr. Alfred C. Kinsey's much publicized *Sexual Behavior in the Human Female*, a scholarly study which some critics thought went beyond the bounds of scholarship into the realm of conjecture. The book came out in September. By the end of the year, 250,000 copies were in print (at $8 each), about the same number as had been sold of Kinsey's report on men, published in 1948.

*Sexual Behavior in the Human Female* was one of the five leading nonfiction best sellers of the year. But lest an observer think the country sex-mad, it is noteworthy that the four others all concerned religion. The top seller was The Holy Bible: Revised Standard Version. Second was the Reverend Norman Vincent Peale's *The Power of Positive Thinking. Angel Unaware,* by Dale E. Rogers (wife of cinema-cowboy Roy Rogers) was fourth; Bishop Fulton J. Sheen's *Life Is Worth Living,* fifth.

Two extremes engaged American readers in 1953—mountain climbing and deepsea diving. Both subjects produced notably successful books. Maurice Herzog's

**DRAMATIC PHOTO** from Barnaby Conrad's book "La Fiesta Brava" shows Mexican matador Luis Procuna leading bull in perilous "Procunesa" pass

**KNEELING ALONE** on the sand of the bull ring, Spain's great Carlos Arruza lets scimitar-like

horn miss him by inches in pass called "farol" (lantern). This picture is also from "La Fiesta Brava"

*Annapurna* was a thrilling account of a French expedition's conquest of a 26,493-foot peak in the Himalayas. Its counterpart was Captain J. Y. Cousteau's and Frédéric Dumas' *The Silent World,* an adventurous description of the authors' experiences with a camera on the floor of the Mediterranean. After Herzog and Cousteau had climbed down (and up) from their strange worlds, both took to the American lecture platform.

The Korean War came in for its share of attention. Most popular contribution was James Michener's short novel *The Bridges at Toko-Ri,* first published in *Life* magazine. Most controversial was Lieutenant Colonel Melvin B. Voorhees' *Korean Tales,* which the Army disliked because of its unflattering references to our conduct of the war.

Voorhees, a mild-mannered, high-principled ex-newspaper editor from Portland, Oreg., was chief censor of the Eighth Army. His main criticism concerned Army censorship policy. When he refused to submit his book for official clearance, he was court-martialed and relieved of his duties. The case dramatized a thorny problem: who should censor the censor?

All kinds of people wrote books in 1953. Willie Sutton, the notorious bank robber, told his story (with the help of Quentin Reynolds) in *I, Willie Sutton.* The late American concert violinist, Albert Spalding, came up with *A Fiddle, a Sword, and a Lady.* Actor Lionel Barrymore made his fiction debut with *Mr. Cantonwine.* But the amateur who made the biggest splash was Charles A. Lindbergh. The famous flier's *The Spirit of St. Louis,* fifteen years in the writing, tells the story of his life up through his celebrated flight to Paris. Critics acclaimed it, the public bought it, and Hollywood paid $1 million for the motion-picture rights.

Major literary contributions of the year —books that brought their authors more fame than fortune—included Professor Edgar Johnson's scholarly, two-volume *Charles Dickens: His Tragedy and Triumph*; Marchette Chute's *Ben Jonson of Westminster*; and Carl Sandburg's autobiography of his early years, *Always the Young Strangers.*

Fiction in 1953 was somewhat disappointing. Of the five top best sellers, two were playing return engagements. Number 1 was Lloyd C. Douglas' *The Robe,* first published in 1942. As in the case of *From Here to Eternity* (number 5), by James Jones, *The Robe*'s reviving popularity was attributable to a lavish and highly successful 1953 movie version.

The second fiction best seller, Thomas B. Costain's *The Silver Chalice,* was a holdover from the previous year. That left *Désirée* (number 3), a novel about Napoleon's love affairs, by Annemarie Selinko; and Leon Uris' *Battle Cry* (number 4) the only new books to get into the top money.

Among the newcomers of 1953, one was the son of a distinguished old-timer. *The Second Happiest Day,* by John Phillips—the son of novelist John P. (for Phillips) Marquand—trod familiarly, if entertainingly, in papa's footsteps.

Among new works by reliable standbys, the late Marjorie Kinnan Rawlings' *The Sojourner* was a novel of considerable distinction. But the offerings of Pearl Buck, Frances Parkinson Keyes, Van Wyck Mason, James Hilton, and A. J. Cronin—although as popular as ever—drew short shrift from the critics, as did John Hersey's brief but obscure tale of a New England woodchuck hunt, *The Marmot Drive.*

The most original novel of 1953 was Saul Bellow's *The Adventures of Augie March,* a forceful, highly entertaining, but difficult-to-read chronicle of a young

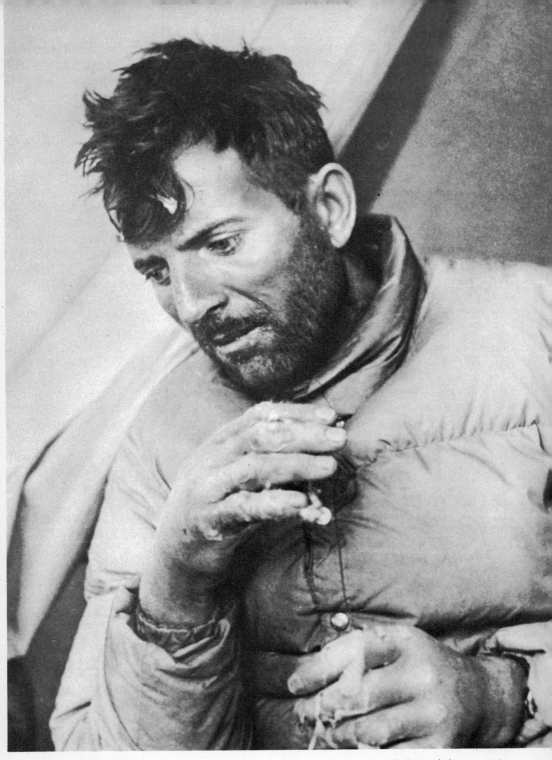

**FINGERS PEELING** from frostbite, author Maurice Herzog ("Annapurna") descends his mountain

man's coming of age in the Depression. Canada-born, Chicago-bred Bellow, 38, had written two previous novels which pleased the critics but left most readers cold. This one—275,000 words long—split them down the middle. It was both praised and condemned—but it was not ignored.

Every year, it seems, American publishers are taken for at least one ride by a literary hoaxer. In the November issue of *The Reader's Digest* appeared a condensation of *The Man Who Wouldn't Talk,* an exciting "true story" of a Canadian intelligence agent in World War II. The author, Quentin Reynolds, an old hand at converting military adventures into literary property, had for his subject one George DuPre, a Calgary, Alberta, businessman. According to DuPre, as a member of the French underground, he had posed as a near-idiot to gather military intelligence for the Allies.

The book had gone into three printings when a Calgary newspaper reporter, himself a former Canadian intelligence man, produced evidence that DuPre had never been in France. DuPre broke down and admitted the hoax. The story, he said, had grown from modest beginnings when he talked before various Canadian luncheon clubs. Finally it got out of control.

Said DuPre's wife: "He was trying to be a hero to me but he didn't need to. I was quite satisfied with him the way he was." Jested publisher Bennett Cerf, whose company, Random House, brought out the book: "It seems that the book should have been called *The Man Who Talked Too Much.*"

Whatever the fate of new books, the old ones did better than ever. The country's booming paper-back industry chalked up a new production record—1061 titles (189 more than 1952) for a total of 259,000,000 copies (7,000,000 more than 1952). The export of American books jumped sharply, too. The $28 million worth of books shipped overseas in 1953 was an increase of 28 percent over the previous year.

Laurel wreaths for the literary "bests" were passed out pretty much according to prediction. The Pulitzer award for 1952 fiction went to Ernest Hemingway for his short novel *The Old Man and the Sea,* and the poetry award to Archibald MacLeish for *Collected Poems, 1917-1952.* Others: *The Era of Good Feelings,* by George Dangerfield (history), and David J. Mays' two-volume *Edmund Pendleton, 1721-1803* (biography).

The National Book Awards for 1953 (given for books published in 1952) went to the young Negro author, Ralph Ellison, for his first novel *The Invisible Man;* to historian Bernard DeVoto for *The Course of Empire,* the best nonfiction; and to the often honored poet Archibald MacLeish for *Collected Poems, 1917-1952.* Quipped one critic: "MacLeish not only collects poems but prizes."

There were cakes and ale, along with the solid literary fare, in the 1953 literary world. The American Booksellers Association donated 200 books to President Eisenhower's White House library—including a collection of campaign speeches by Adlai Stevenson. Georges Simenon, the prolific French detective-story writer now living in the U.S., signed a contract to deliver twenty books over the next two years. And Dale Carnegie's *How to Stop Worrying and Start Living* was translated into French as *Overcome Your Troubles, Live, What the Devil!*

The most unsolemn cut of all was delivered by the popular religious author and member of a Kentucky monastery, Thomas Merton. Wrote the Trappist, declining an invitation to appear at a book-club dinner: "As you must realize, I don't get around much any more."

**ONE-MAN FACTORY** Georges Simenon poses with a few of the scores of novels (some of them translated into 18 languages) he has produced. He sometimes writes a novel in thirty-three hours

**SPRING IN PARIS** brings out age-old symbols: a park bench, a pair of young parents, another couple for whom parenthood may well be just around the corner

# PEOPLE

LIKE EVERY OTHER YEAR IN HISTORY, 1953 did not consist of great events alone. For the most part, it was lived by little people in the little letters of history that historians often forget. Here are glimpses of the year as it *was*, though not perhaps as it will be recorded.

**January**  In San Mateo, Calif., the sheriff rushed to a radio station to see what had happened to a disk jockey. Listeners said all they were getting on their radios was snores. The radioman blushingly explained that he had fallen asleep while reading a commercial—for mattresses.
★  Herman Perlman, who had done some glass carving during the renovation of the White House, admitted to some secret handiwork that had escaped the Secret Service. On the wall side of one of the presidential bathtubs, where it would not ordinarily be seen, he had sandblasted a message: "In this tub bathes the man whose heart is always

**ARMLESS AND LEGLESS** since birth, 5-year-old Freddie Thomason of Magnolia, Ark., watches limb-fitter attach new "bucket" section for his wooden legs. Normal in all other respects, Freddie is learning to walk, eventually may be able to use artificial arms

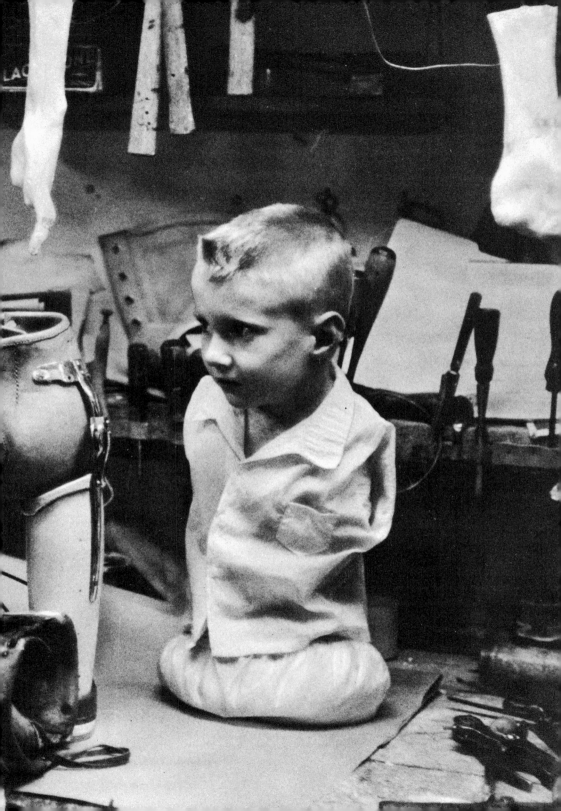

**SEMINARIANS ON THE SIDELINES:**
Students from Grand Halleux Seminary, Belgium,
are entranced by cyclists in Europe's biggest race

clean and serves his people truthfully."

★ The biggest penny value in America passed away when, after seventy-three years, the 1¢-fare East Boston ferry was discontinued.

★ Garry Davis, the young man who years ago had renounced his U.S. citizenship to become a "citizen of the world", was back in America as an "immigrant" and briefly went to jail rather than pay a fine for traffic violations.

★ Representative Carroll Kearns (Rep., Pa.,) hit a new high in skepticism by inspecting the gold buried at Fort Knox, Ky., to make sure the outgoing Democratic administration had left it there.

★ The town council in Sunbury, England, put it rather nicely when it warned contestants in a local beauty contest that they would be disqualified if they wore "false aids calculated to mislead the judge".

★ Jean Connors of San Fernando, Calif., unwrapped a gift from her boy friend and, to her horror, discovered a boa constrictor coiled inside. The beau's explanation was simple: "I just wanted to give her something different."

DEATHS: Mrs. Cornelius Vanderbilt, 83. The dowager queen of New York society since 1910, she was the daughter of a cotton speculator who grew

wealthy during the War between the States. In 1896, against his family's wishes, she married the fabulously wealthy man whose homes in New York and Newport she turned into society's citadels.

OSA JOHNSON, 58.    Widow of big-game hunter Martin Johnson, and a famous explorer in her own right, she was preparing for another trip to Africa when she died.

FLETCHER HENDERSON, 55.    One of the great jazz figures of all time, noted equally as pianist and arranger.

**February**    A valiant moonshiner named C. L. Grimes walked fourteen miles to beg police to confiscate his entire liquor supply. It had given him severe cramps and, he said, "if it did this to me, it would probably kill anybody else".

★    Conducting a symphony at the New Orleans Municipal Auditorium, Leopold Stokowski was irritated by the clangor of a Dixieland band playing just beyond a steel partition. Russ Papalia, the leader of the Dixieland group, gave a prompt rejoinder: "Does he ever stop to consider that he's disturbing us?"

★    To a chicken thief who had made off with almost all her stock, Mrs. Ebb Hargrave of McLeansboro, Ill., directed this newspaper ad: "Will the person or persons who took all my hens and left the old rooster come and get him. He is lonesome."

★ Thirteen second-string Communists, convicted in New York of conspiring against the United States, turned down an offer to be deported to Russia rather than serve jail terms in America.

★ Traffic-counters in Washington registered what Republicans considered a significant fact: peak traffic in the morning occurred twenty minutes earlier than during the Democratic regime.

DEATHS: WILLIAM ALLEN MAGEE, 108. A bugler to General Sherman, he was one of the last survivors of the Yankee armies in the War between the States.

MICHAEL S. JACOBS, 72. The best-known fight promoter since Tex Rickard, "Uncle Mike" made millions from exclusive contracts with Joe Louis and other top-draw boxers.

WALTER B. PITKIN, 74. His book *Life Begins at Forty* became a household stand-by. Pitkin wrote more than thirty books after he himself passed the age of forty.

KARL RUDOLF GERD VON RUNDSTEDT, 77. A Prussian career officer in the German armies, he became a field marshal under Hitler and led Nazi troops into Poland, France, and the Ukraine.

FRITZ KUHN, 55. The former *Führer* of the German-American Bund was deported to Germany in 1945, lived there in obscurity, and died in December, 1951. But not until 1953 did word of his death come to the attention of the outside world.

BEN AMES WILLIAMS, 63. He was the author of more than 500 novels, short stories, and serials. Among his last and most famous novels: *Leave Her to Heaven, House Divided, The Strange Woman*.

STEVE HANNAGAN, 53. One of Amer-

"HOME, JAMES!"

ica's truly great press agents, respected for his honesty in a trade beset by deceptions. He brought fame to Miami Beach, Sun Valley, and the bathing beauty. At the time of his death he was helping to promote the sale of Coca-Cola in Africa.

JAMES L. KRAFT, 78. Inventor of a cheese-pasteurization process (in 1915), he founded the vast food company that bears his name.

**March** The General Accounting Office revealed that the presidential pay for January 20, end of Truman's and beginning of Eisenhower's terms in office, had

been split right down the middle, giving each man about $135 for the day's work.

★ At a prize fight in Lowell, Mass., lightweight Neil Kind hopped into the ring, doffed his robe, discovered he had neglected to put on his trunks.

★ A California appellate court struck a blow for bedeviled adults when it ruled that a child of four could be held liable in a civil suit. The suit (for $10,000) had been brought by a 55-year-old baby-sitter against a youngster who, she said, had thrown her to the floor and broken both her arms.

★ The youngest woman ever to head a U.S. armed service—Lieutenant Colonel Julia E. Hamblet, 36—became Director of Women Marines.

★ Washington came up with another classic story of bureaucratic confusion when a man told a Senate committee that he had reported to the wrong State Department office and had worked there two years, being paid regularly from the wrong payroll.

★ The respected *Tailor and Cutter*, British fashion magazine, decided that Adlai Stevenson should be included among the best-dressed men of the year because, while running for the presidency as a Democrat, he had dressed like a Republican.

**SOUP'S ON:** Bemedaled Sir Winston Churchill attends London Lord Mayor's traditional dinner, held in the Guildhall

**ACTIVE FEMALE:** Undaunted by her 70th birthday, famed party-giver Elsa Maxwell eats a hot dog with girlish abandon

★ After questioning people all over the country, a manufacturer announced that 158,000 women in the United States smoke pipes.

DEATHS: JAMES J. JEFFRIES, 77. Long retired from the ring, to many experts he was still the greatest heavyweight champion of them all.

IRENE BORDONI, 59. Remembered for her French flair in singing songs of the post-World War I era, Miss Bordoni actually was born in Corsica.

RAOUL DUFY, 75. Together with Picasso and Matisse, Frenchman Dufy, with his delicate dabs of color, helped revolutionize painting early in the twentieth century.

**April** Perhaps the most-quoted comment of the year was Lady Astor's when she saw Senator McCarthy taking a drink at a Washington shindig: "I wish it were poison."

★ When Alex Hansen died in a Chicago hospital, he seemed destitute. From his $14-a-month pension he had saved only $1 in a local bank. But in his rented room relatives found a telegram. It said Hansen had just won $56,000 in the Irish Sweepstakes.

★ The Canadian Legislature approved a bill lumping together Toronto and twelve of its suburbs into one "greater" city, with a population of 1,191,000. Toronto thus became No. 7 in the North American size parade, after New York, Chicago, Mexico City, Philadelphia, Los Angeles, and Detroit.

★ Changing times in circus fads were apparent as Ringling Brothers and Barnum & Bailey opened in New York. As the star attraction, the big top offered a 5-year-old lad from Brussels who played the "Poet and Peasant" overture on a xylophone.

★ The year's most provocative classified ad ran in the Albany (Ore.) *Greater*

*Oregon.* It read: "If the man who went rushing out the front door of my house the other night without any clothes on will call at my office, he can have his clothes and no questions asked."

Clara Kinsey, wife of the famous Dr. Alfred Kinsey, revealed a sad fact of her marriage. "I don't see much of him any more," she said, "since he got so interested in sex."

DEATHS: JIM THORPE, 64. He was the greatest athlete of the century. A Sac and Fox Indian, Thorpe was an All-American football player, winner of both the decathlon and pentathlon events at the 1912 Olympics, and outstanding in every other sport to which he turned his attention. But he died almost broke.

KING CAROL II, 59. Known as the "playboy king", he ruled Romania from 1930 to 1940, later traveled the world with his mistress, Magda Lupescu (whom he married in 1947), and wound up at Estoril, gayest city in Portugal.

MALVINA C. THOMPSON, 61. As a secretary, she was famed throughout the world. Her boss: Mrs. Franklin D. Roosevelt.

**May** After a long trip through Europe, the novelist Edna Ferber, a New Yorker herself, returned to her home town, took one look, and termed it the most "disgustingly filthy" city of the world, a "scab on the face of our country".

★ Japanese Crown Prince Akihito also took a look at New York and termed it "the most wonderful masterpiece ever created by human beings".

★ In a town in Central Africa, censors ruled that an old Tarzan film could not be shown in the local movie house. It wasn't, they said, suitable for an African audience.

★ Albert Einstein, receiving a $1000 award for "original and nonconformist thinking", accepted it and the words of

**PERSISTENT BRIDE** Barbara Hutton allows her fifth husband Porfirio Rubirosa to show suitable affection at start of their 1953 marriage

praise accompanying it by saying: "I shall carefully refrain from disputing [the praise]. For who believes that there is still such a thing as genuine modesty?"

★ The deliberately obscured son of famous parents, Jon Lindbergh, while on an exploring trip near Yosemite National Park, discovered one of the largest underwater caves in the West.

★ At Ford Ord, Calif., parents and relatives of men in service were invited for a special feed to show them how well the boys were being treated. There was only one hitch: after the banquet, 200 of the diners came down with food poisoning.

DEATHS: ROBERT F. WAGNER, 75. Author of the New Deal labor-relations act that bore his name, he served in the U.S. Senate from 1927 to 1949 as

**UNHAPPY TWO-YEAR-OLD,** Carel Bouwens kisses his horse good-by—temporarily—on learning no one under four can ride in show he hoped to enter

a Democratic senator from New York.
PETER DE ROSE, 53. Composer of such favorites as "Wagon Wheels", he was also known for the radio program on which he appeared for many years with his wife, May Singhi Breen.

**June** After Dr. Wallace Howell had been paid $100 a day to bring rain scientifically to the New York area, amusement-park owners got together to pay him some more—to make it stop raining.

★ Two years after winning the title of "Mr. America", Roy Hillihgenn was on his way out of the country. Reason: he actually was a South African who had come to America five years before on a one-month visa.

★ In England, a hot jet pilot was warned officially to confine his flying to less dangerous planes. The pilot: Philip, Duke of Edinburgh, husband of the Queen.

★ On his way to get a gold pin for fifty-three years of driving without an accident, Dr. Boetius Hansen of Niebull, Germany, ran into a police car.

★ Sara Delano Roosevelt, 21, grand-daughter of Franklin D. and heiress to $50 million, married Anthony di Bonaventura, 23, the pianist son of an immigrant barber.

★ In New York a Supreme Court decision returned a city job as washroom attendant to Bonaventura Pinggera, 57, who had admitted to membership in the Communist party during the '30's. Said the court: "It is a bit difficult to visualize how a washroom attendant in his official capacity can give aid to his country's enemies."

DEATHS: ALBERT SPALDING, 64. A widely admired violinist and composer, known as America's first great native concert instrumentalist.
FRANK S. LEAVITT, 62. Under the *nom de ring* of Man Mountain Dean, he won fame as a wrestler.
WILLIAM FARNUM, 77. One of the greatest and most handsome of the silent screen's matinee idols, he ended playing bit parts in the talkies.
ROLAND YOUNG, 65. Another veteran player, happily remembered for such roles as *Topper* and *Ruggles of Red Gap*.
DOUGLAS SOUTHALL FREEMAN, 67. Richmond newspaperman who brought the history of the War between the States to brilliant life in his epic volumes *Robert E. Lee* and *Lee's Lieutenants*.
RENÉ FONCK, 59. Perhaps the top ace of World War I, the French flyer officially downed seventy-five German planes and was credited unofficially with more than 125.

**July** To quash canards against the weatherman, a Baltimore forecaster offered to bet 2 to 1 on the accuracy of his predictions. Statistics showed he had been 87 percent correct.

★ The most positive method of removing government officials turned up on the Ivory Coast of Africa when officials announced that a senator, Biaka Boda, had been served for dinner by his irate, cannibalistic constituents.

★ Nearing the end of his round-the-world trip, Adlai Stevenson finally got behind the Iron Curtain in East Berlin. Trying to take pictures, he was held at gun point for half an hour by Red Police.

★ Competing against girls from twenty-five nations, France's Christiane Martel, 18, was awarded the title of Miss Universe. Her measurements, presumably the world's most pleasing: bust, 33 in.; waist, 22 in.; hips, 35 in.

★ For the first time in America a national monument was created to honor the memory of a Negro. The birthplace of the great scientist George Washington Carver was so designated.

DEATHS: HILAIRE BELLOC, 82. Though one of the most prolific and profound writers of his time, author of more than 150 books, he was better known for his nonsense verses than for his studies of historical figures.

MAUDE ADAMS, 80. Renowned for her stage portrayal of Peter Pan, she won fame as one of the great actresses of all time. In the late 1930's she emerged from retirement to head the drama department of Stephens College in Missouri.

TSA-TOKE, 107. This Kiowa Indian chief could look back on one of America's bloodiest chapters, the massacre of General George Custer's troops at the Little Big Horn, where Tsa-Toke had been an army scout.

JAN STRUTHER, 52. Best-selling novelist (*Mrs. Miniver*), the British-born writer was also admired for her poetry.

**August** A king-size tax problem caused Bing Crosby to sell fifty-eight of his sixty-five race horses. The price, $42,500, helped him to pay a $1 million tax levied against the estate of his wife Dixie, who had died a year before. Crosby also put up for sale his $300,000 Los Angeles mansion and an estate near San Francisco.

★ Said onetime boxing champion Joey Maxim of his wife's divorce complaint, alleging beatings, "I always came out worse than she did in . . . our fights."

★ A British judge turned down a divorce application in which a wife alleged her husband's conduct had caused her to lose weight. The slimming, the judge ruled, had helped her appearance.

★ Recipient of America's highest military decoration, the Congressional Medal of Honor, was a Japanese-American G.I., Sergeant Hiroshi H. Miyamura, just re-

**LONDON FROST** hits Hollywood tourist Ava Gardner as she tries to make a Grenadier Guardsman disobey orders and glance at her—just once

leased from a North Korean prison camp. His award had been kept secret to protect him from Red reprisals for his medal-winning feat: killing sixty Communists singlehanded while covering his comrades' retreat.

DEATHS: ABNER C. POWELL, 92. A veteran of big-league baseball, originator of Ladies' Day and the rain check.

BERT ANDREWS, 52. A Pulitzer Prize winner and one of the country's most respected newsmen, he was chief of the *New York Herald Tribune's* bureau in Washington.

**September** In Salina, Utah, Communism-conscious residents took a close look at an old sign outside of town—"Welcome Fellow Travelers"—and prudently erased its middle word.

★ Arthur Kull, high-school history teacher in Summit, N.J., resigned his $85-a-week post to become a brewery-truck driver—which paid $52 a week more.

★ In Topeka, Kans., Miss Jerry McConkey, a schoolteacher, announced she was going to marry Jerry McConkey, a schoolteacher. In Salt Lake City a man named Willard Smith met a man named Willard Smith in the waiting room of a maternity ward and discovered that both wives had had a fourth daughter and had named her Christine.

★ One of the longest picketing stints on record ended for Alexander Orr when the A.F.L. auto mechanics' union finally signed a contract with a Chicago auto firm. Orr had been pounding his picket beat for twelve years, walked some 40,-000 miles, wore out twenty-four pairs of shoes. Said he: "It was beginning to get kind of monotonous."

★ The year's winner of the Miss America contest was a 20-year-old college student from Ephrata, Pa. Her name: Evelyn Margaret Ay. Her measurements: bust, 37 in.; waist, 24 in.; hips, 36 in.

★ A near neighbor of Miss Ay was chosen Mrs. America: Mrs. Erna Snuder, 24. Her measurements: 34 in., 23 in., 34 in.

★ Helen Traubel, Wagnerian soprano, dropped from the roster of New York's Metropolitan Opera, started a successful night-club singing tour.

★ In Kings Mountain, N.C., a church social function was swamped when a typographical error caused the announcement to promise "all-night sinning".

★ The Tokyo telephone company began to do something about a backlog of applications for phone service, some dating back to 1906.

★ Honoring Sophie Tucker's fiftieth year in show business, an all-male New York audience roared when "the last of the red-hot mamas" remarked, "This is the first time I've been in a room alone with enough men. The heck of it is, it comes too late."

DEATHS: JONATHAN M. WAINWRIGHT, 70. The general who stayed on with the beleaguered garrisons of Bataan and Corregidor, spent World War II in a Japanese prison, and emerged to find himself a hero.

LEWIS STONE, 73. Best known for his portrayal of Judge Hardy in the Andy Hardy movies, he had been a stage and screen star for more than fifty years. He died from a heart attack, brought on by chasing prowlers near his Hollywood home.

FATHER WILLIAM AUGUSTUS MAGUIRE, 62. Former Roman Catholic chaplain of the Pacific Fleet, he was credited with having inspired the World War II song: "Praise the Lord and Pass the Ammunition".

**October** Army brass banned Dr. Kinsey's *Sexual Behavior in the Human Female* from service libraries in Europe. Announced reason: it "was not thought to be of general interest" to G.I.'s.

★ Pleased with his first day as Acting Governor of Texas during the absence of Governor Allan Shivers, State Senator Jimmy Phillips leaned back in the gubernatorial chair, reached into Governor Shivers' cigar box, and let out a yip. A mousetrap, apparently placed inside just for the occasion, had snapped shut on his fingers.

★ Fred Bennett, custodian of files in the Evanston, Ill., detective bureau, leafed through one dated 1929 and discovered something he'd never seen before: a commendation, to Fred Bennett, for efficient organization of the files.

★ In Paris, Ill., an all-too-clever publicist for a variety show starring Dorothy Lamour sent out a flood of postcards saying, "Darling, don't forget our date at 8 P.M. . . . Dorothy." Results: one wife flagged down a locomotive being driven by her husband to demand an explanation, another took steps toward a divorce, a third smashed a window.

★ In New York City, a Columbia University student, warned by police to get his jalopy off the street, pushed it into the East River.

★ In the richest divorce settlement of recent years, Winthrop Rockefeller offered to hand over $5.5 million to his estranged wife Barbara (Bobo) Rockefeller, a girl from the other side of the social tracks.

★ Ira Hayes, an Arizona Indian, one of the men immortalized in the epic picture of the flag raising on Iwo Jima, was arrested as a drunk and vagrant in Chicago. Hollywood personalities scheduled him for TV appearances, finally secured for him a job as a chauffeur.

DEATHS: CLARENCE SAUNDERS, 72. His name was unfamiliar, but his revolutionary grocery-selling technique (self-service, begun in The Piggly Wiggly stores) became a national byword and elevated him from a $4-a-week clerk to millionaire.

JAMES EARLE FRASER, 76. As a sculptor and designer, he turned out two works known probably to every American: the buffalo nickel and the statue "End of the Trail".

FRANK MUNN, 58. For twenty-three years his Irish tenor had won him fame as the "golden voice of radio".

NIGEL BRUCE, 58. Veteran of many a motion picture, he had become best known and loved for his perfect portrayal of Dr. Watson in the Sherlock Holmes films.

**November** General of the Army George C. Marshall, 72, came home with a new honor: the Nobel Peace Prize, for his plan to rebuild the economy of Europe— the Marshall Plan. A duplicate prize went to Dr. Albert Schweitzer, the 78-year-old Alsatian Bach scholar and medical missionary to Africa.

★ Notified that her husband, actor George Sanders, had filed for a divorce after a running feud with her, glamorous Zsa Zsa Gabor told reporters: "Nothing that George could ever do would surprise me. He does what his psychoanalyst tells him to do."

★ A defendant in a drunken-driving case in Detroit explained why he had taken the wheel of his car despite his condition: "I was too drunk to walk."

★ In Norway, citizens of the town of Paradise began doing something about the road into their town when they discovered that a highway project was making it much easier for motorists to reach the town of Hell.

★ Kenneth Griffin, a truck driver facing a bigamy trial in Los Angeles, told why he had married four women in less than a year, although he had still another wife in Chicago: "I had to have something to do on my days off."

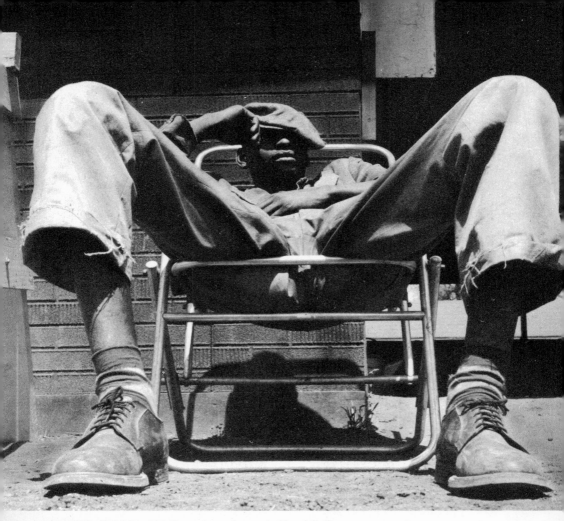

**INERT MALE:** Outside a horse barn at Churchill Downs race track near Louisville, Ky., this swivel-jointed barn hand takes his ease in the afternoon sunshine

★ In Omaha, a robber rushing from an insurance company he had just held up hailed what he thought was a taxi, clambered into a police car.

★ The oddest hold-up weapon of the year appeared in Johannesburg, South Africa, where four men robbed a filling station while holding the attendant at bay with a live lobster.

★ In Washington, a meeting of the Association of the Ice Manufacturers of the United States was interrupted by an unexpected and distinguished guest, President Eisenhower. "I want to look in the faces of the people who are now the bosses in this industry," the President explained, "and see if they look as coldhearted as my boss used to look—because my job before I went to West Point was in the ice business."

DEATHS: HARRISON WILLIAMS, 80. A utilities executive who at one time was estimated to control a sixth of all public utilities in the nation, he once rebuffed a suggestion that he stop working when his personal fortune reached $680 mil-

**LOOK MA!** German tight-rope specialists in death-defying performance over rocky chasm in Wetterstein Mountains, Bavaria

lion. "I want to make it an even billion," he said.

EMMERICH KALMAN, 71. Hungarian-born composer of such light operettas as *Sari* and *Countess Maritza,* who will probably be best remembered for one melody: "Play Gypsies, Dance Gypsies".

**December** At the International Live Stock Exposition in Chicago, a 1005-pound Hereford named Lone Star took top honors and was sold for a record $20,100—$225 a pound.

★ Even the great George Bernard Shaw had his off moments. Executors of the late playwright's estate said that one unpublished Shaw play, *Why She Would Not,* would not ever be published or played. It was not, they said, good enough.

★ A Baltimorean charged with turning in false fire alarms explained why he did it: "I don't like to see firemen sitting around. If they don't get exercise, they get stale."

★ Ageless Marlene Dietrich created the style furor of the year when she showed up for the first night of a three-week night-club singing engagement in Las Vegas, Nev., wearing a $6000 gown transparent from the waist up.

★ As a publicity stunt for a Chicago travel agency, Pamela Martin, a 23-year-old advertising artist and writer, broke by eight hours the world's record for circling the globe in regularly scheduled commercial airliners. Her record-breaking time for the 22,000-mile trip: 90 hours, 59 minutes.

★ From a public-health-service official came an estimate of how much time the average man spends shaving or getting his hair cut during his lifetime: 427 days.

★ The Army, unsuccessful in trying to force members of the Women's Army Corps to wear khaki-colored underthings, had to back down again. Instead of cotton stockings, W.A.C.'s would be issued nylons.

★ Pat O'Brien, veteran of many a film role as a good-natured Irish cop, had to call in real cops in Santa Monica, Calif., when someone stole his brief case. In it were honorary police badges from more than a score of cities.

★ Mrs. Della May McKeon, 67, had kept a faded photograph ever since she became too ill to work in 1931 and moved into a two-room apartment with her son, a maintenance man. In a Pittsburgh courtroom, the old photo proved Mrs. McKeon's identity and her right to $479,000 from the estate of a wealthy aunt.

★ To win a $2.80 bet, an English golf pro, Charlie Macey, brightened the Yuletide season by making 12,000 hops on a pogo stick in one hour and thirty-five minutes.

DEATHS: MARJORIE KINNAN RAWLINGS, 57. Unable for a decade to make a go of writing fiction, she turned her pen to the scrub country of Florida. Result: *The Yearling,* for which she received the 1939 Pulitzer Prize.

DR. ROBERT A. MILLIKAN, 85. Awarded the 1923 Nobel Prize for measuring the charge carried by an electron, he was best known for his work on radiations from outer space, called cosmic rays.

FRANK D'OLIER, 76. First national commander of the American Legion, he later achieved business eminence as president of the Prudential Life Insurance Company.

**OVER A CENTURY APART:** Mrs. Christine Nelson, 107, at ground-breaking ceremony for Downey, Calif., church, greets her great-great-grandson. This young American was one of nearly 4,000,000 babies born in the U.S. in 1953, a new all-time record. He helped swell total population to about 161,-200,000. More than 35,000,000 U.S. babies were born in decade ending in 1953. Upward trend of birth rate plus steady decline in mortality rate promise a population of 200,000,000 in the U.S. by 1970

# PICTURE SOURCES ——————————————————

*SLIM AARONS:* 345.

*RAY ATKESON:* 389.

*CONSTANCE BANNISTER:* 126-7 (10 photos from *We Were Spies Behind the Iron Curtain* by Constance Bannister, Edward Stern & Co., Philadelphia).

*MRS. MARIE BARTLETT:* 196-7.

*MARY ELINOR BROWNING:* 310 (t, bot), 311.

*COMBINE:* 54, 165, 166-7, 170-1, 184-5, 202-3.

*BARNEY COWHERD:* 444.

*BLACK STAR:* Bern Keating 79, T. Satyan 189, Horace Bristol 259, Nilsen Hilgren 300, Ross Madden 308, Gene Cook 360 (t, bot), 361 (t, bot), Lilly Tass 403, Joe Clark 409.

*EASTFOTO:* 242-3, 251, 252-3, 255 (2 photos).

*EBONY:* David Jackson 78, Isaac Sutton 83.

*EUROPEAN:* 82, 194.

*DAILY MIRROR:* 437.

*DAILY NEWS:* 65, 97, 329.

*ROYAL DANISH MINISTRY FOR FOREIGN AFFAIRS:* Lennart Larsen 302-3.

*DEPARTMENT OF DEFENSE:* 239.

*E. P. DUTTON & CO., INC.:* 423.

*EASTMAN KODAK:* 335.

*E.C.A.:* Vagn Hansen 159.

*HARRISON FORMAN:* 254, 272.

*ROBERT FUHRING:* 368-9.

*GLOBE:* Larry Barbier, Jr., 279, 352.

*BOB GOLBY:* 348.

*GRAPHIC HOUSE:* 285, 445.

*P. E. GUERRERO:* 392, 395.

*HARRIS & EWING:* 69.

*HERBLOCK:* 143.

*HOUGHTON, MIFFLIN CO.:* 419, 420-1 (from *La Fiesta Brava* by Barnaby Conrad).

*ILLUSTRATED:* 174-5, 182-3, 432-3.

*INTERNATIONAL NEWS PHOTOS:* 14, 29, 80-1, 95, 112, 124, 140, 178, 179(r), 199, 208(t-lt), 220-1, 248, 264, 280-1, 284, 301, 327, 328, 330, 334, 364, 380(t, bot), 391, 404, 408, 434.

*F. L. KENNETT:* 397.

*KEYSTONE:* 219.

*J. J. LANGUEPIN:* 378, 379.

*LIFE MAGAZINE:* Mark Kauffman 10, George Skadding 37, George Silk 278, John Dominis 288, Mark Shaw 315, Lisa Larsen 322, 376.

*THE LONDON TIMES:* Courtesy The Himalayan Committee and Royal Alpine Club 193.

*LOOK MAGAZINE:* 32-3, Jones 48, Atwood 56-7, 59, Werner Bischof 188, Rothstein 296-7, Slim Aarons 351, Vose 357, Greene (4 photos) 366-7, 388, Lerner 410-1, Hansen 425 and 428-9, Lucy Becker 426-7.

*MAGNUM:* David Seymour 163 and 216, Marcos Chamudes 225 and 226-7, Werner Bischof 266, Myron Davis 362-3, Henri Cartier-Bresson 414.

*METROPOLITAN MUSEUM-* 401.

*PIX:* 181, Dungan 191, Claude Jacoby 214, Feingersh 256-7.

*N.A.C.A.:* 47.

*PARAMOUNT PICTURES:* 260, 354-5.

*PARIS-MATCH:* 211, 271, 435, 407, 208(cn, lt), 209.

*CARL PERUTZ:* 342-3.

*FRED PLAUT:* 400, 416(t and bot), 417,(t and bot-r).

*RAPHO-GUILLUMETTE:* S. H. Roth 316 and 318, Andre de Dienes 325 and 369(r), Ormond Gigli 340, 341, and 344.

*REALITES MAGAZINE,* U. S. Edition: 301.

*SOVFOTO:* 102-3, 105, 108-9, Artkino 113 and 114(bot), 114-5, 120-1, 130-1.

*ST. LOUIS POST DISPATCH:* 36.

*SGT. SHERRARD:* 332-3.

*UNITED NATIONS:* 218.

*UNITED PRESS PHOTOS:* Back endpaper, 18-9, 23, 24, 25, 26-7, 28, 41, 49, 50, 62, 86-7, 122, 132, 133, 139, 140(t, bot-lt), 149, 150, 154-5, 179(lt), 195, 205, 206-7, 213, 232, 234-5, 238, 240-1, 244-5, 247, 292, 319, 323, 326, 415, 430-1, 440, 447.

*U. S. MARINE CORPS:* 398.

*U.S.I.S.:* 126(t).

*DAN WEINER:* 417 (bot-lt).

*WIDE WORLD:* Front endpaper, 12, 13, 15, 16-7, 20-1, 38, 39, 40, 42, 43-4, 52-3, 55, 58, 60-1, 63 (lt, rt), 67, 68, 70, 72, 73, 76-7, 89, 90, 91(t, bot), 94, 98, 99, 118-9, 123, 129, 134-5, 140 (bot-r), 141(bot-r), 142, 144-5, 151, 152, 153, 158, 162, 200-1, 208(t-r, cn-rt, bot), 210, 233, 249, 262-3, 265, 268-9, 274, 275, 289, 293, 314, 331, 336-7, 339, 381, 382, 384-5, 393.